Illustrator® 9 For Dummies®

Cheat Sheet

Selecting and Moving Shortcuts

To Do This	Macintosh Shortcut Key	Windows Shortcut Key
Activate Selection tool last used (Select, Direct Select, or Group Select)	⌘+any tool (except Selection tools)	Ctrl+any tool (except Selection tools)
Toggle between Select and Direct Select (or between Select and Group Select)	⌘+Ctrl+Tab	Ctrl+Tab
Add to or subtract from selection	Shift+click with any Selection tool	Shift+click with any Selection tool
Select All	⌘+A	Ctrl+A
Deselect All	Shift+⌘+A	Shift+Ctrl+A
Move selection in one-point increments	Any arrow key	Any arrow key
Move selection in 10-point increments	Shift+press any arrow key	Shift+press any arrow key
Constrain movement to 45-degree angles	Shift+drag with any Selection tool	Shift+drag with any Selection tool
Lock selected artwork	⌘+2	Ctrl+2
Lock all unselected artwork	Shift+option+⌘+2	Shift+Alt+Ctrl+2
Unlock all artwork	Option+⌘+2	Alt+Ctrl+2
Hide selected artwork	⌘+3	Ctrl+3
Show all hidden artwork	Option+⌘+3	Alt+Ctrl+3
Group selected artwork	⌘+G	Ctrl+G
Ungroup selected artwork	Shift+⌘+G	Shift+Ctrl+G

Painting Shortcuts

To Do This	Macintosh Shortcut	Windows Shortcut
Toggle between Paint Bucket and Eyedropper tools	Press Option while using Paint Bucket or Eyedropper tool (tool changes from one to the other when you do so)	Press Alt while using Paint Bucket or Eyedropper tool
Sample specific color from gradient	Shift+click with Eyedropper tool	Shift+click with Eyedropper tool
Add appearance of other object to Appearance palette of currently selected artwork	Shift+option+click with Eyedropper tool	Shift+Alt+click with Eyedropper tool
Swap Stroke and Fill colors of an object	Shift+	Shift+X
Set Stroke and Fill colors to Black and White	Press	

D1318889

Hungry Minds™

For Dummies®: Bestselling Book Series for Beginners

Illustrator® 9 For Dummies®

Cheat Sheet

Path Editing Shortcuts

To Do This	Macintosh Shortcut	Windows Shortcut
Toggle between Pen tool and Convert Anchor Point tool	Option+Pen tool	Alt+Pen tool
Move anchor point while drawing	Click+Spacebar with Pen tool	Spacebar+Pen tool
Create closed path while drawing	Option+drag with Pencil tool or Paintbrush tool	Alt+drag with Pencil tool or Paintbrush tool
Connect path to end of another path (both paths must be selected)	⌘+drag with Pencil tool	Ctrl+drag with Pencil tool

Type Shortcuts

To Do This	Macintosh Shortcut	Windows Shortcut
Align text to left, right, or center	Shift+⌘+L, R, or C	Shift+Ctrl+L, R, or C
Justify text	Shift+⌘+J	Shift+Ctrl+J
Increase font size	Shift+⌘+. (period)	Shift+Ctrl+. (period)
Decrease font size	Shift+⌘+, (comma)	Shift+Ctrl+, (comma)
Reset Horizontal Scaling to 100 percent	Shift+⌘+X	Shift+Ctrl+X
Increase/decrease kerning/tracking	Option+right arrow/left arrow	Alt+right arrow/left arrow
Reset Tracking/Kerning to 0	Shift+⌘+Q	Shift+Ctrl+Q
Select entire word	Double-click word	Double-click word
Select entire paragraph	Triple-click a word in the paragraph	Triple-click a word in the paragraph

View Shortcuts

To Do This	Macintosh Shortcut	Windows Shortcut
Fit page in window	⌘+0 or double-click Hand tool	Ctrl+0 or double-click Hand tool
View at 100%	⌘+1 or double-click Zoom tool	Ctrl+1 or double-click Zoom tool
Change any tool into the Hand tool	Spacebar (when not editing text)	Spacebar (when not editing text)
Change any tool into the Zoom In tool	Option+⌘+Spacebar	Alt+Ctrl+Spacebar
Pixel Preview	Option+⌘+Y	Alt+Ctrl+Y
Outline View	⌘+Y (also toggles preview)	Ctrl+Y
Show/Hide Smart Guides	⌘+U	Ctrl+U
Zoom In	⌘++	Ctrl++
Zoom Out	⌘+-	Ctrl+-
Reposition Zoom marquee	Drag with Zoom tool; then press Spacebar and continue dragging	Drag with Zoom tool; then press Spacebar and continue dragging

For Dummies®: Bestselling Book Series for Beginners

Illustrator® 9 FOR DUMMIES®

by Ted Alspach and Matt LeClair

Foreword by Shane Tracy

Hungry Minds™

HUNGRY MINDS, INC.

New York, NY ◆ Cleveland, OH ◆ Indianapolis, IN
Chicago, IL ◆ Foster City, CA ◆ San Francisco, CA

Illustrator® 9 For Dummies®

Published by
Hungry Minds, Inc.
909 Third Avenue
New York, NY 10022
www.hungryminds.com
www.dummies.com (Dummies Press Web site)

Library of Congress Control Number: 00-101849

ISBN: 0-7645-0668-4

Printed in the United States of America

10 9 8 7 6 5 4 3

1B/QX/QS/QR/IN

Distributed in the United States by Hungry Minds, Inc.

Distributed by CDG Books Canada Inc. for Canada; by Transworld Publishers Limited in the United Kingdom; by IDG Norge Books for Norway; by IDG Sweden Books for Sweden; by IDG Books Australia Publishing Corporation Pty. Ltd. for Australia and New Zealand; by TransQuest Publishers Pte Ltd. for Singapore, Malaysia, Thailand, Indonesia, and Hong Kong; by Gotop Information Inc. for Taiwan; by ICG Muse, Inc. for Japan; by Intersoft for South Africa; by Eyrolles for France; by International Thomson Publishing for Germany, Austria and Switzerland; by Distribuidora Cuspide for Argentina; by LR International for Brazil; by Galileo Libros for Chile; by Ediciones ZETA S.C.R. Ltda. for Peru; by WS Computer Publishing Corporation, Inc., for the Philippines; by Contemporanea de Ediciones for Venezuela; by Express Computer Distributors for the Caribbean and West Indies; by Micronesia Media Distributor, Inc. for Micronesia; by Chips Computadoras S.A. de C.V. for Mexico; by Editorial Norma de Panama S.A. for Panama; by American Bookshops for Finland.

For general information on Hungry Minds' products and services please contact our Customer Care Department within the U.S. at 800-762-2974, outside the U.S. at 317-572-3993 or fax 317-572-4002.

For sales inquiries and reseller information, including discounts, premium and bulk quantity sales, and foreign-language translations, please contact our Customer Care Department at 800-434-3422, fax 317-572-4002, or write to Hungry Minds, Inc., Attn: Customer Care Department, 10475 Crosspoint Boulevard, Indianapolis, IN 46256.

For information on licensing foreign or domestic rights, please contact our Sub-Rights Customer Care Department at 650-653-7098.

For authorization to photocopy items for corporate, personal, or educational use, please contact Copyright Clearance Center, 222 Rosewood Drive, Danvers, MA 01923, or fax 978-750-4470.

For information on using Hungry Minds' products and services in the classroom or for ordering examination copies, please contact our Educational Sales Department at 800-434-2086 or fax 317-572-4005.

Please contact our Public Relations Department at 212-884-5163 for press review copies or 212-884-5000 for author interviews and other publicity information or fax 212-884-5400.

Hungry Minds™ is a trademark of Hungry Minds, Inc.

About the Authors

Ted Alspach: Ted Alspach is the author of over two dozen books on graphics and publishing, including the best-selling *Illustrator Bible*. Considered one of the leading authorities on vector-based graphics, Ted is currently the Illustrator Senior Product Manager at Adobe Systems, Incorporated.

Matt LeClair: Matt LeClair has been involved in the computer graphics industry for more than a decade as a designer, artist, and educator. His writing and artwork have appeared in *MacUser* and *Implosion Magazine*. He co-authored *Photoshop in a Nutshell (First Edition)* and *Digital Prepress Complete* and served as technical editor for *Print Publishing: A Hayden Shop Manual*. Not content to be just another anonymous face behind a computer, Matt is also a fashion model for Gallagher International and is a yellow belt in tae kwon do.

Dedication

Ted's Dedication: To all the people who are experiencing Illustrator for the first time, may this serve as a guide to the wonders which are vector graphics.

Matt's Dedication: To my parents, Henry and Ethel LeClair, who taught me never to give up no matter what the odds are against you.

Authors' Acknowledgments

Ted would like to thank Matt LeClair for stepping in during crunch time to make sure this book is the definitive work on getting started with Adobe Illustrator, Jeanne Criswell for her patience and talent in shaping this book into the fine weapon of pulpy death you now hold in your hands, Mike Roney for not strangling me, and everyone at IDG Books Worldwide who made *Illustrator 9 For Dummies* so darn good. In addition, huge kudos to everyone at Adobe who worked on the revolutionary Illustrator 9.0 (be sure to Option/Alt+click that item called About Adobe Illustrator to see the in-house artwork while you view the credits).

Matt would like to thank: Emily Stephens for being the absolute best of a hundred thousand million girlfriends; Liz Fowler, coolest housemate ever (sorry about all the dishes and the mess in the living room. . .); Tim Plumer, whose excellent technical editing kept us from looking like fools way too many times; Steve Kurth for his most excellent artistic contributions; Donnie O'Quinn for laughter in times of great stress; Dustin Ruoff for always being there; Greg Paquette and all the gang at Accolade for their ongoing support; my students (at least the ones who gave me good reviews!) for putting up with me for hours on end and pretending to be interested; and, as always, the Curti gang — Mike, Caritha, Sofia and Matt — for helping to put things back into perspective.

And of course, big thanks to all the folks at IDG Books Worldwide, especially the ever-patient Senior Project Editor Jeanne Criswell and Senior Copy Editor Barry Childs-Helton, and all the poor folks in production who had to deal with the godzillions of graphics we threw at them.

Publisher's Acknowledgments

We're proud of this book; please register your comments through our Online Registration Form located at www.dummies.com.

Some of the people who helped bring this book to market include the following:

Acquisitions, Editorial, and Media Development

Senior Project Editor: Jeanne S. Criswell

Senior Acquisitions Editor: Michael L. Roney

Copy Editors: Barry Childs-Helton, Rebekah Mancilla, Zoë Wykes

Proof Editor: Teresa Artman

Technical Editors: Tim Plumer, Jr., Craig Dearing

Permissions Editor: Carmen Krikorian

Editorial Managers: Rev Mengle, Leah Cameron

Media Development Manager: Laura Carpenter

Editorial Assistant: Candace Nicholson

Production

Project Coordinator: Regina Snyder

Layout and Graphics: Amy Adrian, Angie Hunckler, Shelley Norris, Kristin Pickett, Jacque Schneider, Rashell Smith, Brian Torwelle, Jeremey Unger, Erin Zeltner

Special Art: Steve Kurth, Joe Lamere

Proofreaders: Corey Bowen, Betty Kish, Susan Moritz, April Perez, Marianne Santy, Sossity R. Smith

Indexer: Richard T. Evans

Special Help

Steve Arany, Valery Bourke, Leah Cameron, Craig Dearing, Amanda M. Foxworth, David Gregory, Shelley Lea, Mary SeRine

General and Administrative

Hungry Minds, Inc.: John Kilcullen, CEO; Bill Barry, President and COO; John Ball, Executive VP, Operations & Administration; John Harris, CFO

Hungry Minds Technology Publishing Group: Richard Swadley, Senior Vice President and Publisher; Mary Bednarek, Vice President and Publisher, Networking and Certification; Walter R. Bruce III, Vice President and Publisher, General User and Design Professional; Joseph Wikert, Vice President and Publisher, Programming; Mary C. Corder, Editorial Director, Branded Technology Editorial; Andy Cummings, Publishing Director, General User and Design Professional; Barry Pruett, Publishing Director, Visual

Hungry Minds Manufacturing: Ivor Parker, Vice President, Manufacturing

Hungry Minds Marketing: John Helmus, Assistant Vice President, Director of Marketing

Hungry Minds Online Management: Brenda McLaughlin, Executive Vice President, Chief Internet Officer

Hungry Minds Production for Branded Press: Debbie Stailey, Production Director

Hungry Minds Sales: Roland Elgey, Senior Vice President, Sales and Marketing; Michael Violano, Vice President, International Sales and Sub Rights

◆

The publisher would like to give special thanks to Patrick J. McGovern, without whom this book would not have been possible.

◆

Contents at a Glance

Cartoons at a Glance

By Rich Tennant

"YES, I THINK IT'S AN ERROR MESSAGE."

page 7

"I COULDN'T SAY ANYTHING—THEY WERE IN HERE WITH THAT PROGRAM WE BOUGHT THEM THAT ENCOURAGES ARTISTIC EXPRESSION."

page 61

page 267

"OK, TECHNICALLY, THIS SHOULD WORK. JUDY, TYPE THE WORD 'GOODYEAR' IN ALL CAPS, BOLDFACE, AT 700-POINT TYPE SIZE."

page 233

"Are you sure that's the best way to apply a stroke to a path?"

page 199

page 317

Cartoon Information:
Fax: 978-546-7747
E-Mail: richtennant@the5thwave.com
World Wide Web: www.the5thwave.com

Table of Contents

Foreword

Did you ever consider sending in a drawing of that little guy on the matchbook cover from one of those art school come-ons? Do you still remember how much fun you had finger-painting in second grade? Do you ever dream of using your computer to realize a new kind of creative freedom and expression, but you struggle even to draw a straight line?

If you're like me, you sometimes see in your mind's eye something you wish you could share with others, but somehow you were standing in the snack line when God handed out raw drawing ability. Luckily, drawing-and-painting programs can help anyone draw a straight line — and a whole lot more — and Adobe Illustrator 9.0 is the best.

Illustrator's wealth of features may seem daunting at first. I know I was a bit intimidated. But with *Illustrator 9 For Dummies*, that feeling quickly disappears. Before long, the tools that made me nervous were opening my mind to a new creative freedom. In no time at all, I was using transparency to create graphics for the Web; the Styles palette to create consistent artwork across related projects; and Pixel preview mode to know right away whether the color I chose was going to look good on my Web page, rather than relying on trial and error.

Charting a clear path through the complexity of Adobe Illustrator, Ted and Matt have created a book that can help anyone get comfortable with the program. Step-by-step instructions and explanations on how to use the tools — along with tips that make using Illustrator easier — give you a boost in accomplishing the most with this software.

Illustrator 9 For Dummies won't overwhelm you with *everything* there is to know about Illustrator. Instead, this book gives you a reliable foundation upon which to build. And that, my friends, is the key. Whether you're an experienced graphic designer or a newbie, this book can help you realize and share your artistic vision.

Shane Tracy

Worldwide Product Support Manager, Illustration

Adobe Systems, Inc.

Introduction

Welcome to *Illustrator 9 For Dummies*. You are reading this because you want to find out more about Adobe Illustrator. That is a very smart move! Adobe Illustrator is *the* industry-standard drawing tool for print and the Web. Not only does it outsell both of its competitors combined, it is one of the most powerful graphics-creation tools ever created. When you use Illustrator, all you need to produce graphics on a par with the best you've seen in print or on the Web is (a) knowledge and (b) artistic ability. Artistic ability is a challenge you can handle on your own. The other half is what this book is all about.

Like some tragic hero, Illustrator's great power is also its terrible curse. With its 20+ palettes, 50+ tools, and scores of menu items, its sheer depth is enough to make the most hardened graphics expert go shaky in the knees. But don't be fooled by Illustrator's vastness. There's a unique, consistent logic underlying it all. Once you get a few basics down, all the rest falls nicely into place.

This book's mission is to get you past Illustrator's "intimidation factor" and into its "wow factor." To go from being befuddled and mystified by Illustrator's nigh-infinite options to creating the kinds of graphics that others look at and say, "Wow, how did you do *that!*"

About This Book

This book is written to make your journey into Adobe Illustrator flexible and self-paced. Each chapter is as self-contained as possible. You can hop in anywhere you want, with a minimum of flipping to other parts of the book to find out what you missed. If your goal is to find out more about the Pencil tool, for example, you can skip everything else and go directly to Chapter 8 without getting hopelessly lost. On the other hand, if you're determined to find out as much about the program as possible, you can read the book cover to cover. We organized the book so the chapters move from simpler concepts to more complex. The early chapters make a good base for understanding the later ones.

This book is both a reference book and an on-site trainer for Adobe Illustrator. To find out more about a specific feature, find it in the index or in the Table of Contents and read up. To get a more in-depth feel for the feature, follow the step-by-step instructions that accompany the information on the major features.

By and large, human beings get more out of *doing* than out of reading about doing. Adobe Illustrator is a classic case in point. Don't bother to memorize anything in this book. Instead, pick up a concept, work with it in Illustrator for a while, and then come back to the book when you're ready for something new! Above all, have fun with it! Adobe Illustrator is one of the coolest programs on the planet. With a little practice, you can be creating illustrations that knock your socks off.

What You Don't Need to Read

Each and every word in this book has been carefully crafted to carry the maximum amount of information. If you skip even one of them, you miss out on information that is essential to your livelihood. So give every word your full attention, especially the ads in the back of the book — that's where the secret Illustrator power techniques are buried! (Uh-huh. And you access them by playing the CD backwards.)

Just kidding! But you knew that.

Actually, feel free to skip any information that seems far afield from what you need to know. The stuff that no one should ever *really* have to know (but which is nonetheless utterly fascinating) is clearly labeled *Technical Stuff*. Technical Stuff won't help you sleep better at night, but it just might give you a little background on why Illustrator behaves the way it does (which could save your computer from being modified with a ball-peen hammer). Besides, it's fun to know more than anybody else!

Foolish Assumptions

We're going to make just the following two basic Foolish Assumptions about you, gentle reader:

- **You have time, patience, and a strong desire to learn Adobe Illustrator 9.** Illustrator has a steep learning curve at the start; but once you get the basics, you find the program pretty straightforward. Getting over that first hump is going to take a little endurance and can get pretty frustrating at times. Be patient with yourself and with the program. All shall be revealed in the fullness of time. Until then, this book is intended to help you get over that hump.

- **You have access to a computer with Adobe Illustrator 9 available on it.** This is a hands-on book. It isn't meant to be read like a novel. *If this is your very own copy of the book,* attack it with highlighters and sticky notes, scribble in some marginalia, or even force it open till it lies flat on your desk. Then — after you collect all the loose pages and glue 'em back in — you can have both hands free to work at the computer as you follow along.

How This Book Is Organized

In this book, you find 21 chapters organized in six parts. Each part reflects a major Illustrator concept; each chapter chomps a concept into easily digestible morsels. The whole thing is arranged in a logical order, so you can read straight through if you are so inclined. Or you can jump in at any point to find the exact information you need. To help you do that, we provide here an overview of what you can find in each of those six parts.

Part 1: Driving People Crazy — Illustrator's Bum Rap

Here's where you get the absolute basics of Illustrator. What it is. What it does. Why it's worth the effort. The wonders of blank pages, paths, and the beguiling Pen tool all make their debut here. By the time you finish this part, you have a good overview of the entire program.

Part II: Drawing and Coloring Your Artwork

This part is where the fun begins — you roll up your sleeves and start creating illustrations. Whether or not you can draw using old-fashioned paper and pencil (ewww — how "twentieth century"), wait'll you see what you can create!

Part III: Taking Your Paths to Obedience School

With Illustrator, you can really unleash your creativity. Unfortunately, unleashed creativity often results in an unruly mess. This part looks at how to tame the mess, through changing parts of graphics, organizing graphics into separate layers, and using many other techniques that prove that organization and creativity are not mutually exclusive. You don't even need a smock.

Part IV: Weaving Beautiful Typestries

Illustrator is truly a wondrous modifier of written symbols, so we devote an entire section just to working with type. We cover everything from the most basic formatting to complex type treatments.

Part V: Getting Art to Print, to the Web, and to Other Applications

Illustrator doesn't exist in a vacuum. Just about everything you create there is destined to go someplace else — to the printed page, to the Web, or to another application. Here you get the briefing on how to get your artwork out of Illustrator and into the rest of the world.

Part VI: The Part of Tens

No *For Dummies* book is complete without its Top Ten lists, and this book is no exception! Here are ten tips to help you use Illustrator more effectively, ten techniques for creating complex, beyond-the-basics artwork, and ten ways to customize Illustrator (chrome hubcaps optional). Save this part for dessert.

About All Those Little Icons

Scattered throughout this book you find some nifty little icons that point out bits of information that are especially useful, important, or otherwise noteworthy.

This information can help you do something faster, easier, or better; save you time and money; or make you the hero of the beach. Or at least make you a little less stressed during a production crunch!

Watch out! This icon means that danger lurks nearby; it tells you what things you should avoid and what things you must absolutely never do.

Here's some utterly fascinating technotrivia that most people never need to know. This information is the kind you can drop into a conversation at a party to remind people how much smarter you are than everyone else. (Assuming you plan to go home alone.)

 This information is stuff that you use on a regular basis in Illustrator. So write it down on your hand so you can refer to it at any instant. Just don't wash that hand! Or better yet, bookmark the page or remember the advice you find there.

Where to Go From Here

Illustrator is a graphics adventure waiting for you to take it on. This book is your guide for that adventure. If you're ravenous to know everything now, you can rush through the text as fast as you can, starting with Chapter 1, and charge right through to the end. Or you can take your time, pick a point that interests you, explore it at your leisure, and then come back to a different place in the book later. Whatever works best for you, this book is your ready-willing-and-able guide for the journey. You have but to start your computer, launch Illustrator, turn the page, and let the adventure begin.

Part I
Driving People Crazy — Illustrator's Bum Rap

The 5th Wave   By Rich Tennant

"YES, I THINK IT'S AN ERROR MESSAGE."

In this part . . .

Here you meet the main character of the book: Adobe Illustrator 9. You get a look at its illustrious past, its remarkable powers, its place in the universe, and (most importantly) what it can do for you. You probe the difference between vectors and pixels. You hover above the various parts of Illustrator and watch what they do. By the end of this part, you uncover a straightforward and easygoing program behind the complex, sometimes intimidating exterior of Illustrator.

Chapter 1

Introducing the World of Illustrator

*I*f there were any truth in advertising (or at least in product naming), Adobe *Intimidator* may be a more appropriate name for Adobe Illustrator. The program's dozens of tools, hundreds of commands, and more than 20 palettes can transform confident, secure individuals into drooling, confused, and frustrated drones.

The situation doesn't have to be that way, of course. Sure, all that stuff is scary. Even more frightening to some is the prospect of facing the giant white nothingness of the document window — the endless possibilities, the confusion over where to start. This chapter helps you get past that initial stage and move forward into the mystical state of *eagerly awaiting* (instead of fearing) each new feature and function.

From Humble Origins to Master of the Graphics Universe

As its box proudly proclaims, Adobe Illustrator is the "Industry Standard Graphics Creation Software for Print and the Web." But the software didn't always enjoy that standing. Illustrator evolved from a geeky math experiment into the graphics powerhouse it is today.

A brief history of Illustrator

Until the mid-1980s, "computer art" was limited to blocky-looking video games, spheroid reflections, and the movie *Tron*. Then something happened to change all that — PostScript, a computer language created especially for printers. Adobe Systems created PostScript specifically to help printers produce millions of teeny-tiny dots on the page, without running out of memory (graphics files *are* notoriously huge).

In 1987, Adobe released Illustrator 1.1, which was designed primarily to be a *front end* for PostScript — a way to make its capabilities actually usable. At that time, the concept of artwork that is scalable to any size *without loss of quality* (one world-beating advantage of creating art within Illustrator) was brand new. Illustrator gave companies the opportunity to have electronic versions of their logos that could be printed at *any* size.

In the more-than-a-decade since Version 1.1, Adobe Illustrator has become the Web-ready, giant application it is today. Millions of people around the world use Illustrator — and its *thousands* of features, big and small, meet a wide variety of graphics needs. Oddly enough, the one aspect of Illustrator that *hasn't* changed is the intimidation factor. Version 1.1 had several tools, many menu items, a neurosis-inducing Pen tool, Bézier curves, and that way-scary blank document when you started it up. Version 9 still has nearly every feature that 1.1 did, and adds a staggering array of new features — transparency, layers, appearances, patterns, effects, and on and on. Illustrator 1.1 was a playful little kitten compared to the tigerish Illustrator 9!

Illustrator's place in the cosmos

Professional graphic artists have a toolbox of programs that they use to create the books, magazines, newspapers, and Web sites that you see every day. Any professional will tell you, you need the right tool for the job to do the job well. The right tools (in this case) are software products — drawing programs, paint programs, as well as products for page layout and Web-authoring. *Drawing programs* like Adobe Illustrator are the best tools for creating crisp, professional-looking graphics such as logos, working with creative type effects, and recreating photographs from line drawings. *Painting programs* (often called *image editing programs*) such as Adobe Photoshop provide tools to color-correct, retouch, and edit digital photographs and recreate "natural media" effects such as hand-painting. Page layout programs such as Adobe InDesign or QuarkXPress let you combine graphics that you create in Drawing and Paint programs with text for print publishing. You can use Web-authoring tools (such as Macromedia Dreamweaver or Adobe GoLive) to combine graphics, text, sound, animation, and interactivity for presentation on the World Wide Web.

While each tool performs a fairly specific (if wide-ranging) task, There is some cross-over between applications. For example, Illustrator has some limited image editing capabilities, but very few people ever use them. Since you can edit images with complete control and freedom in Photoshop, why use the wrong tool for the job? QuarkXPress lets you run type along a curve, but Illustrator has so many tools for creative type effects that you'd be silly to do them anywhere else.

Using Illustrator on its own, you can create an astonishing variety of graphics and type effects. When you combine it with paint, page-layout, and Web-authoring programs, you have the tools you need to create print and Web publications that match the quality of anything you see in the stands or on the screen today.

In the field of professional graphics and publishing, each software program has to perform only a few basic functions: graphics creation, image editing, page layout (for print), or Web layout.

Illustrator is the *de facto* standard in graphics creation. Adobe has products in the other categories (two in the page-layout category). One benefit of using Illustrator is that it works very well (as you may expect) with the other Adobe products, most of which have a similar interface and way of working. If you know one Adobe product well, chances are you'll have an easy time of figuring out other Adobe products.

Illustrator excels at creating and editing artwork of all types. In fact, you can use Illustrator to create and edit nearly anything that isn't a photograph. (For more about the differences between photographs and artwork created with Illustrator, see Chapter 2.)

Starting Up Illustrator and Revving It a Little

To get Illustrator running, either choose Illustrator from the Start menu (in Windows on a PC) or double-click the application's icon (on a Mac). (The latter method also works in Windows, if you're a Mac user who happens to be using Windows. Don't worry; we won't tell a soul. Honest.)

The Illustrator startup process displays the *splash screen* — an image to look at while the program is cranking up. You're in luck; this one is a lovely picture of Venus, from Botticelli's famous painting, rendered by using Illustrator. Look at her enigmatic smile — she's inviting you to enter the creative and exciting world of Illustrator! To accept her invitation, choose File⇨New and answer the riddles of the New Document dialog box, shown in Figure 1-1.

Figure 1-1:
The New
Document
dialog box.

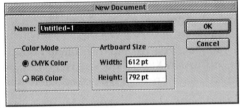

Before you start a new document, you have to answer a few questions in the New Document dialog box about the name, color mode, and page size you plan to use.

What's in a Name (field)?

You can give your new document a name in the Name field. If you don't, then Illustrator names it Untitled-1, and every new document you create is titled sequentially — Untitled-2, Untitled-3, and so on, until you quit the program. When you relaunch, you'll be right back at Untitled-1. If you don't give a name to the new document, you get another chance when you save it. The only advantage to giving the document a name right now is a bit dubious: If you accumulate a whole bunch of unsaved files (*not* recommended!), you can tell them apart.

CMYK or RGB?

CMYK or RGB? In Illustrator, this question is a bit more significant than the ubiquitous question, "Paper or plastic?" To understand why you have to answer Illustrator's question, you need a little more history and some tech-nobabble. (Sorry, we'll try to keep this brief.)

Illustrator has been around for a long time. It was around when putting color images on the World Wide Web was impossible (the world was Webless), and *interactive multimedia* was little more than a buzzword. In those days, the main reason for creating documents in color on the computer was so you could print them out in color. Color printing almost always uses a *CMYK* process — for Cyan, Magenta, Yellow, and blacK inks (the *K* stands for black because RGB has dibs on *B;* it stands for *blue*). These four colors, blended in different amounts, produce the full range of colors you see in printed material. So back then, Illustrator used only CMYK colors because nobody needed to do anything in color besides print.

Then along came interactive multimedia — in effect, the "lights, camera, sound, and action" for computer users. Shortly after that came the World Wide Web. Because images used for multimedia and the Web appear only on the computer screen, a need emerged for RGB images. *So what's RGB, already?* Okay, we're getting to that: Computer screens create the colors you see by using electrons to make a coating of phosphors glow *Red*, *Green*, or *Blue* (hence RGB) in different intensities. If you're creating content for multi-media applications or for the Web, you need RGB images that look good onscreen. You probably don't give two hoots about CMYK. So Illustrator, trying to please everyone, added the capability to create colors in RGB.

Unfortunately, this new feature didn't quite please *everyone.* In fact, it upset some people quite a lot. And left a wake of money wasted, deadlines blown, marriages ruined, lives lost. (Well, okay, that's a little exaggeration, but *only* a little.) CMYK and RGB just didn't get along.

Some side effects of a typical CMYK/RGB goof were minor. If you accidentally used CMYK colors for an image displayed on the World Wide Web (for example), your colors would look a little different from what you expected, but that's all. The mistake wouldn't cost you anything. Printing out that image, however, was an entirely different matter.

Printing in color meant using the standard *four-color printing process:* Every image had its own percentage of cyan, magenta, yellow, and black, so four sets of films were made (one for each of those colors); the final printed image combined the colors). Each set consisted of only four single-color plates (C, M, Y, and K) — and that's all you'd expect to print out. But if your Illustrator file contained any RGB elements (even a few pixels' worth), you had big trou-ble: Three additional films would print out — frequently at a cost of $100 or more per film — for *every* page that contained *any* RGB colors. One mistake like that could cost thousands of dollars, if you weren't paying attention. And a lot of people weren't. They'd never had to worry about RGB colors in an Illustrator file before. (You can bet they did after that!) To prevent this sort of uproar from happening again, Adobe wisely removed the capability to com-bine CMYK and RGB colors in the same document. That's why you have to specify CMYK *or* RGB before you start a new document. Sure, it's a hassle, but you're *so much* better off having this hassle now, rather than spending money for it later!

So which do you choose, CMYK or RGB? You may think it safe to assume that RGB is for multimedia or the Web and CMYK is for print. Okay, that's a *safe* assumption, but not necessarily the *best* assumption. For the sake of your creativity, choose RGB in the following situations:

- ✔ **You're creating for the Web or for multimedia.** In this situation, you're always creating work that is going to be viewed in RGB and have no practical reason whatever to use CMYK.

- ✔ **You're creating for print BUT do not need precise CMYK colors.** If you don't have to specify exact CMYK values while you work, choose RGB. (You can convert to CMYK, using the File⇨Document Color Mode command, *before you go to print* — just don't forget to, okay?) We know that approach sounds like asking for trouble, but we can give you two good reasons for using RGB this way:

- Some of Illustrator's coolest features (including many Effects commands) only work with RGB color.

- When you work in RGB, you can use the full range of colors — *millions* of them — that are possible on the computer. (CMYK only supports mere *thousands* of colors.) If you are creating content for both print and the Web, creating the image in RGB gives you the maximum color range possible in both CMYK *and* RGB.

For the sake of accuracy, choose CMYK in these situations:

✔ **You need precise CMYK colors.** Some artists who create for print use a *swatch book* of printed CMYK colors. They use only the specific CMYK colors they see in the book because they feel (and rightly so) that this is the only way to get a good idea of what that color will look like when it finally prints. If your designs have to meet such specific requirements, then always work in CMYK. Some companies specify the exact CMYK colors they want in their publications. If you're working on a project for one of those companies, use CMYK.

✔ **You're creating for grayscale or black-and-white print.** In RGB, shades of gray exist by default as blends of red, green, and blue. If you're printing with black ink, this blending is a hassle because you always have to work with three colors instead of one. In CMYK, however, you can create shades of gray as percentages of black ink, ignoring all other colors (which you may as well do if they won't be visible anyway).

Page Size

You set your page size by typing values into the Height and Width fields. Your page size truly matters only when you're printing your document directly out of Illustrator. Otherwise, it just exists as a point of reference, a guide to show you how far things are apart from each other. One great thing about Illustrator is, for the most part, size doesn't matter. When you create graphics for the Web you can determine the size of the graphic when you save it. When you are creating graphics for print, most of the time you'll be creating graphics to be imported into page layout applications such as QuarkXPress, PageMaker, or InDesign. In this case, you scale the graphic to the size you need it in your page layout. In either case, the Web browser or page-layout application recognizes your Illustrator drawing, ignoring the page size.

Page size is good for two things: proofing and conceptualization. Often you'll want to print your artwork on paper directly from Illustrator to get an idea of what it looks like. In this case, set the Paper Size to the size paper you have loaded in your printer. While creating graphics, keep in mind the size of the page or browser window you are creating for — in this case, set the Height and Width to whatever the target output is. For example, if you are creating for the Web, you may want to set the size to 640 pixels by 480 pixels, a fairly standard size for computer screens. Keep in mind that this is just to help you visualize the final artwork. Actually you can change the size of the artwork to be anything you want, and that is one of the great things about creating in Illustrator.

By default, Illustrator measures image size in *points* (1 point = 1/72 inch). If that unit of measurement is unfamiliar to you, be sure you type the unit of measurement along with the number when you specify values for page size. When you open a new document, it comes up showing a width in points — say, for instance, 612 pts. If you want to specify a width of ten inches or 30 centimeters, just type (respectively) **10 in** or **30 cm** in the Width field. If you don't know the standard abbreviation for a unit of measurement, you can type the whole word out (for example, **10 inches** or **30 centimeters**). Illustrator understands what you mean and does the conversion for you! And it will do so wherever you enter a unit of measurement, not just in the New Document dialog box. Smart, very smart!

When you have answered the three magic New Document questions, click OK, say *Open sesame!* (just kidding), and behold: A blank page opens, inviting you to realize your creative potential. You're ready to start illustrating. If blank-page syndrome doesn't faze you and you want to dig into the good stuff right away, thumb over to Chapter 2.

Exploring the Illustrator Workspace

Between figuring out what the 200+ menu items *do* and rearranging palettes (until you have a tiny little area on your document in which you can actually *work*), you may find the Illustrator environment a bit daunting. (If you do, you're far from alone.) The next sections are an overview of all that stuff that's preventing you from getting any work done (that stuff is what the geeks call the *UI* — pronounced "you-eye" — for *user interface*).

A graphic handyman's Toolbox

The Illustrator Toolbox (that alien artifact in Figure 1-2) is the place most people start when they use Illustrator. (*Right — hand me the pliers and the plunger.* . . .) After showing you twenty-four tools, six odd-looking buttons, and a gang of giant square things, the Toolbox pretends that's all there is to it. Actually, the Toolbox has over 50 *hidden* tools (just when you think you've seen them all. . .). You can call up most tools in Illustrator by clicking (once) the tool you want in the Toolbox. The cursor then changes to either something that looks like the tool, or in the case of special tools (Rectangle, Ellipse, and others), a cross-hair cursor.

The tools live in *toolslots,* subdivisions within the Toolbox. Many toolslots contain more than one tool. To find out whether that's the case, you click and hold the mouse pointer on a tool in its toolslot. Frequently you see a bunch of other (usually related) tools materialize by the toolslot you clicked (as shown with the Pen tool in Figure 1-2). You can use those other tools by dragging to the tool you want to use and releasing the mouse button.

 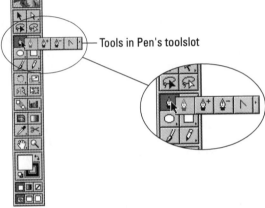

Tools in Pen's toolslot

Figure 1-2: The Illustrator Toolbox. Click and hold the pointer on a toolslot to display all its tools.

TIP

Drag over to the little bar to the right of the extra tools in the toolslot and let go of the mouse button when the little bar becomes highlighted (refer to Figure 1-2). A separate little window appears containing all the tools from the toolslot. You can place this window anywhere on the screen. This procedure can save your sanity if you're constantly switching between two tools that share a toolslot. To get rid of this *toolslot window,* click the tiny white Close box in its upper-left corner.

As you gaze at the Toolbox, notice that it doesn't have a Close or Expand box along its top. One possible explanation for this is that you go to the Toolbox for just about everything you do in Illustrator, and it's nigh impossible to work without it. If you really want to, though, you can hide the Toolbox by selecting Hide Tools from the Window menu at the top of the screen. To bring back the Toolbox, go to the Window menu again and select Show Tools.

You can hide the Toolbox temporarily — along with everything else but your artwork and menus — by pressing the Tab key. While this feature can be unsettling if you don't know about it (if you hit the Tab key by accident, everything disappears except your graphics!) it's still mighty useful — especially if you're working on a small computer screen. You can work with everything hidden, hit the Tab key when you need to, select the tool or palette item you need, and get back to work unfettered by the things you aren't using! This approach is a lot faster than selecting Show or Hide from the Window menu whenever you want to do something different!

When you pause the mouse pointer over any tool, the name of the tool appears, followed by a letter. Well, no, the letters aren't grades given to the tools for their usefulness; the letters let you know which keys to press if you want quick access to the tools. (For instance, press **P** to get the Pen tool or **T** to get the Type tool.)

Palettes to suit any artist

Illustrator has a ton of palettes. You may think of a palette as something more closely associated with a painter than an Illustrator, but nonetheless, Illustrator has twenty or so of them. As with a painter's palette that holds the paints she's using most, an Illustrator palette provides quick access to the most frequently used commands and features. The contents of palettes are organized according to what they do. The Character palette contains commands to format text, while the Color palette lets you create and change colors. While Illustrator has dozens of palettes, you rarely need to have them all open at once. When entering text, for example, you'd want the Character palette open, but you probably wouldn't need the Gradient palette open, since the Gradient palette only controls gradients.

You open a palette by choosing it as a menu item. Most of these are under the Window menu (such as Window⇨Show Colors) but more are hiding under other menus. To close a palette, click the tiny white box in its upper-left corner.

Fortunately, Illustrator can both *tab* and *dock* palettes to keep them more organized, giving you a wee bit of space in which you can actually draw and edit your artwork. *Tabbing* lets you stack palettes in one area so they overlap like index cards. *Docking* connects the top of one palette to the bottom of another, so that both palettes are visible, but taking up as little space as possible.

By default, Illustrator displays the palettes shown in Figure 1-3. Notice that each set of palettes offers you several tabs. (For instance, the Swatches, Gradient, and Stroke palettes are tabbed together in one set.) Initially, you only see the Styles palette; the Swatches and Brushes palettes are hidden behind the Styles palette. To see either of those palettes, click the tab for the one you want to view.

Figure 1-3:
The Styles, Swatches, and Brushes palettes are tabbed together in one set.

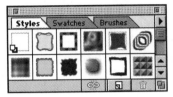

You can combine palettes by any method that you feel works for you. To move a palette from one set to another, click and drag that palette's tab from one set into another — or out by itself (which creates a new set). Illustrator doesn't limit you; you can combine any palette with any set. You can even put all of Illustrator's palettes into one set if you really want to — but we don't advise doing so. The tabs all overlap so you can't tell what's what.

Another way to combine palettes is by *docking* them together, as shown in Figure 1-4. Unlike tabbed palettes, docked palettes are all out there in plain sight; you can see more than one palette in a set at the same time. To dock one palette to another, drag the tab of the first palette to the bottom of the other palette. A dark line appears on the bottom of the second palette when it's in docking position. When you release the mouse button, the first palette docks with the second one.

Figure 1-4:
The Layers palette docked to the Swatches palette, just underneath.

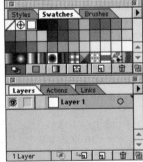

Many Illustrator palettes have their own menus, accessed by clicking the triangle in the upper-right corner of the palette, as shown in Figure 1-5.

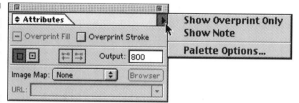

Figures 1-5:
Palettes
also have
their own
menus.

Items in the palettes' pop-up menus relate specifically to each palette. This makes them easy to ignore and easy to figure out — after you master the individual palette.

Menus with the finest cuisine

Illustrator menus are organized fairly well. Some menus are immediately obvious. You find commands having to do with type under the Type menu and commands for viewing your document under the View menu. Other menus are a little less intuitive and only make sense after you start using them. For instance, once you realize that *any one onscreen "thing" in Illustrator is an object,* you discover that items in the Object menu *relate to* objects (see Figure 1-6). Other menus take a little more work and experimentation to understand. For instance, the Filter menu and the Effects menu have many items that appear identical, yet do very different things. Believe it or not, all these menus are arranged to make figuring out and using Illustrator as easy as possible. Honestly. No, *really.* (Stop laughing.)

Figure 1-6:
The Object
menu
contains
items that
deal specifi-
cally with
objects
(what a
concept).

To use an item in a menu, drag down to that item and release. *Something should happen when you do that (no explosions or tsunamis — as far as we* know), depending on which menu item you select. Even the way a menu item appears on a menu can be a handy tipoff — for example, the following characteristics:

✔ **Submenus.** Many of Illustrator's menus have several submenus in them, indicated by a little triangle to the right of the menu item. To access a menu item in a submenu, drag down to the title of the submenu and then over to the item you want to use (see Figure 1-7).

✔ **Keyboard commands.** Most menu items in Illustrator have keyboard shortcuts (key combinations listed at the right) that can activate them.

✔ **More info needed.** An ellipsis (...) indicates that when you click the item, a dialog box appears, requesting additional input from you.

✔ **Unavailable commands.** A grayed-out menu item means Illustrator won't let you do anything with that item just now.

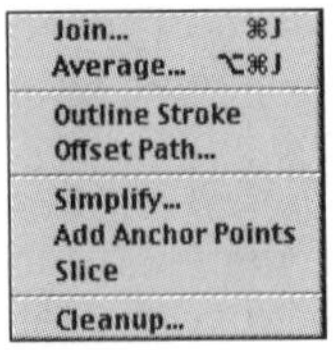

Figure 1-7:
The Path submenu in the Object menu.

Mac and Windows issues spring eternal

Okay, we know some loyalties in this area are fierce — can't we all just get along for a while? Regardless of which system you use or like, you work in Illustrator pretty much the same way. A few little differences are important enough to mention, especially if you jump between the two systems:

✔ **The .ai extension.** Windows users often need *filename extensions* after their filenames or the system refuses to look at the files. The Illustrator file extension is .ai. That's right, just *.ai* (as in *aieee!* but without the *eee*). Most file types (on Windows systems) have three-letter extensions; Illustrator uses two. (Think of the situation this way — they could have used *.ill*.) Windows folks should save Illustrator documents with the **.ai** extension for maximum compatibility with all flavors of Windows. Having the wrong extension on the file can cause problems. If you were to put *.aif* on there, for example, Windows would try to open the file as a sound file, fail, and give you an error message!

Windows users are accustomed to using two- and three-letter filename extensions. Mac users don't have to, but they really should get in the habit of doing so. For starters, that keeps the peace when you send files and lets you instantly identify what the file is. Illustrator lets you save files in an alphabet soup of file formats, such as PDF (.pdf), TIFF (.tif), EPS (.eps), or JPEG (.jpg) Each of these formats has its own unique properties and purposes. When you see .eps on a file, chances are good that it's a graphic created for use in a page-layout program. When you see .gif, you know it's a graphic created for display on the Web. File extensions can tell you a lot about your files even before you open them!

✔ **Right-click versus Ctrl+click.** While in Illustrator, Windows users can right-click most places in Illustrator to display a *context menu* (see Figure 1-8). Mac users, who don't have a right mouse button, press the Ctrl key while clicking the mouse button. Context menus (clever creatures!) are *context-sensitive;* they recognize what the mouse is near when you click and give you options you can apply. . . the following, for example:

- Right-click (or Ctrl+click) the Ruler, and a context menu shows up, offering to help you change the Ruler's unit of measurement.

- Right-click (or Ctrl+click) text, and you can change the font, size, and a slew of other options.

- Click a path, and up come the options related to paths, and so on.

All the items found in context menus appear in the regular menus, too, so you never really *have* to use context menus. They are among those little luxuries (like a steering-wheel-warmer on a cold day) that make Illustrator so nice to use.

Figure 1-8:
A context menu appears when you Ctrl+click (Mac) or right-click (Windows).

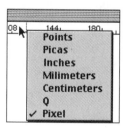

Defining the Document Area

Illustrator uses a traditional art table as metaphor; it's what you see when you create a new file (in fact, you can see it in Figure 1-9). You have the page you are working on (the Artboard), and the table the page sits on (called the Scratch area, but traditional artists will recognize it as a pasteboard). When you create a new document, the Artboard appears as a rectangle in the middle of a white expanse. (The actual size and shape of the Artboard depends on what you enter for height and width when you create a new document.)

Artboard   Scratch area

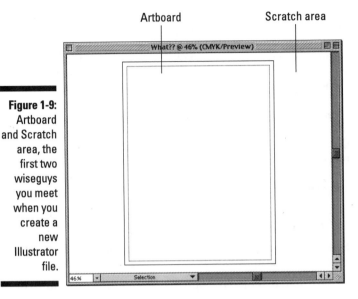

Figure 1-9:
Artboard
and Scratch
area, the
first two
wiseguys
you meet
when you
create a
new
Illustrator
file.

The Artboard serves as a guide to show how large your artwork is (relative to the page size you chose when you created the document). Many people find it easier to create with a specific page size in mind. If you come from a traditional graphic-arts background, you may find the idea of an Artboard and Pasteboard (or Scratch area) reassuring. You can create elements and leave them in the Scratch area, ready for you to grab and add to the artwork you are making on the Artboard. As to how the Artboard affects your art — well, it doesn't. It's only a guide to help you get your bearings. Elements in the Scratch area will still print if you print to large enough paper. If you save your Illustrator artwork as an EPS file to bring it into a page-layout program (or as a GIF to use on the Web), anything in the Scratch area saves with it.

If you don't find the Artboard useful as a guide, you can hide it altogether by choosing View➪Hide Artboard.

For printing a document, you may find the Page Tiling feature a little more significant than the Artboard. Illustrator smartly recognizes the printer that your document is currently selected to print to — and creates a *Page Tile,* a rectangle the size and shape of the largest area the selected printer can print. You can recognize the Page Tiling feature by a thin, dotted line that appears just inside the Artboard if you set page size to the size of your printer paper.

Most printers show a printable area slightly smaller than the page size. Anything outside these guides doesn't print. Even so, remember that this guide is based on *your* printer; what's inside someone else's printable area may not be the same.

Opening Existing Documents

To open any existing Illustrator document, choose File➪Open and then select the document you want (using the Open dialog box shown in Figure 1-10).

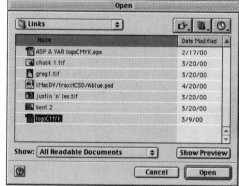

Figure 1-10:
Use the
Open dialog
box to
select the
file you
want to
open.

Another way to open a document is by double-clicking the file itself. If you double-click an Illustrator file when Illustrator isn't running, the program launches for you automatically. (Glad it's not a missile.)

Viewing Illustrator Documents

Illustrator provides versatile options for viewing documents — including controls for zooming, scrolling, and hiding (or showing) certain document features. You can get close up to the smallest areas of your artwork and make changes so minute that they aren't visible to the human eye — but you *feel better* knowing that your graphic is microscopically perfect. Or you can view your document at the actual size it's going to be when it prints, to get a good feel for your artwork's effect in the real world. Or you can view your onscreen objects as their "skeletons" of essential points and paths, with no strokes or colors to distract you from the true essence of your artwork. A view of any phase is available, from points-and-paths to perfect printout. Bottom line: You have to see what you're doing to know what you're doing. Illustrator gives you that capability.

Zooming in and out of artwork

You can view your artwork at actual size (approximately its size when it prints), much larger than that, or much smaller. Changing the zoom amount changes only the image's onscreen appearance — not the image's actual size, the way it prints, or its appearance in another application. Zooming is like using binoculars to watch a neighbor violate the bylaws of the homeowners' association. Those unapproved maple saplings (and the sap who's planting them) don't actually change size; you just zoom in on them from a discreet distance.

The Zoom tool

 The Zoom tool is the magnifying glass in the lower-right corner of the Toolbox. When you click the Zoom tool and move it over the document, a plus sign appears in the center of the magnifying glass. Clicking the Zoom tool makes the details of your artwork appear larger in the document window. You can click until you zoom in to 6400 percent (sixty-four times larger than actual size). Figure 1-11 shows a document viewed at actual size and zoomed in to 400 percent.

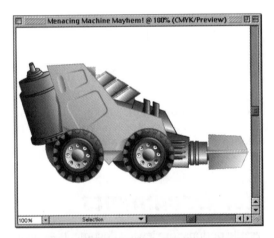

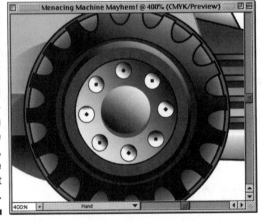

Figure 1-11: Two views of the artwork: actual size and zoomed to 400 percent. If you print while zoomed in, the image still prints at actual size.

The Zoom tool is actually two tools in one. When you hold the Option or Alt key down, the magnifying glass contains a minus sign. Holding down the Option or Alt key and clicking your image with the Zoom tool causes your image to appear smaller. You can zoom out as far as 3.13 percent (where everything is really tiny). Figure 1-12 shows the art from Figure 1-11 as it would look at 25 percent actual size.

Figure 1-12:
The artwork
from Figure
1-11 at 25
percent of
its actual
size.

Speed zoom ahead

Zooming is something Illustrator users do often enough to warrant the multitude of keyboard commands associated with this function. In order of usefulness, the following items represent some of the most useful *speed-zoom* techniques:

- ✔ **Use any tool to Zoom In.** Press ⌘+Space [Ctrl+Space] and the tool you're using changes to the magnifying glass with a plus sign in it. Click the area where you want to zoom in. After you release the keys, the Zoom tool switches back to the tool you were previously using. This shortcut is *really* handy.

- ✔ **Use any tool to Zoom Out.** Press ⌘+Option+Space [Ctrl+Alt+Space], and the tool you're using changes to the magnifying glass with a plus sign in it. Click the image to zoom in. After you release the keys, the Zoom tool switches back to the tool you were previously using. This shortcut is as handy as the temporary Zoom In tool.

- ✔ **Go to Actual Size.** Press ⌘+1 [Ctrl+1] to return to actual size. You can also double-click the Zoom tool to do this.

- ✔ **Go to Fit In Window view.** Press ⌘+0 [Ctrl+0] to zoom to the level at which your page fits into the window. You can also double-click the Hand tool to do this.

✔ **Zoom in and out.** Press ⌘+Plus [Ctrl+Plus] to zoom in one level or ⌘+Minus [Ctrl+Minus] to zoom out one level.

✔ **Activate the Zoom In tool.** Press Z to change to the Zoom In tool. If you actually read to the bottom of this list, geekiness from someone you know is starting to rub off on you. We strongly advise taking a few days off — away from your computer (and from said geek).

Scrolling around your document

You can use the *scroll bars* (those gray stripes along the right and bottom of the document window) to move around your document, but they limit you to moving horizontally or vertically — and only one of those directions at a time. If you're *really* cool (and you know you are), you can use the Hand tool to move around your document in *any* direction.

To use the Hand tool, choose it from the Toolbox. Then click and drag anywhere in the document. The artwork moves in the direction you drag. At first, this action may seem slightly awkward — but power corrupts. After a few minutes of pushing your art around, you never want to go back to those nasty scroll bars.

You can use any tool as the Hand tool. To change a tool into the Hand tool, hold down the spacebar as you click the tool. Then click and drag just as you would with the Hand Tool. Let go of the spacebar, and the tool you were using returns to its original form. This trick works with any tool but the Text tool. (If you try it with that tool, you just type space after space after space.)

Using the Navigator palette

Illustrator's handy Navigator palette (see Figure 1-13) helps you move about your document. If the Navigator palette isn't showing, choose Window➪Show Navigator. The Navigator palette displays your entire document in a tiny window. A red rectangle indicates where the edges of the document window are, relative to the artwork. This rectangle corresponds exactly to the document window. If you change the shape of the document window, the red rectangle changes shape correspondingly.

Don't confuse the view rectangle with the Artboard (represented in the Navigator by a black rectangle around your artwork, even after you choose View➪Hide Artboard).

Drag the red rectangle around in the Navigator, and the part of the image that is inside the rectangle miraculously appears inside the main document window, as if you'd moved it there with the Hand tool. Hold down the ⌘ [Ctrl] key and click and drag inside the Navigator palette to drag out a new view rectangle. When you let go, that area fills the document window, as though you'd used both the Zoom tool and the Hand tool simultaneously.

You can also zoom by dragging the Zoom slider in the lower-right corner of the Navigator palette or by typing a different viewing percentage into the readout box at the lower-left of the palette. In addition to zooming, the Navigator palette is scalable. If the preview you have is too small to provide a useful degree of detail, click and drag the Resize tab in the lower-left corner of the palette. The thumbnail changes scale accordingly.

Figure 1-13:
The Navigator palette, displaying the artwork from Figure 1-11.

The Navigator palette can slow down your system if you have either a slow system to start with or complex artwork. Every time you make a change to your artwork, zoom, or view a different part of your artwork, the Navigator needs to update its thumbnail image. Hiding the palette eliminates the slowdown.

Looking at the guts of your artwork

(Ewww.) Typically, what you see in your document window is pretty much what's going to print (the view in Preview mode). However, what you see isn't what the printer and Illustrator look at. Instead, they see all your Illustrator artwork and objects as a series of outlines, placed images, and text (the view in Outline mode). If you want to view your document in this skeletal form, choose View➪Artwork. Outline mode is a great diagnostic tool; it helps you understand how a document was made. Figure 1-14 shows artwork in both Preview and Outline modes. Outline mode also makes it easier to select objects that are very close together.

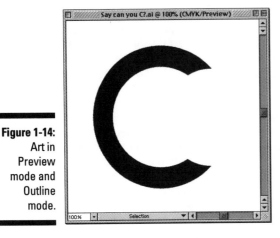
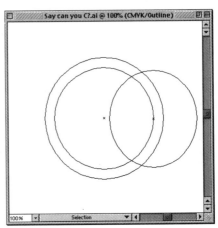

Figure 1-14:
Art in
Preview
mode and
Outline
mode.

Notice that in Preview mode, the artwork appears to be the letter *C*; Outline mode shows the three circles (two white circles on top of a black circle) that create that appearance. Graphics like this can be tricky to work with; if you don't know how the object is made, you may assume (mistakenly, but logically enough) that you actually *have* a C-shaped object instead of three circles. As soon as you start making changes to it as though it were really a C, Illustrator starts acting completely illogical. Jumping into Preview mode lets you see the secret truth behind the graphic, helping you to understand how the graphic was made.

The first three versions of Illustrator didn't let you work in Preview mode. Artists of the time had to envision the art in their minds — or bounce briefly into Preview mode for a peek. (If that kind of thing makes your head throb, be glad you never picked up Illustrator before 1993.)

Saving Illustrator Documents

The instant you accomplish something you like, you should save it. And you should save every few minutes, even if you haven't done something you like, because if you don't, you'll lose all the work and have to recreate it if you crash, accidentally quit, or accidentally shut off the power supply to your computer. Unlike applications such as Microsoft Word or Adobe InDesign, Illustrator has no auto-save feature. Anything you don't save is lost. Just remember that old TLA (three-letter acronym): SOS. It stands for Save Often, Silly! Saving only takes a second, and it saves not only your artwork, but also your time and sanity.

To save a document, choose File⇨Save. If you haven't previously saved the document, the Save As dialog box (shown in Figure 1-15) appears; reward its promptness by naming your file something appropriate, witty, and deep. Or type something hurried-but-meaningful like **gasdfoiu** or **jkl23** so you can challenge yourself later to puzzle out what that @#*! document is. (Just kidding.)

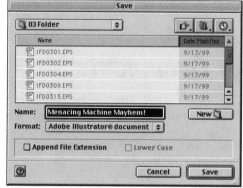

Figure 1-15:
The Save dialog box, in which you name your masterpiece.

If you've already saved your document, the Save command updates the existing file. If you're not sure whether you previously saved, look at the title bar. If it says Untitled-1, then you *probably* haven't saved (only a creepy sense of humor would pick *Untitled 1* as a title just to befuddle the rest of us).

Changing Your Mind

One of Illustrator's most powerful features may be strikingly familiar: the Edit⇨Undo command that gives you a way to take back the goof you just made. But that's so *common* these days; in Illustrator, Edit⇨Undo is a *multiple undo* — it makes you the Master of Time! You can take your artwork back through time, step by step, all the way to when you first opened the document! If you make a mistake (or several), just select Edit⇨Undo (or type ⌘/Ctrl+Z) repeatedly, until you get back to the way things were before they went so wrong. To redo the last thing you undid, select Edit⇨Redo or press ⌘/Ctrl+Shift+Z. (A time machine with a reverse gear — way cool.)

Imagine creating with wild abandon — moving points, changing colors and line thicknesses, running filters — because in Illustrator, you can change your mind after the fact. Think of what you could obliterate from time — the misplaced stroke that looks like a bad tattoo, the missed goal that kept your team from the playoffs, the blind date that went so horribly wrong — well, okay, it only works in Illustrator. At least it works somewhere.

You can take a graphic back to the way it was when you first opened it. Only one exception applies: If you close a file and then open it again, you can't go back to anything you did before you closed the file. You can, however, save a file and then go back to things that happened before you saved it — if you left the file open *after* you saved it! In that case, the only thing that can't be undone is the Save command, meaning you still have a file on your hard drive that exists exactly as it did when you hit Save. This method can be useful if you have to create multiple revisions of the same document.

Printing Illustrator Documents

If you're computer is hooked up or networked to a printer, you can print just about anything you create in Illustrator. Before you print, however, make sure your artwork is within the Page Tiling boundaries (that dotted gray rectangle that shows up when you select View⇨Page Tiling). Only items within these boundaries print. The dotted lines on the page indicate the trim area; if your image is outside the dotted lines, it won't print.

To print your artwork, choose File⇨Print. The Print dialog box appears. Click OK; soon a sheet of paper emerges from your printer *with your artwork on it.*

Closing Documents and Quitting Illustrator

To close an Illustrator document, choose File⇨Close. The document closes without a fuss. If you haven't saved before closing, a dialog box appears, asking whether you want to save changes made to your artwork. To quit Illustrator, choose File⇨Quit. If you haven't saved before quitting, a dialog box appears and asks whether you want to save your changes. (Consistent good manners — aren't they wonderful?)

Chapter 2

Following the Righteous Path

*B*eing new to Illustrator typically means being new to paths. Paths are the heart and soul of Illustrator — its primary way to create graphics. Nearly all computer-generated graphics are either pixel-based or path-based (a.k.a. *vector*-based — more on that later). Getting a firm grip on the differences between the two graphics types can help you create graphics of *any* type.

Pixel-based images (created in Adobe Photoshop, Corel Painter, as well as by scanners and digital cameras and others) use a fixed grid of tiny colored squares (kind of like the tiniest mosaic tile) to create images on your screen. Your computer monitor's *resolution* is a measure of how detailed an onscreen image can be, based on how many pixels the screen can provide per square inch. To give you some idea of how small these pixels are, every square inch of the average monitor contains 5184 of them! Even so, monitors have a relatively low resolution; they don't use very many pixels per inch compared to high-resolution printing — which can require 90,000 pixels in a square inch — or more!

In spite of their astonishing quantity, pixels work just like mosaic tiles (or like the dots in a Seurat painting). Because images are a bit less distinct from farther away, putting squares of different colors together results in a continuous picture when seen from a distance; the individual squares are (in effect) invisible. The more squares used to create a square inch of the image (that is, the higher the resolution), the more continuous and realistic the picture is.

In addition to their staggeringly small size, the range of colors a pixel can have is equally astonishing. A single pixel can display only one color at a time, but that color can be any of 16.7 million!

Path-based (often called *vector-based*) graphics are much simpler — and in some ways, easier to comprehend — than their pixel-based cousins. Think of an image in a coloring book: you have a shape defined by a line. Inside the line you can add color. (But don't color *outside* the lines!) Using this simple method of shapes and color, you can create just about any picture you can imagine. That is basically the bottom line of path-based images. Just shapes filled with color, or not. In Illustrator, the shapes can be any size and complexity, and the lines can be as thick or as thin as you want to make them. They can even be invisible. And the shapes can be filled with an astonishing variety of colors, even patterns and gradients (even pixel-based images!), but the same basic coloring-book principle still applies. The coloring-book principle may seem very limited, but you'll be astonished at the things you can do with this idea in Illustrator!

Whether Paths or Pixels Are Better

It depends. (How's that for a definitive statement?) The conclusion depends on some other factors. Paths are better for some things and pixels for others, and each approach has its strengths. The key to determining whether to use paths (which Illustrator creates) or pixels (from a program such as Photoshop) is to be familiar with the capabilities of each method. Figure 2-1 shows path-based artwork next to pixel-based artwork.

Figure 2-1:
Path-based artwork (left) and pixel-based artwork (right).

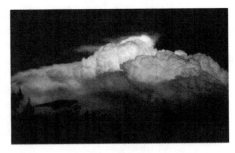

For example, paths are generally better for type, logos, and precision graphics. Pixels are generally better for photographs, complex backgrounds, textures, and simulated lighting effects. Quite often, however, the proper *combination* of paths and pixels results in the best final illustration possible. Determining what combination to use is a lot easier when you're hip to the advantages and drawbacks of both paths and pixels.

Paths: The ultimate flexibility in graphics

Paths are used to define shapes. Any shape, really, from a simple square or circle to the shape of South America. Because paths are the *outline* of these shapes, and not the shapes themselves, they take up very little storage space. A path-based square that measures 15 feet by 15 feet takes up no more room in your computer than a 1-inch-by-1-inch path-based square. (Believe it or not.)

How is this accomplished? Through math, mostly. No, no, don't skip ahead; we won't rattle off equations or lapse into binomial-speak (even if we knew for sure what binomials are). Looking at how Illustrator draws a square can help you make sense of all this information. To Illustrator, a square is simply a set of four locations — one for each of four points (the corners) — as well as any Fill or Stroke information (what color the square is). So *where* the points are doesn't matter; what matters is that you've got four of 'em and that they make a square when you connect the dots.

Okay, what about complex outlines? Glad you asked. (You *did* ask, didn't you?) A semiaccurate representation of South America with a limited amount of detail would probably need dozens of points to define the shape of the continent. In this case, there's nary a straight line anywhere — from point to point, it's nothing but curved lines. And because they need more info to describe them, those curved lines take up about twice as much disk space as straight lines. Even so, a tiny little 1-inch-high illustration of South America could be enlarged to 15 feet tall and still have *exactly the same file size* because the illustration still has *exactly the same number of points*. Only the math that determines the location of those points has been changed to put them farther apart.

Figure 2-2 shows South America next to a square that physically appears to be about three times as large as South America (well, three times as large as the illustration of South America). Which one is bigger in terms of file size? South America is. It has more detail and, therefore, more points.

What's so cool about paths is something we previously alluded to: You can make paths much larger or smaller in physical dimensions without increasing the file size or losing image quality. You can rotate a path, flip it (which Illustrator calls *reflecting*), skew it (which Illustrator calls *shearing*), or distort it in a number of ways without changing the file size or detail. (Here's the secret: *All you're really changing is the location of the points.*) This near-effortless scalability makes Illustrator a perfect choice for creating logos that must appear not only on tiny business cards, letterhead, Web pages, and various documents, but also as banners, billboards, or signs.

Figure 2-2:
Although the South America shape looks smaller than the square, the South America shape is actually a larger Illustrator file because more points are used to define the continent's shape.

Pixels: Detail and realism to spare

Pixel-based images tend to be used for photorealistic illustration because photorealism is virtually impossible to create in a path-based image. Digitized photographs represent about 75 percent of the pixel-based images in use today. Most of the rest are Web graphics and other onscreen images.

Think of it this way: Even a low-resolution pixel-based image can have 5,184 squares of color per square inch, each of which can be any of 16.7 million different colors. In a path-based image, every different color (with a few exceptions) must be defined by a separate path. To equal the number of different colors you can create in a pixel-based image, you'd have to draw so many paths that . . . well, imagine covering a basketball with confetti, one piece at a time. For this reason, pixel-based images are the hands-down choice over path-based graphics if you're creating incredibly detailed images — or recreating the continuous tones found in nature, such as the smooth darkening of the skin as you follow the line from someone's cheek to the shadow under the chin. To portray realistically in Illustrator all the colors you find in someone's face, you'd have to draw so many paths that . . . well, this time imagine covering a mannequin's face with confetti, one piece at a time. . . .

On the other hand, paths have it all over pixels if you want to maintain the quality of a graphic image despite enlarging and reducing its size. Think what you'd have to do to increase the size of artwork made with mosaic tiles. You'd have to increase the number of tiles, unless somehow you could enlarge the tiles that were already there. But if you did that, then the tiles would be obvious from a distance. Same deal with pixel images. You have to add more tiles (pixels) or you see the pixels you already have showing up onscreen as big squares. And when you add pixels, you make the file size larger while reducing the quality (worst of both worlds) because you can't get away with just tossing in any old pixels. An artisan might be able to add tiles to her mosaic and preserve its image quality, but the computer is just guessing about what tiles to add. Though it does a pretty good job, there is just no way to enlarge a pixel-based image without reducing the quality, as shown in Figure 2-3. Likewise, shrinking the image means throwing away pixels — which degrades the image because it then has fewer pixels available for showing detail.

An image with thousands of pixels can be displayed onscreen or printed much larger with high quality than an image with only 900 pixels. Of course, all those pixels take up a whole lot more storage space on your hard drive. Path-based images have no such limitations, however.

How Paths and Pixels Compare

This is it — the definitive answer you've been looking for: Pixels let you create graphics that are very complex, such as photography. Their file sizes are large, but smaller than if you tried to create the same quality of graphic using paths. Pixel-based graphics that need to print or display at large sizes require larger file sizes than the same graphics printed or displayed at smaller sizes. Path-based graphics let you create fairly simple graphics, and their file sizes are typically much smaller than their pixel-based counterparts. A path-based graphic can be displayed or printed at any size, from microscopic to billboard, without any change in file size, yet always at maximum quality.

A comparison of path and pixel documents

The best way to show advantages of each format is to take a look at the same graphic created with both paths and pixels. The illustration, shown in Figure 2-4, is a logo created with paths. It's the logo for a country to use on all of its manu-factured goods, as well as on signs, brochures, and other places.

One thing you notice right away is that the logo is text-heavy. Paths tend to represent text fairly well. A big advantage in creating this logo with paths is its scalability; you can enlarge or reduce it to virtually any size without changing the image quality. Compare Figure 2-5, which shows a pixel-based version of the logo. (Looks like a clone, doesn't it? But looks can be deceiving . . . .)

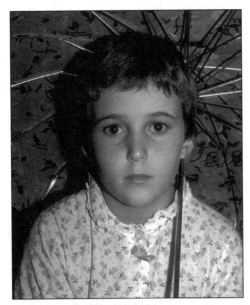

Original

Reduced to 900 pixels

Figure 2-3:
The effects
of reducing
and
enlarging
the image.

Re-enlarged

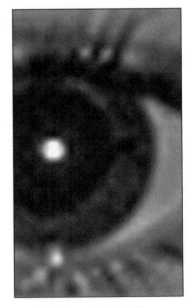

Enlarged to 2000%

Figure 2-4:
A logo for Oddland, created with paths and weighing in at 188K.

Figure 2-5:
The same Oddland logo we know and love, created with pixels.

If you use a high enough resolution, the pixel-based logo looks as good — but its file size is 1.2 MB (almost 10 times the size of the path-based logo). Maybe that isn't a problem if you have a hard drive the size of New Jersey, but watch what happens when you change the size of the logo. If you enlarge the path-based version, you get the image on the left in Figure 2-6.

Figure 2-6:
A section
of the
Oddland
logo,
enlarged to
five times its
original size.

All we had room for in Figure 2-6 was a smidgen of the logo — the whole thing would be over 20 inches square — but note how the edges remain perfectly smooth and crisp in the path-based version. And the file size is still only 188K! On the other hand, if you enlarge the pixel-based version, you get the image on the right. The same bit of the pixel-based version is having a *really* bad hair day. Worse, the whole logo at this size would become the Giant File That Ate New Jersey — over 25 MB in size — more than 100 times the file size of the path version!

Just for laughs, consider what happens when you try to use Illustrator to create photographic reality. Figure 2-7 is a photograph of a little girl, one of the residents of Oddland. This document was created entirely with pixels.

The path-based illustration is a different matter entirely. To recreate this image as paths, it was necessary to trace the pixels with Adobe Streamline (software that recreates pixels as paths that can be used in Illustrator). A graphic like this would take weeks to create in Illustrator by hand. As Figure 2-8 shows, paths are hard-pressed to achieve the look of the pixel-based original, so they give up in despair.

Figure 2-7:
This young lady looks good in all pixels. In the close-up of her left eye (enlarged 500 percent) you start to see blurring, but only when you get this close.

 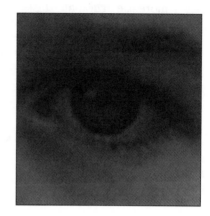

Figure 2-8:
Oddland's young resident as a path-based document (trying miserably to match the pixel-based detail) and the same enlargement of the left eye.

The big limitations and upcoming solutions

From the preceding figures, you can probably see some limitations of both pixels and paths. Depending on the type of artwork, detail is lost if you use the "wrong material" to create images. Fine detail can be present in pixel-based images only at very high resolutions (many, many pixels) and in path-based images only with an unreasonably large number of paths.

As computer processing power increases, however, paths are likely to find more use in graphics tasks that used to be pixels-only affairs. For instance, new technologies enable paths to contain smooth, flowing gradations (such as Illustrator's Gradient Mesh). Although the sheer number of paths needed to create the continuous tones of photographs is prohibitive — even today — look for that capability to emerge as computers get faster and can deal more quickly with larger numbers of paths.

When to use paths and when to use pixels

Just this once, it's okay to put your thumbs on the table — rules-of-thumb, that is. Table 2-1 shows some attributes that are best created with paths, and some that are best created with pixels.

Table 2-1	What Paths and Pixels Are Especially Good For
Use Paths if Your Artwork Contains	*Use Pixels if Your Artwork Contains*
Large amounts of type	Photographs
Geometric shapes	Complex textures
Thin lines	Soft-edged details

Often, for best results, you may have to combine pixels with paths (or vectors) in the same artwork. Fortunately, Illustrator is a perfect tool for doing that. The File➪Place command allows you to bring pixel-based artwork into Illustrator to combine it with vector-based artwork. See Chapter 18 for complete details.

Paths and the PostScript Language

The PostScript printing language, present on many printers, uses paths to print smooth-edged images. This happy circumstance is one reason that Illustrator can make such good-looking artwork; most printers are designed specifically for printing out path-based images.

Dot-matrix printers of the '80s gave way to laser printers and inkjets, and with them came a dramatic increase in speed (not to mention blessed quiet). When you add PostScript to the mix, the printing process is even faster.

Which is faster — a square or a square?

For basic shapes, path-based artwork prints much faster than pixel-based art-work. For instance, a 5-inch-by-5-inch path-based square prints in a fraction of the time it takes to print the same pixel-based square. Why? The printer only needs the four corner locations for the path-based square. For the pixel-based square, the printer needs to see each and every pixel that's on the way to the printer (imagine counting sand grains with tweezers, really *fast . . .*).

PostScript: The evolution of Bézier curves

The PostScript language handles paths in much the same way Illustrator does — using points that are connected by lines. It's almost identical to the connect-the-dots games you did as a kid. Instead of processing each pixel, the PostScript code says, "Connect this point to that point, that point to this one over here, and so on." All it takes is another bit of code to say, "Now fill that shape with solid red" or some other color.

This approach makes a great deal of sense for objects with flat sides, but curves are another matter entirely. You'd need to connect a nigh-infinite number of dots to make a perfect curve. Here's where PostScript (and Illustrator) get really clever. Instead of using straight lines between points, PostScript uses curves between points: *Bézier curves*, named after their cre-ator, world-famous mathematician Pierre Bézier (pronounced bezzy-*ay*).

The idea behind Bézier curves is that you need no more than four points to define any curved line: One point to say where the path begins, one point to say where the path ends, and two *control points* in between. Where you put each control point (relative to the end points) determines how much the line curves — and in what direction — on its way to meet the end point.

Fortunately, Illustrator spares you and me the headache of having to work out the math; you have a little magnet-like handle onscreen (the *Bézier con-trol point*) that changes the direction of the curve. Okay, actually *using* it may be far from intuitive, but it does give Illustrator the capability to generate complex shapes with curves — using the PostScript language, no less.

What's my vector, Victor?

You often hear the words *vector graphics* used to describe the kind of art cre-ated in Illustrator. According to *Webster's Unabridged Dictionary* (2nd Edition), a *vector* in mathematics is "a quantity, such as a force or velocity, having direction and magnitude" and "a line representing such a quantity, drawn from its point of origin to its final position." In artists' terms, a *vector* is a line of a specific size drawn in a specific place. So vector graphics are simply graphics made with lines! At bottom, every Illustrator graphic is just a bunch of lines. Those lines may have other information attached to them (such as color and width), but no matter how fancy they get, underneath they're still just lines.

So why not call such graphics line art? Unfortunately, that term was already taken. Line art is a specific type of pixel-based graphic. We could call such illustrations Illustrator illustrations, but that term is a little alliterative (is there an echo in here?) and not quite accurate. You can also create vector graphics in CorelDRAW! and Macromedia Freehand. So this book follows convention, using *vector graphics* to describe the kind of graphics you create in Illustrator. Pretty soon you'll be doing the same!

Gray's Anatomy of a Path

Not to put too fine a point on it, paths can be a thorn in your side while you're getting up to speed with Illustrator. At first, points may seem a necessary evil (with "evil" the key word here) — but the more you know about how they're constructed, the easier for you to modify them. Eventually you may even stop cursing at your poor, defenseless monitor.

In Illustrator, it's polite to point

Each path consists of a series of points. These are called *anchor points* because they anchor the path. Another type of point is called a *direction point* (a point that determines the direction and distance of a curve), but when most people refer to a "point" in Illustrator, they mean an anchor point. It only appears in a curved path. A path has at least two anchor points to determine where it starts and where it ends. Figure 2-9 shows a path and the locations of its anchor points.

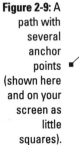

Figure 2-9: A path with several anchor points (shown here and on your screen as little squares).

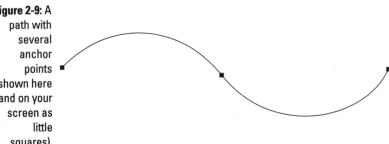

You can handle the truth

For basic shapes with straight lines, points are all that paths need. But as soon as you want curves on a path, you need *direction points* (also known as *handles* among Illustrator insiders). Direction points are connected to anchor points by *direction lines.* They control how a path curves. Figure 2-10 shows the same path, but with direction points showing.

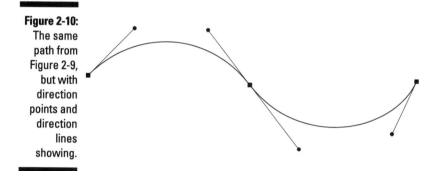

Figure 2-10: The same path from Figure 2-9, but with direction points and direction lines showing.

Handles work like magnets for the paths that extend from points. The farther you drag a handle away from the path, the more that path curves toward the handle. Figure 2-11 shows a few variations of a path between two points. In each of these variations, only the handle on the left has been moved.

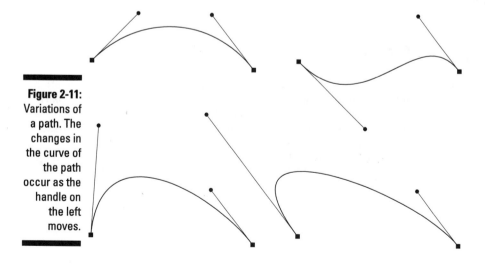

Figure 2-11: Variations of a path. The changes in the curve of the path occur as the handle on the left moves.

You can move the handles of paths by using the Direct Selection tool (the hollow arrow at the top of the Toolbox). Click the curve you want to adjust to select it. This action makes the direction points visible. Direction points are invisible unless the curve is selected with the Direct Selection tool. Once the direction point is visible, click and drag the handle. Figure 2-12 shows a circle with handles showing. Even basic Illustrator shapes use handles to create curves.

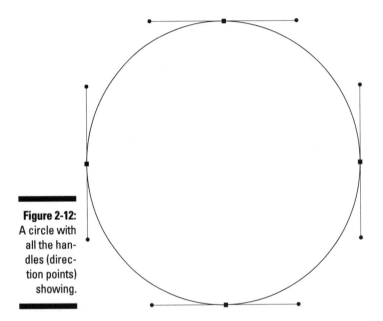

Figure 2-12:
A circle with all the handles (direction points) showing.

Drawing Basics

Illustrator has a full arsenal of drawing tools, ready to take on any illustration task imaginable. But with this power comes a *wee* bit of difficulty. Well, okay, a *fair* bit of difficulty. Illustrator's drawing tools (the Pen in particular) can be a hassle to use at first. However, once you nail the concept of paths (discussed in the previous section) and follow a few simple rules, you can be using Illustrator's tools just as they were meant to be used — in next to no time. (Check out Part II for a guided tour.)

Chapter 3

Doing Everyday Things with Illustrator

The hard part for new users of Illustrator is figuring out just what it does. The program is so vast and has so many capabilities that aren't immediately obvious or self-explanatory. Even seasoned Illustrator veterans often discover that they've been using many convoluted steps to accomplish something they could have done with a single hidden command. This chapter is a tell-all exposé of everything that you can do in Illustrator. At least, as tell-all as you can get in a single chapter. You'd need an entire book to cover such a complex program! But by the end of this chapter, you should have a good overview of the features of Illustrator and know where to look to find the things you need to get the job done.

Picking Up Stuff and Moving It Around

Any time you want to do something to an Illustrator object, you must select it first. After you get the whole select-then-do thought lodged in your brain, many of Illustrator's functions come to you much more easily.

Illustrator has a wide variety of ways to select things, including three tools, a bunch of keyboard commands, and several menu items. Fortunately, even if you only know one or two of these methods, you can be off and running with

Illustrator selections in no time, just like a pro. Using the selection tools enables you to select virtually anything in your document.

Chapter 6 details the process of selecting paths and objects. In this chapter, you find all the ways of selecting, from tools and commands to menu items.

Discovering Selection tools

Illustrator has five Selection tools. You choose a tool according to the type of object(s) you want to select. The Selection tools are as follows (we love a parade):

✔ **Selection tool.** This solid black arrow is *the* regular Selection tool. The Selection tool is for selecting entire paths or groups by clicking them or dragging around them. If the object you click or drag around is part of a group, all the paths and objects in that group are selected as well. The Selection tool, found at the top left of the Toolbox, is plain but powerful.

✔ **Direct Selection tool.** Also known as the hollow arrow, the Direct Selection tool is for selecting portions of paths — single points or segments — by clicking or dragging said points or segments. You can also use the Direct Selection tool to select other objects, such as placed images or text. The Direct Selection tool, found at the top right of the Toolbox, selects only the portions of the path that you click or drag.

✔ **Group Selection tool.** This tool looks like a hollow arrow with a "+" beside it. It selects "up" through paths and groups. It's a little odd but here's what happens: The first click selects the entire path you click. Click the selected path again and you select the group that the first path is in. If you keep clicking, you continue to select groups of groups, all containing the group that the first group is in. The Group Selection tool shares a tool slot with the Direct Selection tool. Just click and hold on the Direct Selection tool, and the Group Selection will spring out from behind it.

✔ **Lasso tool.** This tool selects any objects that are partially touched by (or included within) the area you drag. The Lasso tool is the flexible version of the Selection tool. You can find the Lasso tool in the upper left of the Toolbox, directly beneath the Selection tool.

✔ **Direct Lasso tool.** This tool looks like an anemic loop of string — until you start using it to select points and path segments within an area you designate by dragging the mouse pointer. The Direct Lasso tool is a go-anywhere version of the Direct Selection tool.

Illustrator provides two primary ways of using the Selection, Direct Selection, and Group Selection tools: either by clicking-and-releasing the object or group you want to select, or by dragging a marquee around the objects you want to select. *Marquee* is techno-speak for the dotted line that's created when you drag with these tools (and all this time you thought it had to do with movie theaters).

You can tell when an object is selected in Illustrator: Any selected object shows its "guts" onscreen — the path used to create the object, as well as any points needed to create the path. Text and placed images also show points (and sometimes paths) when they're highlighted, even though they aren't made up of paths and points (weird, isn't it?). Figure 3-1 shows a pair of "star" illustrations; the star on the left is unselected and the one on the right is selected.

Figure 3-1:
The object on the left is unselected; the object on the right is selected. Note the points and paths that appear on a selected object.

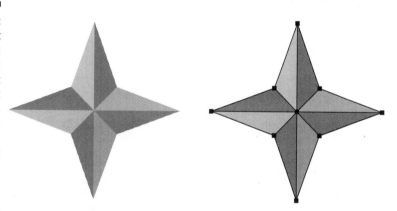

Once an object is selected, you can do any number of things to it, such as change its color, move it, transform it, or even delete it. You may want to consider which tool you use to make the selection. One key difference between the arrow-shaped selection tools and the lasso selection tools is that the arrow tools also *move* objects that are selected; the Lasso tools do not. If you're attempting to use an arrow tool to drag a marquee around an object and happen to click the object first, you move the object instead of selecting it. No marquee appears.

Moving and transforming objects

To move a selected object (or objects), just follow these steps:

1. **Select the object you want to move, using one of the Selection tools.**

2. **Using the Selection tool or the Direct Selection tool, click and drag the selected object to the position you want to move it to.**

Using the Selection or Direct Selection tools to click and drag an object that is already selected doesn't add to the selection or release the selection, but this action does allow you to move what is currently selected.

3. Release the mouse button after the object is in position.

The object is all settled in at its new location.

Instead of dragging with the mouse, you can use the arrow keys to "nudge" anything that is selected a little bit at a time. This trick works no matter what tool you have selected in the Toolbox!

 Illustrator power-users call the other things you can do to an object transforming it. These actions include rotating, resizing, reflecting, and skewing objects. Illustrator puts all these transformation tools together in the middle of the Toolbox. Regardless of which transformation tool you use, the process, shown in Figure 3-2, is much the same as for moving objects. Just follow these steps:

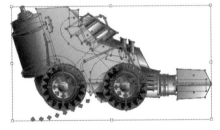

Figure 3-2:
Rotating an
object.

1. **Select the object you want to transform using one of the Selection tools.**

2. **Choose the Rotate tool (or any transformation tool) from the Toolbox.**

3. **Click the selected object and drag.**

As you drag, the outlines of the object show how the object will be transformed after you release the mouse button.

4. **Release the mouse button when the object's preview appears the way you want to change the object.**

As soon as you release the mouse, the object is transformed.

Distorting paths

Moving and transforming paths makes them look different, but you can tell that the moved or transformed path is pretty much the original path in a different position, at a different angle, or maybe at a different size. Distorting paths, however, can make them look drastically different from the way they look originally.

Illustrator provides a number of different ways that paths can be distorted, but the majority of these fall into the category of filter-based distortions. These distortions, found under the Filter➪Distort menu, can create all sorts of interesting (and some downright ugly) effects. Figure 3-3 shows how an innocent path can become grossly distorted in a number of ways by using some of the different distortion Effects.

Figure 3-3:
The original path (left) is (to the right) Punked, Scribbled, Zig-Zagged, and Roughened.

The Distortion Filters are fun to experiment with, because there are no "right" settings for them, they produce immediate and profound changes to your artwork, and they all have *previews* which show you what is going to happen to your artwork before you make any permanent change to it.

To use a Distortion Filter, follow these steps:

1. **Select your artwork using any Selection tool.**

2. **Choose Filter➪Distort➪Punk & Bloat (or any of the other Distort filters).**

   A dialog box opens, showing a Distort filter that has a Preview checkbox. Put a check mark in this box to make the filter show you what it is going to do to your artwork.

3. **Using the slider (a little triangle under a straight line), set the amount of the distortion.**

   Drag the slider to the left; watch what happens to the artwork. Drag it to the right and look again.

4. When you get something you like, click OK.

If the filter produces no pleasurable results, click Cancel to exit the filter without changing your artwork.

For more information on distortions and other ways to mess up (er, _enhance_) your artwork, see Chapter 12.

Organizing Objects

Illustrator provides many tools to help you organize your artwork. You can move objects above or behind each other, group objects together, and distribute objects to layers for heavy-duty organization.

To move an object behind all the other objects in a document, as shown in Figure 3-4, follow these steps:

Figure 3-4:
Moving an
object
behind other
objects.

1. Use any selection tool to select the object you want to move behind another object.

2. Choose Object⇨Arrange⇨Send to Back.

The selected object moves behind all the other objects in the document.

Selecting Object⇨Arrange⇨Bring to Front moves the selected object in front of all the objects in the document.

This procedure is the basic movement of objects back and forth in a document. You can also _group_ a set of objects so they always stay together (and are all selected at once, all the time). To group a series of objects, follow these steps:

1. Select the objects you want to group together.

To select more than one object, either drag a marquee around the objects, or hold down the Shift key and click each of the objects you want to include in the group.

2. Choose Object⇨Group.

The objects are grouped together. The next time you click any one of them with the Selection tool, all of them are selected.

You can group two or more groups together to form a bigger group, and you can select paths along with a group (or several groups) and create a group out of them.

The next step up from grouping is putting related paths and objects in *layers*. Using layers is like placing your artwork into separate sheets of clear plastic. A single layer can have as many pieces of artwork on it as you want. You can select all the pieces of artwork in a layer at once. You can lock the layer to keep them from being selected while they still remain visible. You can hide a layer (and everything on it) to get rid of artwork as if you had deleted it, but still have the option of bringing it back whenever you want. Layers are created, selected, and hidden (and that's just for starters!) using the Layers palette shown in Figure 3-5.

Figure 3-5:
The Layers
palette.

You can do all sorts of amazing things by organizing your artwork into layers, so we devote a big section specifically to layers in Chapter 11.

Using the Fun Stuff

Have you ever looked at an illustration and just scratched your head and thought, "How did they do *that?*" Here's a secret. Chances are, it wasn't that hard. There are a slew of features in Illustrator that let you do really cool things with little difficulty. The only catch to them is that you have to be able to run before you can walk. In Illustrator, this means being able to create simple shapes, color them, and move them in front of or behind one another (covered in Chapters 4, 5, and 6).

Once you've got those things down, you are ready to move on to the fun stuff! You'll be amazed at the things you can do with a simple command or two.

Transparency

When you draw a shape in Illustrator that is filled with a solid color or a gradient, the shape covers up any objects beneath it. You can move the object behind other objects in the document by selecting it with the Selection tool and using Object⇨Arrange⇨Send to Back, but you can't see *through* that shape to the objects behind it.

Transparency breaks those rules by enabling you to fade an object away (from 0%, or completely transparent, to 100% or completely opaque, or any degree in between) to reveal the objects hidden beneath it. Figure 3-6 shows this basic transparency at work with a partially transparent ellipse appearing above a logo.

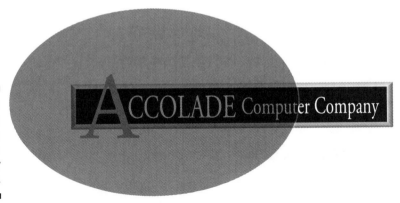

Figure 3-6:
The ellipse on top of the logo is set to be partially transparent.

Transparency, in its most complex form, can be used to see more through one part of a shape than through another part or to blend the colors of a shape with the colors beneath it in strange and interesting ways. Chapter 10 covers transparency in depth.

Blends

Way back in the '90s, *morphing* was all the rage in movies, TV shows, and commercials. No, it wasn't a funny dance to a Garth Brooks tune. Morphing averaged two images together in a series of steps so that the first image appeared to be magically turning into the second. Usually it was a human turning into a wolf, or some other exciting animal. Illustrator lets you use a similar technique called *blending* to transform one object into another in as many steps as you want.

Blending lets objects change color, shape and size over distance, resulting in some truly exciting effects. Illustrator's blends are "live," meaning that you can blend between objects, and still edit them after you create the blend. The objects in between change automatically to match the changes you make to the original objects. This allows you to tweak the way the blend looks without having to start over. Figure 3-7 represents a blend occurring between a small black circle and a larger gray triangle. Only rightmost and leftmost objects were created by hand. the other objects are an average of the two created by the Blend tool. Blends are covered in a more detail in Chapter 12.

Figure 3-7:
A blend
between
two objects.

Masks

An Illustrator *mask* is a path used to hide objects outside itself. For instance, you can mask out everything in an Illustrator screen but one little area, so only that area shows. Creating an Illustrator mask is quite simple, as shown in Figure 3-8. Just complete the following steps:

Figure 3-8:
Masking
artwork.

1. **Create a path to use as a mask on top of some other art.**

   The fill and stroke of the path don't matter because the path itself becomes invisible, along with anything outside the path.

The art beneath the mask can be as complex and have as many parts as you want. The top path masks all paths beneath it. You can use any tool to create this path (such as the Pen, Pencil, or Rectangle).

2. **Using any of the selection tools, select both the path you just created and the object(s) you want to mask.**

3. **Choose Object⇨Mask⇨Make.**

Anything selected that is outside the masking path is hidden, and the masking path itself becomes invisible. Nothing is actually deleted when you make a mask; it is just hidden. You can restore your artwork to its unmasked state by selecting Object⇨Mask⇨Release.

Compound Paths

Compound paths join two or more paths together in such a way that one path makes part of another invisible. Compound Paths sound complicated, but really, if you've ever typed anything in any computer program, you've been using them all along without knowing — many letters are really compound paths! Any letter that has a hole in it (such as *B* or *O*) is a compound path; If you want to place text over something else and see things through the holes in the text, use compound paths as demonstrated in Figure 3-9.

Figure 3-9: A compound path laid over a piece of background art (which is visible through the two round holes).

The figure-8 is a single compound path, made up of three paths. The two paths in the middle are *holes* — areas made transparent so you can see the background artwork through them.

As you may imagine, text characters have lots of holes in them — so they're all compound paths. A typical character such as a lowercase *a* is made up of two paths; the "hole" in the middle is one of those paths. So if you want to magically transform a bit of text into a graphic object made of paths, select the text with a selection tool and then choose Type⇨Create Outlines. Shazam! The text changes from a text object into a series of compound paths (which you can then edit as you edit any other path).

You can make any number of overlapping paths into a compound path by selecting them and choosing Object⇨Compound Path⇨Make. If you want to turn the compound path back into two (or more) individual paths, select the compound path and choose Object⇨Compound Path⇨Release. Figure 3-10 shows what happens when you release compound paths that were originally text objects. When you release the compound paths, the hollow part of the letter fills in, because the purpose of the compound path in the letter is to make those hollow parts of the letter transparent.

Figure 3-10:
Text as text (left), as compound paths (middle), and as compound paths after release (right).

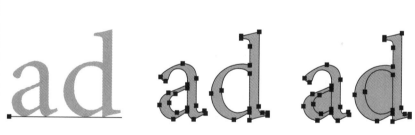

Compound paths work best when you keep things simple. If you stack too many objects on top of each other and try to make a compound path, holes may appear where you didn't expect them. But if you try to keep things to a minimum (only use a few objects, and try not to have more than two objects overlapping in any one place) you'll get splendid results from Compound Paths.

Entering the Wide World of the Web

Illustrator is a Web-happy application. Anything you create in Illustrator can make an appearance on the Web in some form or another. Illustrator gives you mighty powers to create both vector-based and pixel-based images for use on the Web.

We devote an entire chapter (Chapter 17) to the Web because — mark our words — one day it's gonna be big. (Oh. Right. It is already. Sonofagun.) Illustrator does all sorts of Web-specific tasks — such as creating animations, optimizing pixel-based images, and providing a preview of how your artwork looks when viewed in a Web browser.

The following is a laundry list of Web-happy things you can do with Illustrator at no extra charge:

- **Create images without resolution headaches.** When you use a pixel-based graphics program, you must continually worry about whether your graphics have enough resolution to display with the quality you want. In Illustrator, you can always create Web graphics with optimum quality because you decide on the resolution after you complete the image, instead of when you start creating it.

- **Optimize artwork as pixel-based images.** You can save your art as JPEG, GIF, or PNG images, using the Save for Web command to preview how various color reductions and compressions affect the artwork.

- **Export artwork as Flash or SVG vector graphics.** Flash and SVG are new technologies that allow you to display Vector (path-based) graphics on the Web. Before Flash and SVG, only pixel-based artwork could be displayed. Vector graphics on the Web are smaller and better looking than their pixel-based counterparts.

- **Preview artwork as pixel-based graphics.** If you plan to save your artwork as GIF, JPEG, or PNG, you can turn on the Pixel Preview mode while you create it. This makes Illustrator show you your artwork as close as possible to how it will look after it is on the Web. With this mode turned off, the artwork displays as close as possible to how it will look in print.

For more information on any of these topics, see Chapter 17.

Saving the World

Well, maybe saving the world is a little bit of an overstatement, but Saving is arguably the single most important thing you can do in Illustrator. And you may feel as if you *have* saved the world when your client happens to mention — forty hours into the job — that she needs your graphics to work on an Amiga (a relatively obscure computer platform that Illustrator can save to anyway), and you say, "Sure, no problem!" instead of breaking down in tears. Or when your graphics look every bit as good on the Web as they do in print.

Or when your computer crashes and you laugh it off because you didn't lose *any* work. The key to all these heroic scenarios is Illustrator's massive Save features, all found under the File menu: Save, Save As, Save a Copy, Save for Web, and Export.

Save

Choosing the Save command writes the document you are working on to the hard drive. This is the fastest way to save a file, but it is limited. It can only be used on files that were already saved. If you are working on a brand new document, you can't just save it using the Save command. Doing so doesn't change the format; the file is saved in a format that is as close as possible to the format it had when it was opened. So if you open an Illustrator 8 file and hit Save, even if you are working in Illustrator 9, the file is saved as an Illustrator 8 file — in the exact same location as when you opened it. To change the file's format (or to save it to a different location on your hard drive), use the Save As command.

Save As

Save As lets you change the file format of the open document and save it to a different location from where it was originally. Save As also saves new documents that haven't been saved before. When you are creating artwork for print, Save As is the command to use 90 percent of the time; it allows you to save things in the EPS format (short for Encapsulated PostScript). The EPS format is supported by every major page-layout application, PC or Mac. So when you save a file in this format, you are assured almost universal compatibility in the world of print. Save As also gives you the option of saving files in the formats of earlier versions of Illustrator, all the way back to the decade-old version 3.0. This is handy for sharing your files with other Illustrator users who don't have the latest and greatest version of the program, as you do. For more information on the Save As command and file formats in general, see Chapter 18.

Save a Copy

Save a Copy has all the features of the Save As command but adds a twist: You can also use it to save all the information in your current document as a different file on your hard drive — at a different location and sporting a different file format — without changing anything in the current file. You can save multiple versions of the same file (say, one for printout and one for the Web) — and if you need to restore the file to the way it was the last time it was saved using Save or Save As, you have a handy way to do so: the File⇨Revert command. Revert breezes right past the Save a Copy command, allowing you to make a completely different series of changes.

Save for Web

Save for Web, as you probably guessed, allows you to save Illustrator graphics for display on the World Wide Web. Even better, you can use this command to save your files in any of the three most commonly used Web graphics file formats: JPEG, GIF, or PNG. Best of all, the Save for Web dialog box provides a preview of what the file will look like after you save it, as well as what the file size and download time will be, so you can manage the delicate balance between graphic quality and short download time. You use this feature most when you save graphics for the Web. You can find a whole lot more information on the Save for Web command in Chapter 17.

Export

The Export command could be called "Save for Everything Else." It lets you save Illustrator files in an astonishing variety of formats — from the commonplace (such as Adobe Photoshop) to the obscure (such as Amiga IFF). The Export command is most often called upon when you receive a request for a graphic in a specific format that you can't find under the Save As or Save for Web command. Here's where to find every other file format you can use when you save an Illustrator file.

The most commonly used formats found here are Flash, a hot new format for displaying vector graphics on the Web, SVG (Scalable Vector Graphic format), and Adobe Photoshop. Flash (SWF) files can be opened and edited in Flash-savvy applications such as Macromedia Flash; Photoshop format recreates your Illustrator file as a Photoshop file, maintaining the features of the original file (such as Layers and Transparency) as closely as possible. Chapters 17 and 18 provide further information on using Illustrator with these formats.

Using Illustrator for What It Does Best

Illustrator is a powerful tool, but it's limited to certain types of tasks. Knowing what Illustrator does best is key to getting the most out of the software.

Illustrator does anything having to do with path-based artwork extremely well and performs the basics with pixel-based artwork. You *can* use Illustrator for page layout, but it isn't really designed for documents longer than a single page. You *can* also use Illustrator for some basic image adjustment, but that sort of thing is easier with Photoshop.

Any time you want to create art or graphics pieces that need to serve multiple purposes, you probably want to look first at Illustrator. Illustrator's flexibility in transforming artwork is second to none — which means you can, with equal ease, create artwork to appear on a business card, a bottle label, a poster, a billboard, television or film, or on the Web.

Illustrator isn't limited to portraying the way things are in the real world. You can use it to create things that may have no real-world equivalents. Give light bulbs spikes. Create a monster out of eyeballs. (Whoops, a 1950s monster movie already did that. Well, okay, how about a beast with a thousand *noses?*) Whatever you imagine, Illustrator can help you create an image of it. But wait, there's more. After you create your image, Illustrator gives you the means to edit it by adjusting the original or cooking up batches of variations.

Part II
Drawing and Coloring Your Artwork

The 5th Wave™   By Rich Tennant

"I COULDN'T SAY ANYTHING—THEY WERE IN HERE
WITH THAT PROGRAM WE BOUGHT THEM THAT
ENCOURAGES ARTISTIC EXPRESSION."

In this part . . .

This section covers the essentials of creating new graphics in Illustrator. You meet the four types of tools that create new graphics: the basic shape tools that you can use to whomp up stars, rectangles, ellipses, and so forth in a jiffy; the Pencil tool that's handy for drawing free-form lines; the Pen tool that gives you the power to create lines and shapes with astonishing precision; and the Brush tool for painting complex objects on your screen with ease. You find out how to add solid colors, patterns, and gradients to your graphics. Finally, you're tipped off about some cool effects you can create in Illustrator — such as how to fade out your artwork using Transparency; color a single piece of artwork with multiple colors, gradients, or patterns; and otherwise pop your viewers' eyes.

Chapter 4

Shaping Up, Basically

● ●

In This Chapter

▶ Creating objects the easy way

▶ Customizing basic objects

▶ Combining objects to create other objects

● ●

A regrettably large number of people avoid Illustrator altogether because they find the whole point/path thing so intimidating. This situation is unfortunate, but not surprising. When most people look at artwork, they see it as complete shapes, not as the lines that form the shapes (unless they happen to be looking at a Picasso painting or Calder mobile). Working with points and paths forces you to see your artwork in a way many people have never thought of before, which creates enough of a hurdle to scare people away from Illustrator.

Fortunately, Illustrator offers the shape-creation tools as a way to get a running start to clear that hurdle. The shape-creation tools are six tools that let you create basic shapes like rectangles, ellipses, stars, and polygons. With the shape-creation tools, you can create graphics without even thinking about points and paths! (Don't be fooled — the points and paths are still there, but the tools create them all for you with just a single click-and-drag. Ah, progress.)

In this chapter, you discover how to use the shape-creation tools, which offers a good foundation for understanding and using Illustrator's more complex features. You also find out how to combine simple shapes. Indeed, while the shape-creation tools create basic elements, they are by no means limited, especially when used in conjunction with the Pathfinder palette. Some people discover that they can create such an astonishing variety of graphics with the shape-creation tools that they can bypass more complex tools like the Pen and Pencil altogether!

Creating Basic Shapes

Illustrator has six tools for creating shapes. Although you *could* create all those shapes with Illustrator's Pen tool, you'd be tormenting yourself if you did so; Illustrator's specialized tools make the shapes painlessly easy to create. The six tools are named for (and look like) the shapes they create, as follows:

- **Rectangle:** This tool is for creating rectangles and squares. Hold down the Shift key when using this tool to get a perfect square.

- **Rounded Rectangle:** As you may expect, you get rounded corners on your rectangles and squares with this tool. Of course, if you recall high-school geometry, you know that a round rectangle is a contradiction in terms. By definition, a rectangle is a four-sided polygon with each corner forming a 90-degree angle. Oh well. So much for Euclid. For maximum contradiction, use this tool while eating jumbo shrimp.

- **Ellipse:** This tool is for creating ellipses and circles. Hold down the Shift key when using this tool to get a perfect circle.

- **Polygon:** This tool makes objects with any number of sides — from three to 1,000 — each side the same length. You can use this tool for triangles, pentagons, hexagons, and so forth.

- **Star:** This tool is for creating stars with any number of points — between 3 and 1,000.

- **Spiral:** This tool is for creating spirals with any number of winds (that's long *i*, as in *whines*) between –3600° and 3600° (360° is equal to one wind).

The shape-creation tools are located in a single row in the Toolbox, as shown in Figure 4-1. The rectangles reside in the Rectangle tool slot; the others hang out in the Ellipse tool slot.

Figure 4-1:
The six shape-creation tools.

Drawing rectangles and squares

To draw a rectangle, select the Rectangle tool in the Toolbox; then click and drag where you want the Rectangle to go. After you release the mouse button, a rectangle appears. To draw a square, you follow a slightly different procedure, as described in the following steps:

1. **Choose the Rectangle tool from the Toolbox.**

2. **Click and drag with the tool (don't release the mouse button yet).**

3. **Press the Shift key.**

   The rectangle "snaps" into a square.

4. **Release the mouse button (but hold down that Shift key until after you release the mouse button).**

   A square appears.

If you happen to release the Shift key *before* you release the mouse button, the square snaps back into a rectangle.

You can draw a rounded corner rectangle by choosing the Rounded Rectangle tool (hidden in the toolslot with the Rectangle tool) and drawing with that instead of the regular Rectangle tool.

If you want to create a rectangle with exact dimensions (say, 28 points by 42 points), click and *don't* drag with the Rectangle tool. A dialog box appears, as shown in Figure 4-2.

Figure 4-2:
The dialog box that appears after you click with the Rectangle tool.

Type in height and width and then click OK. Illustrator draws a rectangle to those exact specifications.

Illustrator places the rectangle's upper-left corner at the spot where you click with the Rectangle tool. If you hold down the Option [Alt] key at the same time, Illustrator places the rectangle's center at the spot where you click with the Rectangle tool.

Drawing ellipses and circles

To draw an ellipse, choose the Ellipse tool and click and drag in the document window. After you release the mouse button, an ellipse appears. To draw a perfect circle, hold down the Shift key as you draw with the Ellipse tool.

If you hold down the Option [Alt] key at the same time that you click (but don't drag) with the Ellipse tool, Illustrator places the ellipse (or circle) from its center instead of from its upper-left edge.

As with the Rectangle tool, clicking (without dragging) causes the Ellipse dialog box to appear, as shown in Figure 4-3. Here you can type in an exact height and width for the ellipse. These values represent the distance across the ellipse at its widest and narrowest points.

Figure 4-3:
This dialog
box appears
after you
click with
the Ellipse
tool.

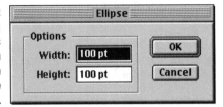

Creating stars, polygons, and spirals

Illustrator has tools specifically designed for creating stars, polygons, and spirals. Like rectangles and ovals, these shapes *could* be drawn with Illustrator's Pen tool, but having a tool for creating them makes the process much easier, faster, and more accurate. Using these tools is fairly straight-forward. As with the Rectangle and Ellipse tools, just click and drag and then release the mouse button when the shape is the size you want. As with the Rectangle and Ellipse tools, just clicking (without dragging) with the Star, Polygon, or Spiral tool opens a dialog box that you can use to specify the shape's exact size (and other attributes).

Need to create stars at various sizes with a certain number of points? Or different sized polygons with the same number of sides? The dialog boxes for the Star, Polygon, and Spiral tools remember the number of sides, points, and winds you enter and use those settings for each subsequent shape you draw, even if you click and drag.

Pulling Polygons

To create a polygon, click and drag with the Polygon tool. When the polygon is the size you want, release the mouse button. The new polygon appears. Because polygons are more complex than ellipses or rectangles, you can get all sorts of special capabilities by pressing certain keys as you draw. To customize the polygon as you create it, hold down any of the following keys as you drag:

- **Shift** constrains one side of the polygon so it's parallel to the bottom of the page.

- **Up/Down Arrow** adds/deletes sides of the polygon as you draw it.

- **Spacebar** moves the polygon around as you draw it.

- **Tilde (~)** creates multiple polygons as you draw. At times there can be so many polygons that they look like one solid figure, but actually each one is a separate entity that you can separate and move wherever you want. This feature can create quite astounding effects, as shown in Figure 4-4. To use this feature, you must release the mouse button before you release the key, or all duplicates disappear. This works when you draw any of the other shapes, too!

Clicking (without dragging) with the Polygon tool opens the Polygon dialog box, as shown in Figure 4-5. Polygons use a Radius value instead of height and width. All sides of the polygon are the same distance from the center; this distance is the Radius value. To create a polygon of a specific width, type in *half the width* you want in the Radius field. You can type in any number of sides, from 3 to 1000.

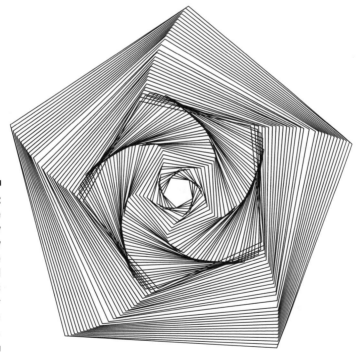

Figure 4-4:
Pressing the Tilde (~) key as you draw with the Polygon tool produces this rather unique effect.

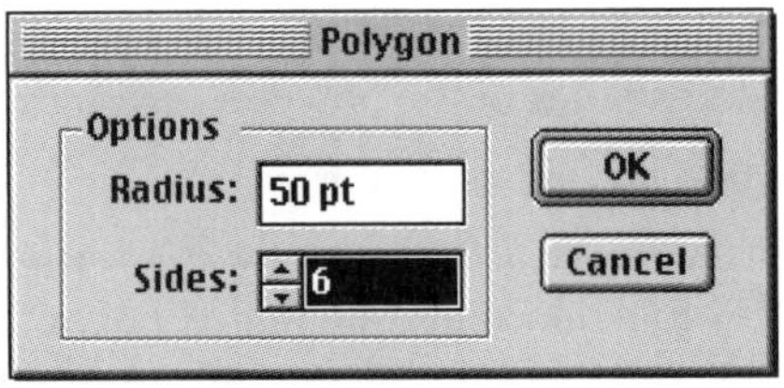

Figure 4-5:
This dialog
box appears
after you
click with
the Polygon
tool.

Seeing stars

To create a star, click and drag with the Star tool. After you release the mouse button, a star is born at the size you dragged. Stars are even more complex than polygons. Fortunately, you also have more keys for customizing options. To customize a star, use the following keys as you drag:

- ✔ **Shift** constrains one side of the star so that the bottom two points of the star are parallel to the bottom of the page.

- ✔ **Up/Down Arrow** adds/deletes points of the star as you draw it.

- ✔ **Command [Ctrl]** constrains the middle points (the inner radius) of the star; the outer ones still move.

- ✔ **Spacebar** moves the star around as you draw it.

- ✔ **Tilde (~)** creates multiple stars as you draw.

Clicking (without dragging) with the Star tool opens the Star dialog box, as shown in Figure 4-6. Stars have two radii that you can set in the Star dialog box. The first radius determines how far the inner points of the star are from the cen-ter. The second radius determines how far the outer points are from the center. In the Star dialog box, you can also set the number of points the star has. After you make your settings, click OK to create the star you speci-fied. After you create a star using the Star dialog box, each star you create by clicking and dragging uses the same specifications, more or less. Regardless of each star's size, it has the same number of points (unless you change them using the up and down arrows), and the first and second radii maintain the same proportions, if not the same size. In effect, if you enter 2 inches for the first radius and 1 inch for the second, the second radius is 50 percent smaller for every star you drag into existence after you establish the settings in the dialog box, regardless of the star's size. (Gads, who knew this galaxy-building business was so finicky?)

Figure 4-6:
The Star
dialog box
appears
when you
click the
Star tool.
You can set
the quantity
and length
of its points.

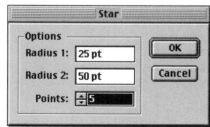

Spiraling out of control

Spirals have fewer keyboard options associated with them than polygons or stars, but the Spiral dialog box is far less intuitive than any of the other shapes' dialog boxes. You're probably better off doing what you can by dragging and using the keyboard. Nonetheless, the Spiral dialog box is worth a look.

To customize a spiral, you can hold down one of the following keys as you drag:

- **Up/Down Arrow** adds/deletes the winds of the spiral as it's being drawn.

- **Command [Ctrl]** winds or unwinds the spiral (the outside moves, but the center stays where it is, making the spiral tighter or looser), which changes the number of winds.

- **Spacebar** moves the spiral around as you draw it.

- **Tilde (~)** creates multiple spirals as you draw.

Click with the Spiral tool (instead of clicking and dragging) to open the Spiral dialog box, as shown in Figure 4-7. In the Spiral dialog box, the Radius option is the distance from the center of the spiral to its outermost point. The Decay option determines how much larger or smaller each coil of the spiral is from the previous coil. Values close to 100% result in a tight spiral, and 100% results in a perfect circle. The Segments option determines just how many coils make up the spiral. Each wind of the spiral is made up of four segments; if you want five coils in the spiral, type **20** in the Segment field.

Figure 4-7:
The Spiral
dialog box,
which
appears
when you
click (but
don't drag)
the Spiral
tool, enables
you to set
the spiral's
tightness.

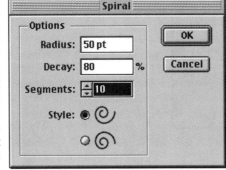

Putting Shapes Together

The basic shape-creation tools are great starting points for creating more complex illustrations, because most complex shapes are just many basic shapes put together. You may be astonished at what you can create simply by combining one basic shape with another. One of the quickest and easiest ways to do so in Illustrator is by using the Pathfinder palette.

The Pathfinder palette has a somewhat misleading name. You may half expect this palette to deliver a guide to lead you through life's journeys . . . or at least locate something. All it really does is combine or separate two or more shapes in a wide variety of ways. You can use the Pathfinder palette to join two or more objects into one object, to remove the shape of one object from another, to cut apart two shapes where they overlap, or to combine objects in many other ways.

To access the Pathfinder palette, choose Window⇨Show Pathfinder. The Pathfinder palette appears, as shown in Figure 4-8.

Using the Pathfinder palette is simplicity itself. Just overlap two or more objects, select them all by clicking them with any selection tool (to select multiple objects, hold down the Shift key while clicking each object) and click the button that does the operation you desire.

Which button to click isn't always obvious; don't worry about that. Simply keep in mind that when you want to combine or separate two or more objects, you're likely to find a button to help you in the Pathfinder palette. Click a button; if it doesn't give you what you want, choose Edit⇨Undo and try a different button.

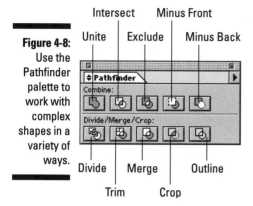

Figure 4-8:
Use the
Pathfinder
palette to
work with
complex
shapes in a
variety of
ways.

The results of the Pathfinder palette depend heavily on which object is in front and which object is behind. To change the stacking order of objects, select a single object with the Selection tool and choose Object➪Arrange. In the Arrange submenu, you can send the object to the back, bring it forward, or move it backward and forward one level at a time.

To get a better idea of how the Pathfinder palette functions, you can use it on two basic objects (in this case, a circle and a star), as shown in Figure 4-9.

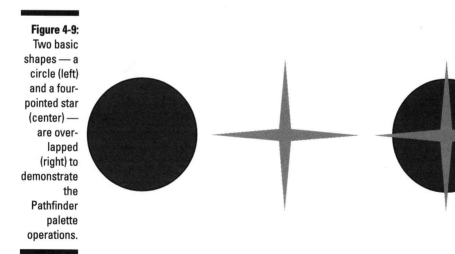

Figure 4-9:
Two basic
shapes — a
circle (left)
and a four-
pointed star
(center) —
are over-
lapped
(right) to
demonstrate
the
Pathfinder
palette
operations.

The following Pathfinder palette buttons create and manipulate complex shapes, as shown in Figure 4-10:

✔ **Unite** joins multiple objects into a single object. The resulting object uses the fill and stroke color of the object that was on top before the objects were united.

✔ **Intersect** cuts away all parts of the objects that don't overlap and unites what is left into a single object. The resulting object uses the fill and stroke color of the object that was on top before the objects were united. Here Intersect joins the circle and star, using the fill and stroke color of the star (which was on top before the objects were united). Intersect only works on two objects at a time.

✔ **Exclude** removes all parts of the objects that overlap and unites what is left into a single object (the opposite of the Intersect option). The remaining object uses the fill and stroke color of the object that was on top before the objects were united. Here Exclude cuts away all parts of the circle and star that overlap, uniting what is left into a single object that uses the fill and stroke color of the star (which was on top before the objects were united).

Figure 4-10:
The circle and star show the results of using (left to right) the Unite button, the Intersect button, and the Exclude button.

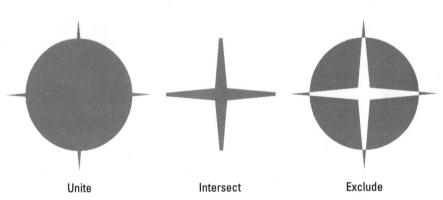

Unite   Intersect   Exclude

The next three buttons in the Pathfinder palette — Minus Front, Minus Back, and Divide — achieve their effects by cutting away specific parts of the image (Figure 4-11 demonstrates the results of using them):

✔ **Minus Front** cuts away all selected objects in front of the backmost object, leaving a hole in the backmost object the shape of whatever was in front of it. The remaining object uses the fill and stroke color of the backmost object. Here Minus Front cuts away the star in front of the circle and unites what is left into a single object, using the fill and stroke color of the circle (which is the backmost object).

✔ **Minus Back** cuts away from the frontmost object all selected objects that are behind the frontmost object. The remaining object uses the fill and stroke color of the frontmost object. This option is the opposite of the Minus Front option. Here Minus Back cuts away the circle from the star and unites what is left (those four forlorn-looking points) into a single object that uses the fill and stroke color of the star (which is the frontmost object).

✔ **Divide** breaks two overlapping objects into separate objects. This operation may look as though it hasn't done anything after you first apply it (left). However, after you divide an object, you can move or color each separate piece individually (right). After the Divide button first breaks the overlapping star and circle into separate objects, they look as if nothing has happened. However, the star and circle can be individually moved or colored (far right).

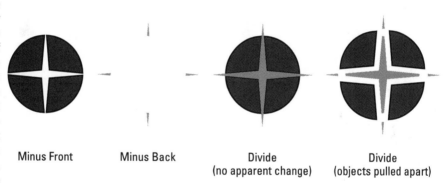

Figure 4-11: The circle and star show the results of using (left to right) Minus Front, Minus Back, and (in the two rightmost images) Divide.

| Minus Front | Minus Back | Divide (no apparent change) | Divide (objects pulled apart) |

The next four buttons in the Pathfinder palette — Trim, Merge, Crop, and Outline — provide the means for tidying up your artwork before sending your creation out into the world. In Figure 4-12, this cleanup crew takes a bow.

✔ **Trim** removes any parts of objects hidden by other objects and also removes any strokes. As with Divide, this command may not produce visible results immediately (it affects only hidden items). However, as you start changing the affected objects, you see a big difference, such as the pie slices (right) that seem to change position. Here the Trim button removes any parts of the circle hidden by the star and also removes any strokes. At first, the command's results aren't visible (left), until you start changing the position of the pie slices of the circle (right) — and they move as separate objects.

✔ **Merge** removes any parts of objects hidden by other objects, removes strokes, and merges overlapping objects that have the same fill colors. This option functions almost the same way as the Trim option, the key difference being that this option merges objects of the same color together into a single object, while trim leaves them as separate objects. Here the Merge button removes any parts of the circle hidden by the star, removes strokes, and merges overlapping objects that have the same fill colors (which the star and the circle do not).

✔ **Crop** divides two overlapping objects into separate objects where they overlap and then deletes everything outside the boundaries of the top-most object. Here the Crop button divides the star and circle into separate objects where they overlap and then deletes everything outside the boundaries of the star (the topmost object).

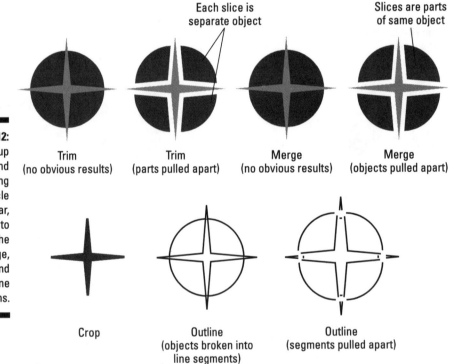

Figure 4-12:
Cleaning up and checking the circle and star, using (left to right) the Trim, Merge, Crop, and Outline buttons.

Each slice is separate object

Slices are parts of same object

Trim
(no obvious results)

Trim
(parts pulled apart)

Merge
(no obvious results)

Merge
(objects pulled apart)

Crop

Outline
(objects broken into line segments)

Outline
(segments pulled apart)

> ✓ **Outline** breaks objects into separate line segments with no fill colors. Of the two outlines shown in the figure, the one on the left shows the visible effects of the command; the one on the right shows the now-separate line segments moved apart.

Creating Objects Using the Pathfinder Command

By combining basic shapes, you can create just about anything you can imagine. So, how do you actually use the Pathfinder command to create such complex shapes? (Details, details.) Consider a couple of examples — a crescent moon and a sunrise.

Crescent moon

A crescent moon seems fairly simple, but if you try to draw one accurately by hand, you can quickly find yourself frustrated. The Pathfinder palette, however, makes drawing a crescent moon almost as easy as smiling and saying, "Green cheese." Just follow these steps:

1. **Choose the Ellipse tool and then draw a perfect circle by clicking and dragging the Ellipse tool while holding down the Shift key.**

   Let go of the mouse button *before* you let go of the Shift key, and a perfect circle appears.

2. **Repeat Step 1, except make the second circle smaller than the first.**

3. **Choose the Selection tool and use it to position the second circle over the first, as shown in Figure 4-13.**

4. **Select both circles (hold down the Shift key and click each circle with the Selection tool, to select more than one object at a time).**

5. **Click the Minus Front button in the Pathfinder palette.**

   Presto! A crescent moon appears!

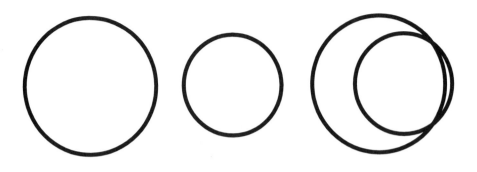

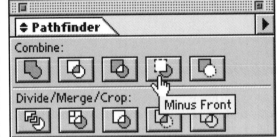

Figure 4-13:
Creating a
crescent
moon.

Sunrise

What better way to follow a crescent moon than with a beautiful sunrise?
(Gotta hand it to Nature.) Just follow these steps:

1. **Click and drag with the Rectangle tool to create a box.**

2. **Click and drag with the Star tool to create a star. As you drag with the
   Star tool, repeatedly press the up-arrow (↑) key.**

   A many-pointed star appears.

3. **Choose the Selection tool and use it to position the star over the
   rectangle, so the two objects overlap, as shown in Figure 4-14.**

4. **Select both the star and the rectangle (hold down the Shift key and
   click each object with the Selection tool, so both objects are selected).**

5. **Click the Minus Back button in the Pathfinder palette.**

   Voilá — a beautiful sunrise! (Well, almost. Still needs colors and a pot of
   fresh coffee.)

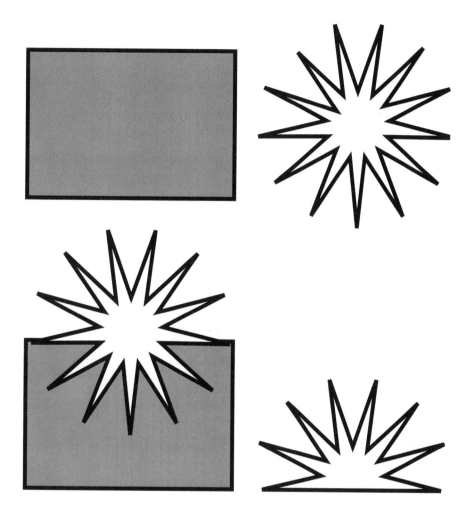

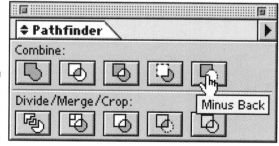

Figure 4-14:
Creating a
sunrise.

Chapter 5

Getting Your Fill of Fills and Strokes

*F*ills and strokes give life to your artwork. If Illustrator were a coloring book, the fills and strokes would be the biggest, best box of crayons ever. Only better, because these colors always stay inside the lines. Better still, they are magic colors. You're not limited to a single solid color within an area. You can have gradients and patterns as well. And not only can you color inside the lines, you can color the lines themselves, make them thinner or thicker, or hide them altogether! Best of all, unlike crayons, these don't make a mess when your big sister grinds them into the carpet because you ran to show Mom your new artwork and forgot to clean up after yourself.

In this chapter, you discover the different boxes of crayons Illustrator has to offer, such as the Color palette and Swatches palette, and how to color your artwork with them using the Fill box and Stroke box. You find out how to create your own colors. Rounding things out, you get to know Illustrator's special colors, gradients, and patterns, which stretch the meaning of what color really is.

Understanding Fill and Stroke

A *fill* is a color enclosed by a path. A *stroke* is a line of color that precisely follows a path. To run the coloring book metaphor into the ground, the stroke is the line, the fill is the "inside the line" that you aren't supposed to color outside of (but you did anyway because you weren't about to let your dumb old parents stifle your creativity!). "Color" is a loose term here; it can mean a solid color, a pattern, or (in the case of fills) a gradient. Figure 5-1 shows a variety of paths with different strokes and fills applied to them.

2-point 100% black stroke
around a 35% black fill

Rainbow Gradient
fill, with a stroke
value of None

25-point Brick
Pattern stroke, with
a Fill value
of None

Figure 5-1:
A bunch of
paths with
different fills
and strokes
applied to
them.

2-point gray (22% black) stroke
around a 100% black fill

Although a stroke can be any thickness, it always uses a path as its center. You can deck out your strokes with solid colors or patterns, but not with gradients (patterns and gradients are special combinations of colors, and yeah, they're lurking in this chapter too, not to worry). The path surrounds the area where you put the color. This area is called the *fill* because it's *filled* with color.

Fills and strokes can obscure the boundaries of your paths, especially when you have very thick strokes on your paths such as the S-shaped bricks in Figure 5-1. To temporarily hide all fills and strokes, choose View⇨Outline. This shows your artwork as just the paths, with all strokes and fills hidden. You can still edit the artwork as you would any other time. The only difference is that you can't see fills and strokes. To show all the colors again, choose View⇨Preview.

The ways to create and modify fill and stroke color in Illustrator are nigh infinite, but the quickest and easiest way to *apply* them is by using the Fill and Stroke box in the Toolbox, which looks remarkably like what you see in Figure 5-2.

Default Fill and Stroke

Fill

Swap Fill and Stroke

Figure 5-2:
Fill and
Stroke in the
Toolbox

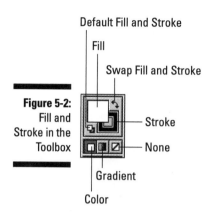

Stroke

None

Gradient

Color

You can change a fill or a stroke, but not both at the same time. You decide whether to affect the fill or the stroke by selecting an object and then clicking the Fill (solid) or the Stroke (bordered) box. The box you click comes to the front; after that, every color change you make happens to whichever one you chose . . . until you choose the other one.

Some very useful features surround the Fill and Stroke boxes. Just to the upper right is a little curved line with arrows on either end. Click this thingamajig to Swap Fill and Stroke colors.

To the lower left of the Fill and Stroke boxes are miniature white (Fill) and black bordered (Stroke) boxes. Click this Default Fill and Stroke button to set the Fill and Stroke boxes to their default colors: white for Fill and black for Stroke.

If you prefer fills and strokes in festive colors, here's the story: Beneath the Fill and Stroke boxes live three square buttons that handle colors for you. Click the first square (the Color button) to change the fill or stroke color to the last color you used. Click the second square (the Gradient button) to change the color of the stroke or fill so that it matches the last-selected Gradient you used. Click the third square (the None button) to use no fill or stroke color at all.

Double-clicking the Stroke or the Fill box summons the Color Picker appears, where you can specify colors in a variety of ways. You can choose a color from a spectrum, using true color field and color slider, or define a color numerically.

Filling and stroking paths with color

You can fill a path with one color and stroke it with another, as shown in Figure 5-3.

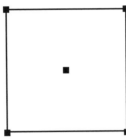 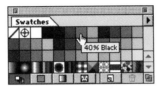 

Figure 5-3:
Filling and
stroking a
path with
two
different
colors.

To fill a path with one color and stroke it with another, just follow these steps:

1. **Using any of the Selection tools, select the path you want to color.**

2. **In the Toolbox, click the Fill (the solid square).**

   Doing so tells Illustrator to apply the next color you choose to the fill (but not to the stroke) of selected paths.

3. **Choose Window⇨Show Swatches.**

   The Swatches palette appears. The squares in this palette function in much the same way as the three squares beneath the Fill and Stroke boxes in the Toolbox. You just click any square in the palette to apply that swatch to the selected stroke or fill. (For more information, see "The Swatches Palette," later in this chapter.)

4. **Click any solid-color swatch.**

   (Well, okay, *any* swatch in the palette works. The ones that aren't solid colors are special colors such as patterns and gradients — but sticking to solid colors is less confusing early on.)

5. **Click the Stroke (the thick-bordered box) in the Toolbox.**

   Illustrator is ready for you to pick a stroke color.

6. **In the Swatches palette, choose a solid color, just as you did for the fill color in Step 3.**

Making a bold stroke

When you follow the steps to color a stroke and don't see any change, you probably have too narrow a stroke. Stroke widths can range anywhere from 0 points to 1000 points (18 inches, or about 46 cm). If the stroke is too narrow to be visible onscreen, you can change the stroke width using the Stroke palette, as shown in Figure 5-4.

Figure 5-4:
The Stroke
palette.

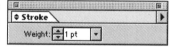

To give the path a different stroke width:

1. **Select the path with any Selection tool.**
2. **Choose Window⇨Show Stroke.**

   The Stroke palette appears.
3. **Enter a new value or choose one from the pop-up menu.**

Filling crossed and open paths

Sometimes a path crosses itself. For instance, a path in the shape of a figure eight crosses itself once. If you fill this path, the two round areas of the eight are full, as shown in Figure 5-5.

Figure 5-5:
A filled
path in the
shape of a
reclining
figure eight.

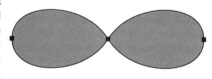

Open paths (the ones that have separate starting and ending points) can be filled, but the results are a little different from what you may expect. When you fill an open path, an *imaginary* path connects the first and last points of the original path. This imaginary path marks off the limits of the fill area. If you apply a stroke to the figure, the stroke doesn't apply to the imaginary path. Figure 5-6 shows open paths with fills in them. We use a dotted line to show where Illustrator creates the imaginary path between two end points.

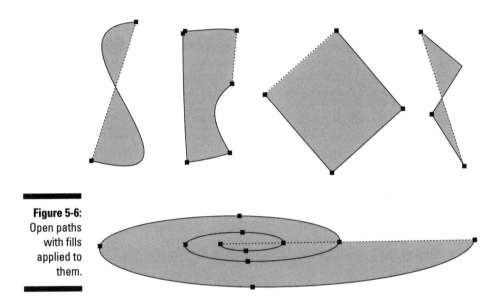

Figure 5-6:
Open paths
with fills
applied to
them.

The Swatches Palette

Illustrator stores colors in the Swatches palette for quick and easy access —
and no matter how fast you grab a color, you never have to worry about
splattering paint. The Swatches palette comes with a whole set of colors premade and ready to use just by clicking them in the palette.

Additionally, Illustrator comes with many Swatch Libraries — sets of colors
created for special purposes — so if your first-grade crayon box never
seemed to have enough colors, you're in luck. And if that's *still* not enough,
you can create your own colors using the Color palette, described later in
this chapter, and add them to the Swatches palette.

Using the Swatches palette (shown in Figure 5-7) is almost as easy as looking
at it. Select an object with any Selection tool, click the Stroke or Fill box in the
Toolbox, choose Window➪Show Swatches so the Swatches palette appears,
and then click any square in the Swatches palette to choose that color. The
selected fill or stroke updates the instant you click the new color. No fuss, no
muss, no melted crayons.

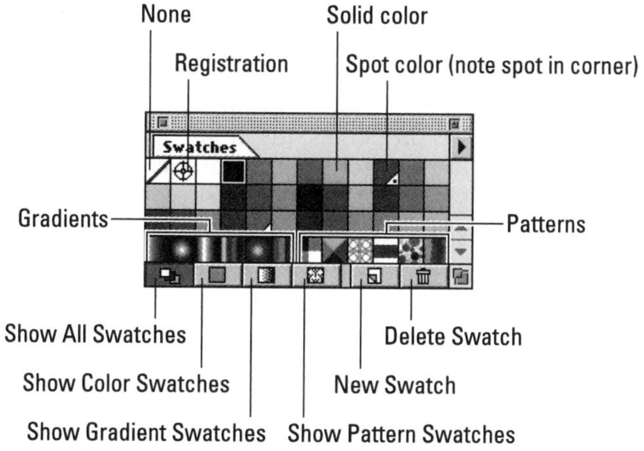
None
Solid color
Registration
Spot color (note spot in corner)
Swatches
Gradients
Patterns
Show All Swatches
Delete Swatch
Show Color Swatches
New Swatch
Show Gradient Swatches
Show Pattern Swatches

Figure 5-7: The Swatches palette.

All the colors in the rainbow and then some

The Swatches palette can contain several different types of color swatches, each with its own range of purposes and uses. Here's the lineup:

- **Process color.** This is your run-of-the-mill, straight-up color with no added bells or whistles. You can make a color for use onscreen or for print by mixing varying amounts of either Red, Green, and Blue (RGB) or Cyan, Magenta, Yellow, and Black (CMYK). For more information on using RGB versus CMYK colors, see Chapter 1. These appear as solid color squares.
- **Spot colors.** (Nope, these aren't just for creating polka-dots or Dalmatians.) Spot colors are used exclusively in printing. The four-color CMYK printing process can only create a limited range of colors from its four basic color ingredients. To compensate, the process can also use spot colors of specified inks that come in a particular color. Many companies make spot colors, but most countries have one dominant company that sets the standards for spot-color printing in that country. (In the U.S.A., it's Pantone; in Japan, it's TOYO.) The range of all colors that a company produces is called its *library*. Very conveniently, Illustrator includes swatch libraries from all the swatch-producing companies. Spot colors show up in the swatches palette with little triangles in their lower right-hand corners, with a tiny spot in the center of the triangle.

✔ **Registration.** Registration is a special Illustrator color that uses 100 percent of all inks — but though it looks like black onscreen, *it's not for artwork.* Registration (as a color, at least) exists for a very specific technical purpose: creating the Registration marks used by commercial printers to get things in proper alignment on press. If you aren't a commercial printer, or have not been specifically told to do so by a commercial printer, you should *never* use Registration. Registration looks like a crosshair in the Swatches palette.

If you used Registration to color your artwork, you'd get an unprintable sticky mess that would probably stink (chemically, at least), waste ink, and never dry.

✔ **None.** This color choice differs from White (which tells a printer to *put no ink in a particular space,* on the assumption that the paper itself supplies the white color). None, on the other hand, is the *complete absence* of color. In a picture, a white object is opaque; it blocks your view of any objects behind it (you can't see the electric outlet behind a white refrigerator). An object whose color is None would be transparent — in effect, invisible. If you want to use a stroke but also want other objects to show through the fill (or let the fill show through the objects), choose None for the specific onscreen area you want to see through. None appears as a white square with a diagonal red line through it in the Swatches palette.

Computers are literalists; selecting None is like telling the computer, *This is what I don't want to see.* Any part of a fill or a stroke that you color as None will use no colors (which is the next best thing to not-being-there).

✔ **Gradients.** Gradients combine two or more colors in a smooth transition that shades from one color into the other.

✔ **Patterns.** If you really love wallpaper, you can use one or more objects in a tiled pattern to fill other objects.

Swatch Options for super colors

Swatches are a quick way to retrieve colors, but they do more. Double-click any swatch in the palette to open the Swatch Options dialog box, shown in all its useful glory in Figure 5-8.

The Swatch Options dialog box can keep you busy with choices and/or give you creative possibilities. Here's the list:

✔ **Swatch Name:** You can give the color a distinctive name (say, Maine Blueberry or Rotten Banana) or change its name (say, to Dollar Green if some wiseacre already named it George).

- **Color Type:** You can change a spot color to its closest CMYK or RGB equivalent. This is a handy option when your client provides you with a logo rendered in spot colors ("Metallic puce? You're not kidding?") and you have to produce an image in CMYK or RGB.

  Unfortunately, you can't go the other way around. Trying to change a process color into a spot color doesn't give you the closest spot color equivalent from the Pantone, TOYO, or any other color library. (For more about color libraries, see the "Swatch libraries" section in this chapter.)

- **Global:** The Global feature is one of the handiest things in Illustrator. After you check this option, Illustrator remembers everything you color with a particular swatch. When you change the color of the swatch, everything that has the old swatch's color updates to the new color. (Mercifully, Adobe didn't call this feature the old swatcheroo.) This feature's a great timesaver when you want to change a color scheme. You don't have to go back, reselect, and recolor everything.

- **Color Mode, Gamut Warnings, and Color Sliders:** These features are especially powerful when used with Global color. They all work just like the Color palette, except they apply your changes only to the currently selected swatch.

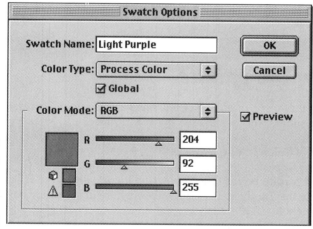

Figure 5-8:
The Swatch
Options
dialog box.

Swatch libraries

Illustrator comes loaded with color choices in the form of *swatch libraries* — sets of color swatches created for specific purposes. (Pantone, for example, has several libraries devoted just to spot colors.) The libraries you get with Illustrator draw from all the major spot-color sources in the world. A Web library provides tried-and-true colors that work best on the

Internet. To start wandering through these libraries, click Window⇨Swatch Libraries. If you turn up a color that you simply must have, add it to your Swatches palette: Open the specific library you need, find the color you want, and click it. Instantly the color shows up in your library and is ready for you to use.

Some libraries contain hundreds of swatches, which can make finding a particular color difficult. Fortunately, swatch libraries have a Find field at the very top of the window. If (for example) a client wants a logo done on a report cover in Pantone 185, just open the Pantone library (by choosing Window⇨Swatch Libraries⇨Pantone). When the swatch library appears, type **185** into its Find field (the empty white rectangle at the top of the palette) to highlight Pantone 185 automatically — you don't even have to press any other key! Click Pantone 185 to add it to your Swatches palette and you are good to go!

The Color Palette

The Color palette is as close as Illustrator gets to a real-world artist's palette. You use it to create new colors by blending. Instead of mixing splotches of pigment and linseed oil with a brush (and getting half of it on your jeans), you move sliders to adjust how much of each component color goes into your new color.

Parts of the palette

The Color palette, shown in Figure 5-9, has several cool features, in addition to the color sliders, that make creating colors easier.

Here's a list of Color palette features:

- **Fill and Stroke boxes.** These function identically to the Fill and Stroke boxes in the Toolbox. They're available here in the Color palette for your convenience.

- **Color sliders and color value boxes.** You can create a new color by dragging these sliders to the left or right. The color in the Fill or Stroke box (whichever is in front) updates to reflect the change, as does any selected artwork. To specify an exact amount of a particular color, type a number into the *color value box* to the right of each color slider.

- **None.** Click the None button to choose a Stroke or Fill value of None.

- **Black-and-white.** You guessed it! Click black to make the color black, and white to make it white. (Wait a minute. Was that a trick question?)

Out-of-gamut color warnings

Fill and Stroke boxes

Color sliders

Color values

Figure 5-9:
The Color
palette is
the closest
you can get
to real
artist's
palette in
Illustrator.

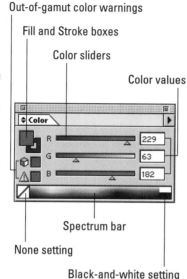

Spectrum bar

None setting

Black-and-white setting

✔ **Spectrum.** In this little rectangle are all the colors you can possibly create. Click anywhere on the Spectrum to choose a color. Well, okay, the spectrum *is* tiny; almost nobody picks exactly the right color on the first click. Use the spectrum to get a color that's in the right ballpark; then use the sliders to make the color precisely what you want.

✔ **Out-of-gamut color warnings.** As you create colors, tiny color boxes appear; their purpose is to warn you if the color is outside the color gamut for print or the Web. (The *gamut* is the total range of colors that a method can create without having to alter them.) For the Web, the gamut is 216 colors; for print, it's a few thousand. If you choose a color outside this range, that color can shift to another color. The *Out-of-web color warning* is a square of color with a little cube beside it; the *Out-of-gamut warning for print* is a square with an exclamation-point-inside-a-triangle beside it. Click the square to choose a color within the gamut that is closest to the color you chose. If you are creating for the Web, you can ignore the print gamut warning — and vice versa if you're creating for print.

To create a new color using the Color palette, follow these steps:

1. **Choose Window⇨Show Color.**

   The Color palette appears.

2. **From the Color palette's pop-up menu, choose a color model.**

   (See the "Modes and Models" section in this chapter for more information.)

3. **Click the Fill or Stroke box in the palette.**

4. **Move the sliders of each component color to the left or to the right, until the color you want appears in the Stroke or Fill box.**

Of course, if you actually want to *use* the colors you create in the Color palette (what a concept), you can do so in a couple of ways:

- **Use the color while you use the palette:** Anything already selected when you create a new Fill or Stroke color is filled or stroked with that color. (For example, you can fill a selected pterodactyl with pteal or pturquoise.)

- **Save the new color for later:** After you create the new color, you can save it to use again later. Here's how:

  1. **Open the Swatches palette by choosing Window➪Show Swatches.**

     The Swatches palette appears.

  2. **Click the Fill or Stroke box (whichever you just created) in either the Toolbox or the Color palette.**

  3. **Drag the Fill or Stroke box onto the Swatches palette.**

     Don't worry, you won't damage the Color palette when you drag away the Fill or Stroke box. Instead, you get a ghostly outline of the box as you drag. Release that outline on top of the Swatches palette to add the Fill or Stroke to the palette.

  After you release the mouse, the color shows up in the Swatches palette for you to use again and again! (Pteal pterodactyls travel in flocks? Who knew?)

With the new color in the Swatches palette, you can double-click it to open the Swatch Options dialog box. Here you can give it a name, make it a global color, or use any of the options described in the "Swatch Options" for super colors section (earlier this chapter).

Modes and models

Whoa. We're not talking about glitzy trends or sexy, well-groomed people. (At least not yet.) *Mode* and *model* are the terms used in Illustrator to define color, *color mode* is the "language" of color that your document "speaks" — either CMYK or RGB. *Color model* is a way of describing how to form the colors in the mode (color-language) your document uses.

All the colors used in the document (except spot colors) exist in one particular color *mode*, no matter what color *model* you use to create them. When you open a new document, you must decide whether to work in RGB or CMYK color (see Chapter 1 for the tale of two color modes). You choose a color model by clicking the pop-up menu for the Color palette (see Figure 5-10 for a mug shot).

Suppose, for example, that you want a shade of gray while you're working in RGB mode. Shades of gray are hard to create in RGB, because you have to drag all three red, green, and blue sliders to get the color you want. To dodge that complexity, you switch your color model to Grayscale in the Color palette. Then you have just one slider to deal with, and you can quickly create the exact shade of gray you want.

Figure 5-10:
Different
color
models
within the
Color
palette.

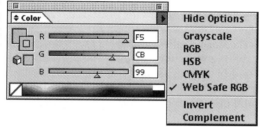

The Color palette is where you create the colors you need, using a variety of color models: Grayscale, RGB, HSB, CMYK, and Web Safe RGB. Each has a specific purpose, but really these different colors exist only to help you visualize the color you are trying to create. The Color palette lets you mix colors in any color model, but as soon as you apply them, they convert to the color mode you are using.

The following list describes these color models and the best ways to use them:

✔ **Grayscale** colors express everything as a shade of gray. This model is handy when you're creating for black and white printing, or just want a quick way to specify a shade of gray. Grayscale is measured in terms of ink values, with black as 100 percent — the most ink possible.

✔ **RGB** colors are based on the three colors (Red, Green, and Blue) used by your monitor to generate all the colors you see onscreen. So these colors are designed for onscreen use, such as when you are creating graphics for the World Wide Web. The amounts you see in the Color Values boxes range from 0 to 255. They correspond to the intensity of the light projected by your computer screen. Computer screens use tiny red, green, and blue phosphors that glow with different intensities to create the colors you see. The higher the value, the brighter the glow. Specifying 255 for all colors gives you pure white; a 0 value for all colors gives you pitch black. These numbers, however, are less important than your practical results: Pay attention to your Fill or Stroke boxes as you drag the sliders, and see the color that results.

✔ **HSB** colors are seen in terms of Hue, Saturation, and Brightness. If you look an HSB color in terms of crayons, Hue is the color of the crayon, such as red or blue or any of 360 choices. Saturation is how red that crayon is, such as brick red versus basic red, for instance. Brightness is equivalent to how hard you press down when you use that crayon. This way of thinking may seem weird, but many painters and traditional artists find it very intuitive.

✔ **CMYK** colors are based on the four colors (Cyan, Magenta, Yellow, and Black) used in process printing. Cyan is a light, bright blue; Magenta is a bright purple color that is almost (but not quite) pink. *Process* printing enables people to achieve a wide variety of colors (including photographic-looking images) using only those four colors. So CMYK colors are designed to specify colors for print. CMYK colors work the opposite of the way RGB colors work; the more of each individual color, the darker the total color becomes. For instance, 0 percent of cyan, magenta, yellow, and black results in white; 100 percent of cyan, magenta, yellow, and black results in black. But nobody who knows better would ever create black for print by using 100 percent of all four colors — that would put way too much ink on the paper, resulting in a sticky mess.

Well, okay, *in theory* you could create black by using 100 percent of cyan, magenta, and yellow — but printing inks (for the most part) are too cheaply made for that approach to work. To create a black that *really* looks black, you have to *add black* to cyan, magenta, and yellow (fortunately, black ink is cheaper than those colors). Try using 100 percent black for black, adding just a little of the other three colors to make it look *really* black. (Such complication of even a basic concept like black may have driven some folks to make graphics only for the Web.)

✔ **Web Safe RGB.** If you're like a lot of us, you're probably used to working with the 16.7 million colors that most computer monitors can display these days (fortunately we get to use 'em without having to count 'em). Out of all those colors, however, only 216 of them display consistently on Windows, UNIX, and Macintosh computers. This reduced range of color is due to differences in operating systems, Web browsers, and color cards. Colors outside this range of 216 can dither when displayed on a system that can't really show them properly. *Dithering* is the computer's attempt to create the missing colors by using dots of two colors that it *can* display — creating an optical illusion that the missing color is there. Dithering usually looks pretty awful, like a patterned fill of cheap corduroy. (See Chapter 17 for more details.)

Use Web Safe RGB when you need colors that look their best on as many different computers as possible. (A corporate logo is a classic example.)

✔ **Invert, Complement, and Hide Options**. The remaining choices aren't color models at all. Invert changes the selected color into its opposite, as if you had taken a color photograph of it and were looking at a negative. To understand Complement, think back to art class and the color wheel: *complementary colors* were the colors on opposite sides of the color wheel. Orange, for example, is the complementary color to blue. (Roughly.) Blue never looks more blue than when it is next to orange, and vice versa. Put another way, choosing Complement chooses the one color that will clash the most with the currently selected artwork. Hide Options collapses the Color palette so that just the Spectrum, Black and White, and None are showing.

Filling with Patterns and Textures

You can fill and stroke any path with a pattern. Patterns fill areas with repeating artwork. Figure 5-11 shows the same path filled with different patterns.

Applying patterns to paths

To fill a path with a pattern, select the path, make sure the Fill box is active by clicking it in the Toolbox, and then click the pattern you want to use in the Swatches palette. The path fills with the pattern you selected.

Figure 5-11:
The same path with several different pattern fills.

You can apply a pattern to a stroke as well as to a fill. Applying a pattern is exactly like applying a solid color (see "The Swatches Palette," earlier in this chapter). Click the object, click the Fill or Stroke box to put the pattern in the proper place, and then click the pattern swatch in the Swatches palette. When you apply a pattern to a stroke, you may need to make the stroke extra thick for the pattern to be visible (see "Making a bold stroke," earlier in this chapter).

Making patterns

You can easily turn most path-based artwork into a pattern, as shown in Figure 5-12 (which hotly pursues the steps required to create a pattern out of paths).

To create a pattern out of paths, just follow these steps:

1. **Create the artwork you want to use for a pattern.**

   For this example, we drew a hammer.

2. **Select the artwork, using any of the Selection tools.**

3. **Drag the artwork from the document window into the Swatches palette and release the mouse button.**

   A new swatch appears in the Swatches palette containing a *very* tiny version of your artwork. (Give it a name; it'll be easier to identify later.)

4. **Double-click the new swatch to open the Swatch Options dialog box.**

5. **Enter the name of the pattern.**

6. **Click OK.**

   The custom pattern appears in the Swatches dialog box.

7. **Apply your custom pattern to any path.**

   Our pattern inside the oval certainly hammers home the point (sorry about that).

Occasionally, you may want to "space out" your pattern artwork, so that the repeated pieces of artwork are farther away from each other. You can easily trick Illustrator into doing this by drawing an invisible rectangle (a rectangle with a fill and stroke of None) over your artwork. The bigger the rectangle, the farther apart the repeated pieces are from each other. Select the artwork and the rectangle before you make your pattern. Illustrator isn't quite smart enough to realize that the rectangle is invisible. The program just sees the paths that make the rectangle and repeats the artwork based on those edges.

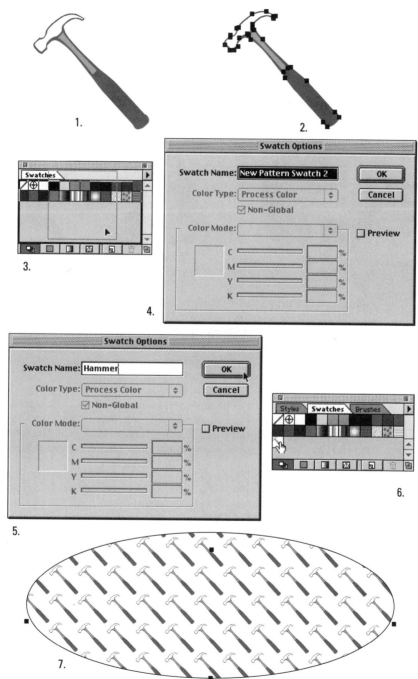

Figure 5-12:
Creating a
pattern.

Using the Gradient Fill

Paths can be filled with colors that smoothly blend from one to another across a distance. These colors are called *gradients*. Gradients can have any number of colors in them, with results that are nothing short of astonishing. Figure 5-13 shows several paths with gradient fills.

Figure 5-13:
Objects with gradient fills.

Filling a path with a gradient involves two steps: creating the gradient and then applying it to a path. However, you can do this in any order. Many times it is easier to create a gradient, apply it to a path, and then continue to tweak it by changing, adding, or removing colors or by modifying the position or angle of the gradient. This method lets you see how the gradient looks on an object instead of in just a small box.

To fill a path with a gradient, select the path and then click a gradient in the Swatches palette. The object fills with a gradient that probably doesn't look a thing like what you want; but that's okay. Using the Gradient tool and the Gradient palette, you can tweak this gradient to your heart's content.

The Gradient tool

 The Gradient tool (which you access with this fashionably shaded button) doesn't actually create anything. Instead, it lets you set the direction and the *duration* (the distance across which the gradient makes its transition from the beginning color to the ending color).

To use the Gradient tool, first use any Selection tool to select an object that is filled with a gradient. Then click and drag across the gradient with the Gradient tool; release the mouse button when you get to the other side. The direction you drag sets the direction of the blend. The place where you click gets 100 percent of the start color; the place where you release gets 100 percent of the end color. The gradient happens as a smooth blend between those two points (as suavely demonstrated in Figure 5-14).

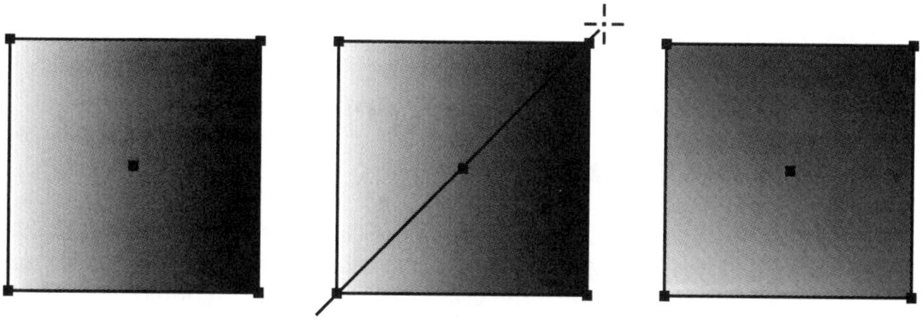

Figure 5-14:
Left: The square (which is selected) shows a gradient applied at default settings. Center: Clicking and dragging with the Gradient tool. Right: The resulting gradient.

The Gradient palette

The Gradient tool can only go so far on its own, especially if you don't like the colors of your gradient! Fortunately, you don't have to settle for the gradients that come in the Swatches palette. You can use the Gradient palette (by choosing Window⇨Show Gradient) to change colors, add colors, remove The Swatches palette appears.colors, and change the way the colors behave (see Figure 5-15).

Figure 5-15:
The Gradient palette: Sleek and simple, and oh-so-powerful!

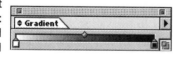

The Gradient palette looks simple compared to other palettes, but don't be deceived! In spite of its humble appearance, this palette lets you create just about any gradient you could ever want. The Gradient palette works with the Color palette and the Swatches palette, so have both of those palettes open whenever you edit a gradient.

The *gradient sliders* slide left and right. You use them to change how gradually (or not-so-gradually) your colors blend with each other. If you want the colors to blend without much nuance over a short distance, drag the sliders closer together. If you want the colors to blend more gradually across a longer distance, move the sliders farther apart.

Gradient-mania (color-tweaking made simple)

When you change a gradient in the Gradient palette, selected objects that are filled with that gradient update to reflect that change. It's a lot easier to see what's going on with the gradient if you make an object and fill it with the gradient before you start making changes in the palette.

To change gradient colors, here's the highly artistic approach (no smock needed):

1. **Click one of the gradient sliders beneath the gradient bar.**

   The color of the slider appears in the Color palette.

2. **Create a different color in the Color palette.**

   As long as the gradient slider is selected, the color updates in the Gradient palette automatically. Is that slick or what?

   As an alternative, you can click any solid color in the Swatches palette and drag it to the Gradient slider in the Gradient palette. The gradient updates with the new color.

Adding colors to the gradient is a lot easier than going to the paint store. Just follow these steps:

1. **Click beneath the gradient bar where there isn't any gradient slider.**

   A new slider appears where you click.

2. **Change the color of the new slider in the Color palette.**

   As an alternative, if the color you want to add already exists in the Swatches palette, just drag the color from the Swatches palette to the Gradient bar in the Gradient palette.

   After you release the mouse button, a new gradient slider appears, and the gradient updates to include the new color.

To remove a color, just click the gradient slider and drag it off the Gradient palette.

On top of the Gradient bar, between every pair of gradient sliders is the *breaking point* slider. This sets the point at which the two colors blend at 50 percent of each color. You can also move this point by dragging it to the left or to the right. Figure 5-16 gives you a look at different ways to change the gradient.

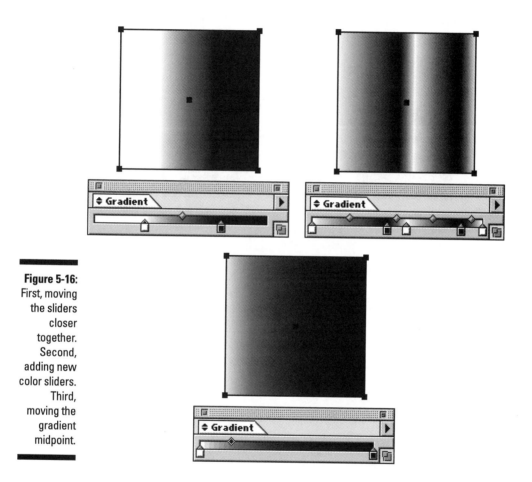

Figure 5-16:
First, moving the sliders closer together. Second, adding new color sliders. Third, moving the gradient midpoint.

The Secret Gradient

If you clicked the gradient swatches in the Swatches palette, you may notice that some gradients look like spheres or sunbursts. You may have tried to recreate one of these gradients, but no amount of clicking and dragging with the Gradient tool, and no amount of moving gradient sliders lets you do that. The trick is in a hidden option in the Gradient palette. Click the little triangle in the upper-right corner of the Gradient palette. A menu with only one item (Show Options) appears. Choose this option to make several more options appear in the palette, as shown in Figure 5-17. The one you want is the Type option — which, when clicked, reveals two choices: Linear and Radial. Choose Radial. You edit radial gradients just as you do linear gradients. The only difference is that radial gradients radiate from the center. The beginning color is the center color. When you click and drag, the spot where you click sets the center of the gradient.

Figure 5-17:
Choosing
Show
Options in
the flyout
menu
to work
with a radial
gradient.

 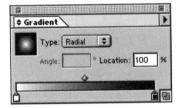

Chapter 6

Selecting and Editing Paths

To change a path in Illustrator, you have to select it. In fact, 99.999 percent of the time you can't make any changes at all to a path unless it's selected. Some exceptions are when you change Document Color Mode (Chapter 1) and when you use the Pen tool to continue on an existing path (Chapter 7). Two things out of the thousands of things you can do in Illustrator isn't a large ratio. Everything else requires that you make a selection.

When you make a selection in Illustrator, you are saying, "From this moment forward, I want what I do to affect this part of the artwork, and nothing else." You are targeting a point, path, object, or objects for change. Using Illustrator's wide variety of Selection tools and commands, you can target everything from a single point to your entire document. And the changes you make — the size, rotation, fill or stroke colors, and so on — simultaneously affect everything that you have selected.

Selecting with Different Methods

Suppose you create a mondo-cool logo. With Illustrator, you can select

✔ the entire logo

✔ any group of paths within the logo

✔ any single path within the logo

✔ any portion of any path or paths

All these possibilities make selecting in Illustrator seem a rather daunting task. As if that weren't enough, Illustrator gives you five different Selection tools, shown in Figure 6-1. In the following sections, you find out about these tools and what happens when you use them.

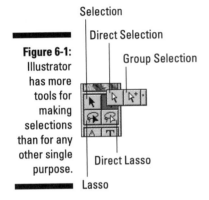

Selection

Direct Selection

Group Selection

Figure 6-1:
Illustrator
has more
tools for
making
selections
than for any
other single
purpose.

Direct Lasso

Lasso

Natural selection

Of the five Selection tools in Illustrator — the Selection tool, Direct Selection tool, Group Selection tool, Lasso tool, and Direct Select Lasso tool — the Selection tool is more-or-less the "main" Selection tool. It simply selects whatever you click. (The names of the other Selection tools aren't quite as accurate in describing their functions, but hey, "Selection tool" was already taken.) To keep the confusion to a minimum, we call the tools by their Adobe-given names — in part so you know what the cute label refers to when you pause the cursor over a tool and see the name in the tooltip.

You use the Selection tool to select objects or groups of objects. When you click a path, you select the entire path. If the path is part of a group, you select that group as well. A *group* is two or more separate objects that are joined together by choosing Object⇨Group. You join objects into a group to get the advantage of selecting all of them at once when you use the Selection tool to select them — which saves all that tedious clicking. (The Object⇨ Group command is just one of the fiendishly clever ways you can organize things in Illustrator — explore 'em all in Chapter 13.)

You can select onscreen items with the Selection tool in two ways:

✔ **Click the object that you want to select.** The object and any other object that is grouped with it are selected.

✔ **Click and drag with the Selection tool.** As you do, a dotted rectangle called a *marquee* appears. Anything inside or touching the marquee is selected, enabling you to select more than one object or group at a time, as shown in Figure 6-2.

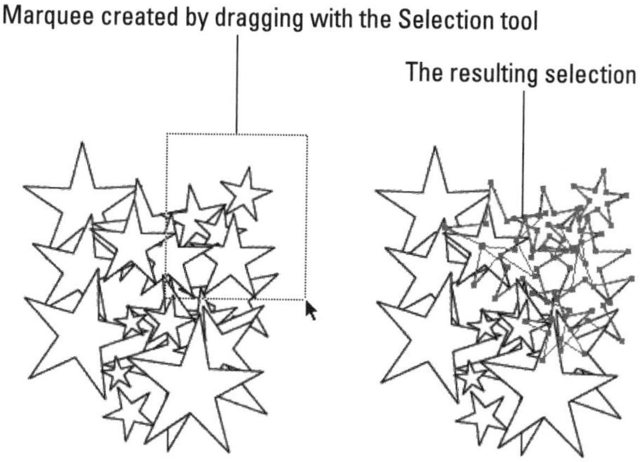

Marquee created by dragging with the Selection tool

The resulting selection

Figure 6-2:
The
Selection
tool selects
objects that
are within
(or touched
by) the
marquee.

If you click another path while one path is already selected, the path you click is selected — and the previously selected path is deselected. If you click an empty area, *everything* is deselected.

Also, if you click inside a path that is filled with None, you can't select that path. To select a path that has no fill, click the path itself. Similarly, when you are in Outline view mode (a way of looking at your paths with all fill and stroke colors hidden, accessed by selecting View⇨Outline), you click your paths to select them. (See Chapter 5 for more info on fills and strokes.)

Direct selection

You use the Direct Selection tool to select individual points, path segments, type objects, and placed images by clicking them one at a time. If you drag a marquee with the Direct Selection tool, then everything the marquee encloses gets selected — all placed images, type objects, and portions of paths. Figure 6-3 shows what is selected when you drag the Direct Selection marquee around several objects. (Note especially the star in the very center of the selected objects at the right of the figure; some of its points are included in the selection, others aren't.)

Marquee created by dragging with the Direct Selection tool

The resulting selection (note that only
what was inside the marquee is selected)

Figure 6-3:
A selection
in progress
with the
Direct
Selection
tool.

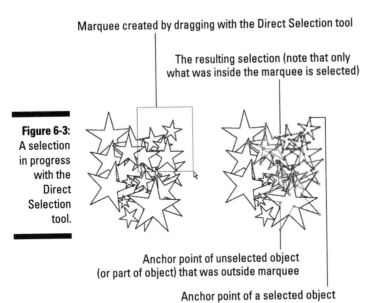

Anchor point of unselected object
(or part of object) that was outside marquee

Anchor point of a selected object

Group selection

Illustrator provides a special tool (called the Group Selection tool) for
selecting — surprise! — groups. But the tool selects groups in a way different
from the plain old Selection tool (which selects everything that is grouped to
the object that you select). The Group Selection tool selects only one subgroup at a time.

A *subgroup* is a group within a group. Remember Statistics 101? (Don't make
that face. What if it froze like that?) Suppose you want to create a graphic of a
pencil. You start with the easy part — the lead (okay, so it's graphite and not
lead — picky, picky). Then you go on to create something harder: that conical
bit of wood that flares out around the lead and eventually becomes the rest
of the pencil. After you get those two pieces positioned together the way you
like, you want to keep them that way — so you group them together. That
way, you only have to click one of them with the Selection tool, and they
move together. Next, you create the rest of the pencil separately. After you
bring all the pieces together, you want to keep them that way — so you group
the lead and the cone with the rest of the pencil (a process that by now
seems hauntingly familiar). All three objects are now a group. The lead and
the cone are a subgroup of that group. You can continue grouping things,
having as many subgroups as you want. Happily, Illustrator remembers the
order in which you group things from the first subgroup to the last big group.
So when you click multiple times with the Group Selection tool, the first click
selects the pencil lead, the second selects both the lead and the wood, the
third click selects the lead, the wood, and the rest of the pencil.

Two oddities of selecting in Illustrator

When selecting in Illustrator, you may find that a couple of oddities crop up. The oddest one is that if you select just a point on a path, the point is all that you've selected — it shows up as solid, while the rest of the points on the path remain unselected and show up as hollow. Then things get weird. Even though only one point is selected, any change that you make to the fill or stroke *affects the entire path.* (For more information on fills and strokes, see Chapter 5.)

Another odd thing is that you can select a line segment, but Illustrator never *shows* you that the line segment is selected. If you click a segment, *all* the points on its path show as unselected (hollow). Nothing appears onscreen to indicate that *only* the segment is selected — but once again, changing the fill or stroke affects the entire path. Consistent? Sure. Weird? Oh yeah.

The Group Selection tool selects only one subgroup at a time, such as an object within a group, a single group within multiple groups, or a set of groups within the artwork. To find out how the Group Selection tool works, follow these steps:

1. **Select the Group Selection tool from the toolbox.**

2. **Click a path that's part of a group.**

   The path is selected entirely (all the points are solid; none are hollow), but the other objects in the group are not selected. (This result is an oddity of the tool. It first selects a single object, even though an object isn't really a group.)

3. **Click the same path again.**

   The next higher level of grouped objects is selected, as well as anything that has already been selected. Each time you click, you select the next higher level of grouping, until finally the all-encompassing group-of-all-groups is selected.

If you continue this crazed clicking, you wind up with groups of groups. For example, if you make several onscreen drawings of pencils, you can group them so that you can move them all at once, draw a pencil box, and then group the pencils with the box. The Group Selection tool lets you select "up" from a single object to the group that the object belongs to, and so on. Figure 6-4 applies this principle to the objects that form a pencil when grouped together.

Figure 6-4:
From top to bottom: Clicking the same path with the Group Selection tool selects first the path, then the group that the path is in, and then the group that the first group is in.

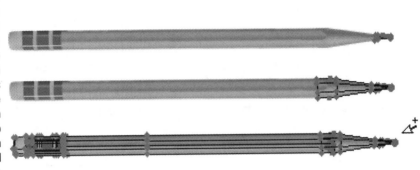

Selecting more or less of what you have

Suppose you want to select a path on the left side of your document, and you also want to select a placed image on the right side of your document, but lots of paths are in between. You can't drag a marquee because then you get all those unwanted paths in the middle. So you select the path on the left and then click the object on the right — and the path on the left becomes deselected. Drat!

The key to selecting more than one item at a time is the Shift key. If you hold down the Shift key and click a path with the Selection tool, you add that path to whatever is currently selected. If two paths are selected, pressing the Shift key and clicking another path results in all three paths being selected. You can also use the Shift key in conjunction with a selection marquee. The process is called *Shift-clicking,* and you can also use it to select *fewer* paths. For example, if you Shift-click one of the three selected paths shown in Figure 6-5, you *deselect* that path, leaving only two selected paths.

Shift-clicking also works with the Direct Selection tool, except this action adds or subtracts single *points* instead of complete paths.

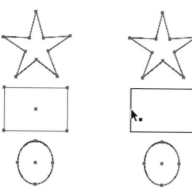

Freeform selections

The Lasso tool and the Direct Select Lasso tool act similarly to dragging out a selection marquee, except this marquee can be any shape, not just rectangular. To use either tool, click and drag around the area that you want to select. When you release the mouse button, all objects or groups touching that selection are selected. (If you are using the Direct Lasso tool, all points in that area are selected.)

Selecting without Tools

Sometimes, selecting objects in Illustrator without using tools is easier or more convenient. Illustrator provides various options in the Edit menu that let you select (and deselect) objects, regardless of the tool you have.

A giant vat of really sticky stuff

By far, the most common selection method in Illustrator is a keyboard command. By pressing ⌘+A [Ctrl+A], you select all the objects in the document. You can also choose Edit➪Select All, but the keyboard command is so useful, you'll probably memorize it in no time at all.

The opposite of Select All is Deselect All — which deselects anything selected in the document (but you knew that). Don't be misled by the name. You don't have to have everything selected to use the command. Even if you have just one thing selected out of a hundred objects, Deselect All deselects it. The keyboard command is easy to remember: ⌘+Shift+A [Ctrl+Shift+A].

Specialized selection functions for important occasions

The Edit menu contains a whole lot of other selection functions besides Select All and Deselect All. Use these functions to select objects that are similar in some way (such as style or fill color) to the object(s) already selected. Figure 6-6 shows the Select submenu.

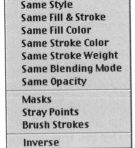

Figure 6-6:
The Select submenu (found under the Edit menu).

Five of the Select submenu options are a bit less obvious:

- **Select Again** reselects whatever was last selected using the Select submenu.
- **Masks** selects paths used as masks in the document.
- **Stray Points** selects paths in your document that contain only a single point.
- **Brush Strokes** selects all paths in the document that have brush strokes assigned to them.
- **Inverse** selects the opposite of what is currently selected. Everything that is currently selected becomes unselected, and everything else becomes selected.

All these commands can be vastly helpful in streamlining the editing process. For instance, if your client loves everything about the image except for that *certain shade* of blue, you can select one object that has that blue color in it, and then choose Same Stroke Color or Same Fill Color. With everything in that color selected, you can edit them all at once! If you're having trouble printing lines of a certain stroke weight, you can choose Same Stroke Weight and increase the stroke weight of all the lines. (See Chapter 5 for more information on fills and strokes.) Other commands select items that have a history of problems printing on certain printers — such as stray points, brushstrokes, and masks. Selecting such items lets you modify them before printing. (See Chapter 16 for more about printing.)

Editing and Adjusting Points

After you go to the trouble of selecting specific points, what are you going to do with them? Well, you can move them and change the kinds of points they are. You can also adjust their handles to change the shape of a curve.

A relocation bonus for points

You can move any selected point to any location. Because points (and not entire paths) are what you're moving, use the Direct Selection tool. Click any point with the Direct Selection tool and then drag the point to move it. You can do this in one step (click and drag at once) or in two separate steps (click and release, and then drag the point). Figure 6-7 shows a path with a point in its original location and then shows the point after it was moved with the Direct Selection tool.

Figure 6-7:
Left: the original path. Right: the path after the selected point is moved using the Direct Selection tool.

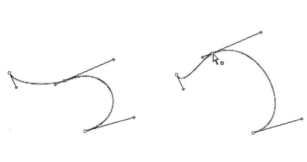

To move points just a tiny little bit at a time — but with precision — use the arrow keys to "nudge" selected points in the direction of the arrow. One keystroke moves the point by an exact, smidgen-sized unit of measurement (1/72 of an inch, or .3528 millimeters) — a unit of measure known in the design and publishing trades as a *point*.

Fine-tuning curves with direction points

If a point has *direction points* (those little gearshift-like line segments) sticking out of it, you can use the Direct Selection tool to adjust the direction points — which adjusts the curves that shoot out from the points where the direction points connect to the curves.

Incidentally, the line that joins the connection point to the curve is called the *direction line.* Don't worry, only you can see the direction lines. They don't print or show up in the graphic when it is on the Web. Their only purpose is to show which anchor point is currently under the control of the direction point.

You probably noticed already that sometimes you see sticking out of points those gearshift-like direction lines and direction points. Other times, you don't. Fortunately, you don't need to increase your therapy to three times a week. (At least not because of this.) What actually happens is that when you click a point or a segment with the Direct Selection tool, you see the handles associated with that point or segment. However, if you Shift+click additional points, you lose those handles. Figure 6-8 shows what happens when you use the Direct Selection tool to click, or enclose in a marquee, a variety of different areas.

Figure 6-8:
Selecting a curving path with the Direct Selection tool reveals its direction points and direction lines.

When you can see the handles that you want to move, click and drag them to move them. Note that missing a handle is *very* easy if you aren't really careful. (And making crude remarks when you *do* miss them is still considered bad form, even if no one else is around.) Figure 6-9 shows the path from Figure 6-8 with the direction points moved to different positions.

Converting anchor points

Illustrator has three types of anchor points: corner points, smooth points, and direction-changing points. You find *corner points* in the corners of squares or triangles. Two path segments join in a corner point when neither of the connecting ends has a direction point associated with it. *Smooth points* are used when two path segments continue smoothly, as in a circle or in a curving path. Both path segments have direction points — linked together so that when you move one point, the other point moves in an equal and opposite direction, preserving the smooth curve. A *direction-changing point* has two direction points that move in different directions, enabling you to impose abrupt changes in direction. (For more on anchor point types, see Chapter 7.)

Figure 6-9:
Believe it or not, this is the same graphic that appears in Figure 6-8; only the direction points have been moved.

You can use Illustrator's Convert Anchor Point tool (which looks like an acute angle located in the same slot as the Pen tool) to change a point from one type into another. (For more about the types of anchor points and their usual behaviors, see Chapters 2 and 7.) To use the Convert Anchor Point tool, put it on a point and then click. What you do next determines the resulting point type:

- ✔ **To get a corner point:** Click an anchor point and release to change it into a straight corner point with no direction points.

  This is a "quick-retract" method of point conversion.

- ✔ **To get a smooth point:** Click an anchor point and drag it to change it into a smooth point with two linked direction points.

- ✔ **To get a direction-changing point:** Click a direction point and drag. It moves independently of the opposite direction point.

Adding and subtracting points (or path math)

Illustrator has two tools that are used specifically for adding points to a path or for removing them. The Add Anchor Point tool adds points, and the Delete Anchor Point tool removes points. Both tools are located in the same slot as the Pen tool.

When you add an anchor point (or even several anchor points) with the Add Anchor Point tool, the path doesn't change shape (as shown in Figure 6-10), but you can move the point or points with the Direct Selection tool or convert them to other types of points using the Convert Point tool.

Figure 6-10:
Left: the
original
path.
Right: the
unchanged
shape with
several new
anchor
points
added (with
the Add
Anchor
Point tool) to
three of the
star's four
arms.

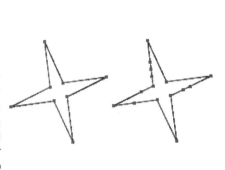

When you remove a point with the Delete Anchor Point tool, the path can change shape — either slightly or dramatically, depending on the shape. Figure 6-11 shows what happens in two different circumstances.

Figure 6-11:
Left: the
original
path. Right:
removing
two differ-
ent anchor
points to
create two
entirely
different
shapes.

Okay, have a squint at Figure 6-11 for a moment. (Ow, that's gotta hurt. Not that hard.) You can probably tell immediately which anchor points were zapped with the Delete Anchor Point tool to change the image on the left into the upper- and lower-right images. In each case, only one point was removed. Powerful creatures, those anchor points.

Chapter 7

Wielding the Mighty Pen Tool

- -

In This Chapter

▶ Using the Pen tool to create four different anchor points

▶ Drawing straight lines with the Pen

▶ Exploring the differences between open and closed paths

▶ Drawing smoothly curved lines with the Pen

▶ Making a seamless transition between curves and straight lines

▶ Drawing some basic shapes with the Pen

- -

*B*ack in medieval times, circa 1982, straight and smoothly curved lines were drawn with elegant handheld implements — such as a Rapidograph pen (an unwieldy tool requiring more practice and skill to use than a three-handed harpsichord), a ruler, and maybe a French Curve. If you never had to use these torturous instruments, consider yourself lucky. We've tried drawing with a Rapidograph pen. Instead of smooth lines, we got bumpy globs of ink and huge splotches that gooshed onto the page each time we paused, changed direction, or heard a hard-hitting tune on the radio. Drawing that way takes a steady hand and a ton of patience — two qualities caffeine-chugging, weaned-on-TV types like us don't have much of.

 Today, if you need a straight line or a curved one — or even if you *want* the appearance of bumpy globs of ink — you want to use Illustrator's Pen tool. This tool is a bit intimidating at first, but once you grasp a few handy, post-medieval concepts, you'll be drawing floor plans, customizing logos, and feeling really, *really* sorry for people who don't have Illustrator.

Unlike its handheld, inky counterpart, the Pen tool is not intuitive. You can't just pick it up and doodle; its functionality is far from obvious. This tool is blatantly unlike any drawing instrument in the real world. But locked within the Pen tool are secrets and powers beyond those of mere physical ink. The Pen tool is a metaphysical doorway to the heavens of artistic exaltation; once you master the path of the Pen, all the riches of Illustrator can be yours. (You may even remain unfazed by such deliciously hokey metaphors. . . .)

Performing with the Pen, the Path, and the Anchor Points

No, this section isn't a retro look at obscure rock bands; it's about telling Illustrator where to go — by creating the paths Illustrator relies on to create shapes and objects. *Paths* are instructions that tell your computer how to arrange straight and curved line segments onscreen. Each path is made up of *anchor points* (dots that appear onscreen). Between every two anchor points is the portion of the path called a *line segment*.

The Pen tool is probably as close as you ever need to get to calling up paths with the PostScript language. Unless, of course, you're an Adobe programming geek — in which case, the thought that you might *need* this book is frightening. So for sanity's sake, we assume otherwise and get right to the point. Make that *points*. Understanding the anchor points that make up paths is critical to using the Pen tool. Anchor points have the following traits:

- At least two anchor points are required for every path. ("One point maketh not a path," saith the sage.)

- Any number of anchor points can appear on a path — dozens, even hundreds, as long as that number is *not* one or zero. ("Zero points make not a path, either, O wiseacre," grouseth the sage.)

- If an anchor point has a *direction point* (a black box you can grab and move with the mouse), then the line segment extending from the anchor point is curved.

  Direction point is the official Adobe term for this handy little black box. You may also hear Illustrator veterans talk about *handles* or *control handles* — same thing.

- If an anchor point has no direction point, then the line segment extending from the anchor point is straight.

- You can use the Pen tool to create *four* types of anchor points (smooth, straight corner, curved corner, and combination corner) to tell the computer how to get from one line segment to another. Care for a closer look? Coming right up.

Smooth anchor points

Smooth anchor points create (as you may expect) a smoothly curved transition from one line segment to another. When you want a line that reminds you of the letter *S* (or some S-words like *sinuous* and *snaky*), use smooth anchor points. Figure 7-1 shows two direction points creating a smooth anchor point on a path. The curve bends to follow the two direction points.

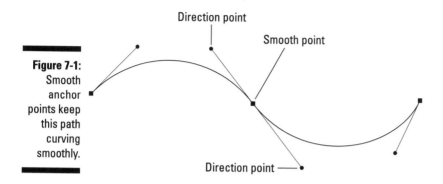

Figure 7-1:
Smooth anchor points keep this path curving smoothly.

If you want to create circles, freeform shapes like puddles, or shapes like those nonslip flower stickers for your bathtub floor, then smooth anchor points are the way to go. Use the Pen tool to create a smooth anchor point by clicking and dragging with the mouse. As you drag, direction points, connected to the anchor point by direction lines, appear on either side of the anchor point (one at the tip of the Pen, the other on the opposite side of the anchor point). Think of those wacky direction points as magnets pulling the line segment towards them. The line segment bends to follow the direction point — just that easy, just that simple. (So far.)

Straight corner anchor points

Straight corner anchor points function as their name suggests, and according to a couple of features that are dead giveaways:

- ✔ One or two straight lines sticking out of them. In Figure 7-2, for example, the anchor point is where you'd find the hub if the two line segments were the hands of a clock.

- ✔ Absolutely *no direction points* sticking out of them (remember, direction points make curves).

Figure 7-2:
Use straight corner anchor points when you need straight paths.

Think of these anchor points as the corner of an angle that you could draw with a pencil and a protractor. (Except you draw them on your computer; nobody bumps your arm so your nice sharp lead breaks off and . . . uh, never mind.) To create straight corner anchor points with the Pen tool, *click and release;* pretend the anchor point is a fish that isn't quite the legal limit and you have to throw it back. *Do not drag.* Promptly release the mouse button the second you hear it click.

You use straight corner anchor points to draw objects with hard angles — rectangles, triangles (note the whole "angle" theme here) — anything that consists entirely of straight lines and *no* curves. Snakes, clouds, and country roads are entirely out of the question.

Curved corner anchor points

This book starts to take a few corners of its own here, so hold on tight. Nice grip.

Think of the *curved corner* anchor point as the *m-curve* anchor point, or the point where the two bumps on a lowercase *m* are joined. If you look at this nice lowercase *m* through a magnifying glass, or a pretty good squint, you can see a corner between the two bumps — with curves coming out of it. The curved corner anchor point may also remind you of a double fishhook turned upside down. You need these points to create not just lowercase *m*s, but also hearts (the Valentine variety, as in Figure 7-3).

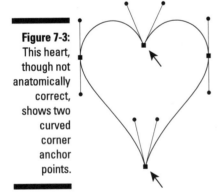

Figure 7-3:
This heart, though not anatomically correct, shows two curved corner anchor points.

Consider the possibilities — clovers, moons (old-fashioned crescents-with-little-noses), and undoubtedly several other shapes you may see in a cereal bowl (except for, say, blue diamonds — those you draw with straight corner anchor points). But beware — curved corner anchor points are a little weird. To create one, you have to modify an existing anchor point — specifically, by following these steps:

1. **Create a smooth anchor point while you're creating a path.**

   This works best after you draw at least one line segment.

2. **Press Option [Alt on a PC] and then click-and-drag the smooth anchor point.**

   A direction point appears — totally independent of the anchor point — on the opposite side of the point. This new handle controls where the double-fishhook corner goes. You can drag the new handle nearer to the first direction point (the one for the original smooth anchor point) — or anywhere else — without affecting that first direction point.

You can also change a smooth anchor point into a curved corner anchor point by pressing the Option [Alt on a PC] key as you drag the smooth anchor point.

Combination corner anchor points

If you want to use the Pen tool to draw rounded corner rectangles — such as classic TV screens, archways, and cylinders — you're going to need *combination corner* anchor points. The combination that identifies this type of anchor point is a blending of two other types: smooth and straight corner anchor points. You can identify a combination corner anchor point by what you find sticking out of it: two line segments and only one direction point. This handle curves one of the line segments and leaves the other segment straight. Keep in mind that the handle is controlling the curved segment, *not* the straight segment, and these points are much easier to use.

As with curved corner anchor points (mutant versions of their straight corner cousins), you can't just say "I want one of *those*" and *poof!* have one appear onscreen. To create the exotic combination corner anchor point, you modify an existing smooth or straight corner anchor point. Which type you modify depends on where you want the curve to go:

- ✔ If you want the curve *before* the anchor point (the existing line segment is curved), then you modify a smooth anchor point.

- ✔ If you want the curve *after* the anchor point (the existing line segment is straight), then you modify a straight corner anchor point.

Figure 7-4 shows how to create a combination corner anchor point in either situation.

Starting with a Smooth Path   Starting with a Straight Path

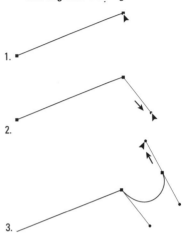

Figure 7-4:
Two ways to
create
combination
corner
anchor
points:
starting
smooth (left)
or straight
(right).

Starting with a smooth path

To create a combination corner anchor point from a smooth one (so that the curve precedes the anchor point), follow these steps:

1. **Click and drag the Pen tool; then, at another location, click and drag again to create a curved line.**

   To get an image that resembles Figure 7-4, start in the upper-left quarter of a blank Illustrator document, click and drag up and to the right for the first drag in Step 1. Start your second drag at a place roughly parallel to your original starting point and about an inch to the right, dragging down and to the right.

   So you can see what you're doing, you have to draw at least one line segment before you change the anchor point. That's the rule!

   When you complete the two drags in Step1, the most recent line segment ends in a smooth anchor point.

2. **Click the smooth anchor point that appeared after you clicked and dragged the second time in Step 1.**

   The direction point (handle) that extended out from the anchor point disappears.

3. **Move the mouse pointer to a place about an inch to the right of the most recent anchor point and then click.**

This click creates a straight path segment (straight because it's free from the influence of the direction point). After you click, the two direction points (handles) disappear from the curved line that you drew in Step 1. The anchor point from which you drew your new straight segment is a combination corner anchor point.

Starting with a straight path

To create a combination corner anchor point from a straight corner anchor point (so the curve comes after the anchor point), follow these steps:

1. **Using the Pen tool, click once and (without dragging) click again in a nearby location in the document.**

   To get an image that resembles the one in Figure 7-4, start in the upper-right quarter of a blank Illustrator document, click once, and then — after moving the mouse pointer to the right and slightly higher — click again.

   A straight path segment appears. You need this line segment so you can see the difference in the path as you change the straight corner anchor point to a combination corner anchor point.

2. **Click the straight corner anchor point you just created; hold down the mouse button and drag.**

   To get an image that resembles the one in Figure 7-4, drag down and slightly to the right.

   A new, single direction point (handle) extends from the anchor point.

3. **Click in another location and drag away from the anchor point.**

   To get an image that resembles the one in Figure 7-4, click a spot in line with the previous anchor point, and then drag up and slightly to the left.

   A curved path segment appears. The anchor point between the straight and curved line segments is now a combination corner anchor point.

Creating Straight Lines with the Pen Tool

Using logic as valid as any followed by Holmes and Watson (not to mention Spock), you can deduce that you use straight corner anchor points to draw straight lines with the Pen tool. Elementary. . . .

Harrumph. Elementary or not, you should jolly well see this marvel in action. To draw a triangle with the Pen tool (see Figure 7-5), just follow these steps:

Figure 7-5:
Drawing a
triangle with
the Pen tool,
using
straight
corner
anchor
points.

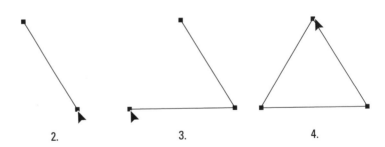

1.   2.   3.   4.

1. **With the Pen tool, click (do not drag) in the document window.**

   An anchor point appears after you release the mouse button. (Cute, isn't it? But lonely; it needs friends.)

2. **Click (don't drag) someplace below and a little to the right of the first anchor point.**

   After you release the mouse button, a line appears between the first and second anchor points. They're joined, open, and ready to rock. You've created a fine-looking path.

3. **Click (uh-uh, don't drag!) someplace a bit to the left of the second anchor point.**

   A stunning-looking angle appears. Maybe it's a skateboard ramp. Maybe it's a less-than sign flopped over, worn out from all those equations.

4. **Put your cursor on the first anchor point and click that puppy.**

   You've created a triangle! Congratulations! Euclid would be proud.

If you make a mistake — such as (ahem) dragging instead of just clicking, you can always undo the last step by choosing Edit⇨Undo. Or do what all the pros do — press ⌘+Z if you're bossing a Mac, or Ctrl+Z on the PC (that even rhymes). For that extra-authentic pro sound, you can mutter something nasty about computers if you goof up.

Well, okay, you've heard this tune before, but once more with feeling: *Do not drag* if you want straight lines. If you drag, you're going to get curves. In fact, *not* dragging to get straight lines is probably harder than dragging to get curves. (If you want to take a break and go drag something, be our guest; you've earned it.)

You can create right angles and 45-degree angles with the Pen tool by holding down the Shift key as you draw.

Open and closed paths

Paths in Illustrator are either open or closed, one or the other, with nothing in between. Open and closed paths differ in the following ways:

- ✔ An *open path* has endpoints. It starts in one place and ends in another place — clearly a line segment, and not a polygon.

- ✔ A *closed path* has no starting point and no endpoint. Like that psychotic bunny in the battery commercial, it just keeps going and going in the same place — clearly the boundary of a solid shape. (Think of complete circles, Möbius strips, and so forth.)

As you draw with the Pen tool, you're creating an open path. If you click the point where you started drawing the path, you close the path.

Creating artwork with the Pen tool is much easier if you set your fill color to None, regardless of the final color you are going to fill your artwork with. When you use the Pen tool with a fill color selected, Illustrator treats every line you make as though it were a completed object by drawing a temporary, invisible line straight from the first anchor point in the path to the last anchor point, then fills the enclosed area with the selected fill color. This is confusing at best, because it hides parts of the path you are creating, and creates an object that appears to change shape completely with every click of the mouse. To avoid this mess, set your fill color to None while you create your path, and change the fill color when the path is complete.

Creating Super-Precise Curves with the Pen Tool

Illustrator's Pen tool is a model of precision and accuracy. With it, you can draw virtually anything (or draw anything virtually). That is, of course, once you master drawing curves.

The Pen isn't designed to be maddening (as far as we know), but using it to draw successful curves *does* seem to require a psychological breakthrough. Illustrator users who struggle to figure out the Pen tool by themselves, without the handy guide you hold in your hands, may slog through months (or even years) of frustration before the breakthrough occurs. They happen upon shapes and curves that work for them — and then they finally "get it."

Therefore, we vow to spare you the pain of all that trial and error. The following sections begin this noble quest, in which we find the knight. . . .

Taming the draggin'

(Sorry about the bad pun.) Where do you want your curve to go? Just drag in that direction. We know, we know, we told you *not* to drag. But in that situation, you were making straight lines. What's even less helpful, dragging is perhaps the most anti-intuitive action imaginable for creating curves. Regardless, we charge into the fray.

If you click and drag with the intent to create a curve, you get what looks like a straight line, as shown in Figure 7-6. (Weird, isn't it?) Oddly enough, the "line" you get is twice as long as the distance you drag, extending in two directions from the spot where you initially click. After you release the mouse button, this "line" is *still* a straight line and still no curve in sight.

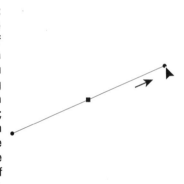

Figure 7-6: In the process of creating a curve, you have to drag out a straight line; the arrow in the figure shows the direction of the drag.

At this stage, what do you suppose is the most natural thing in the world to do? Sure — it's to drag in another direction (typically at a 90-degree angle) from where you last released the mouse. And what are the most natural results? An ugly, curvy bump; a new "straight" line extending in both directions from the second anchor point; and a sudden yearning to direct a few choice expletives at Illustrator.

The problem is the second anchor point. Instead of clicking and dragging at a spot near where you first released the mouse button (a *big* no-no), you always click and drag (you don't *have* to drag, but we get to that later) *away* from where you released the mouse button as shown in Figure 7-7. You understood correctly — *away*. Weird, isn't it?

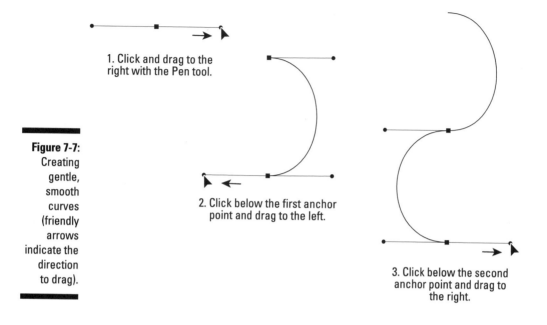

1. Click and drag to the right with the Pen tool.

2. Click below the first anchor point and drag to the left.

3. Click below the second anchor point and drag to the right.

Figure 7-7: Creating gentle, smooth curves (friendly arrows indicate the direction to drag).

To create a lovely, flowing curve for your own purposes, just follow these steps:

1. **Click and drag with the Pen tool.**

   A line extends from the anchor point where you clicked. That's okay; it's supposed to happen that way.

   The line you see is actually a set of *two direction points,* cleverly disguised as lines with little control-handle boxes at each end. Whether you call 'em direction points or control handles, lines or boxes, they don't print out. They're just tools for *controlling* the direction of the line segment that you're drawing.

2. **Without clicking, place your cursor *away* from both the anchor point *and* the direction points. Then click and drag in the direction *opposite* the direction you dragged to create the first anchor point.**

   At this stage, the best approach is to place that second click perpendicular to the direction lines. Note that as you drag, you can actually see the curve between the two anchor points take shape and change. If you drag the same distance that you dragged for the first anchor point, you create an even-looking curve.

3. **Finally, place your cursor away from the second point, still moving away from the first anchor point, and click and drag back in the same direction you dragged for the first anchor point.**

   After you release the mouse button, you see an *S* shape (or a backward *S*, depending on which way you first dragged). Rejoice! If you don't see the *S* or reverse-*S* shape, breathe deeply, count to 10, and try again, exercising superhuman patience and care. When the *S* finally appears, print out a big copy, glue it on the front of your T-shirt, look in the mirror, and repeat this mantra: " . . . truth, justice, and the American way."

Remember that whole song and dance about pressing the Shift key so that new anchor points appear angled at 45 degrees relative to the last anchor point? Well, you can also use the Shift key to *constrain* the angle of control-handle lines to 45 degrees, if you prefer. This action lets you make much more accurate curves than by drawing "freestyle." Just don't press-and-hold the Shift key until *after* you begin dragging with the Pen tool. If you press the Shift key before you drag — and release the key while you're dragging — you get the 45-degree anchor point. If you continue to hold down the Shift key, you get the whole shebang: 45-degree control-handle lines as well as the anchor point.

Following the one-third rule

The optimal distance to drag a direction point from an anchor point is about one-third the distance you expect that line segment to be. So, for instance, if you plan to draw a curve that's about three inches long, drag the direction point out about one inch from the anchor point.

The one-third rule is perfect for creating the most natural, organic-looking curves possible. Breaking the rule can have the following dismal results:

- ✔ If you drag too little, you get curves that are too shallow around the middle of the line segment and too sharp at the anchor points.

- ✔ If you drag too much, you get curves that are quite sharp (like Dead Man's Curve) around the middle of the line segment and too straight around the anchor points (like that curve on the right in Figure 7-8).

Fortunately, on the left, Figure 7-8 shows a "perfect" curve created with the proper use of direction point lines set to one-third the length of the path. Because you can use the Direct Selection tool (the hollow arrow) to adjust the position of the direction points after they're drawn, try to follow the one-third rule whenever possible. Doing so may keep you out of trouble and your vocabulary fit for sensitive listeners.

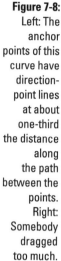

Figure 7-8:
Left: The anchor points of this curve have direction-point lines at about one-third the distance along the path between the points. Right: Somebody dragged too much.

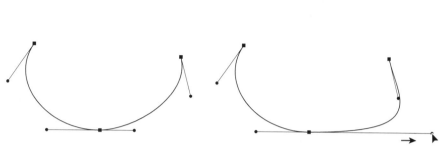

Following rules for the other two thirds

The one-third rule is the most important rule when you're using the Pen tool to draw curves. Of course, you still have to deal with the *other* two thirds of the line segment; that's where a few humble rules can serve you well. Even if you don't plan to follow them right away — because you're still at that awkward, rebellious age — you at least want to be familiar with these rules:

- **Drag in the direction of the path.** Dragging back toward the line segment you just drew results in hard-to-control curves and awkward-appearing line segments between the previous anchor point and the anchor point you're working with. If you need to go back toward the line segment, place an anchor point closer to the previous anchor point you created.

- **Focus on the upcoming segment as well as the current one.** You may notice that the line segment between the prior anchor point and the current anchor point can distract you because it changes as you drag. If you concentrate only on this line segment, the direction point you're dragging out for the *next* line segment probably won't be the right length or angle. You must master the past, present, and future when you use the Pen tool. (Aside from that, it isn't hard at all.)

- **Don't overcompensate for a misdrawn curve.** If you mess up on that last outgoing direction point, don't try to "fix" the line segment with the anchor point you're currently dragging. Instead, focus on the *next* segment; try to ignore the goof-up for now. You can always use the Direct Selection tool to fix the poor thing *after* you finish the path. Chapter 6 has the lowdown on how you can adjust your path after you draw it.

✔ **Use different lengths for each direction point, as necessary.** This rule is the exception to the previous two rules. (You knew there had to be an exception.) If you click and drag and get a segment just right — only to realize that the next segment requires a longer or shorter control-handle line but the same angle — *release the mouse button when the segment is just right.* Then click the same anchor point again (*not* the direction point) and drag in the same direction as you previously dragged. Note that as you change the angle of the direction point on the "other" side (where the previous segment is), you aren't changing the length of that direction point line. And you can match the angle pretty easily because you can see both "before" and "after" versions of the previous line segment.

✔ **Place anchor points at curve transitions.** A *curve transition* is a place where the curve changes. Maybe it changes direction (going from clockwise to counterclockwise or vice versa). Maybe the curve gets smaller or larger. Although you can cheat to achieve similar effects, the results aren't as good — and editing those curve changes can be a nightmare. Figure 7-9 shows a nice curvy path with anchor points placed properly at the transitions.

✔ **Be environmentally conscious in your anchor-point usage.** Don't place anchor points where they're not needed. This rule goes for all types of anchor points. The fewer you have, the easier for you to edit sections of the path (keeping in mind the previous rule, of course).

Holding down the ⌘ [Ctrl] key changes the currently selected tool into whatever Selection tool you used last. This is very handy when you are drawing with the Pen tool, because it lets you move points while keeping the Pen tool selected. Click the Direct Selection tool *before* you choose the Pen tool. If you click, start to drag, and then realize that you clicked in a spot that just isn't going to work, you don't have to stop, undo, and try again. Just press the ⌘ [Ctrl] key. This temporarily changes the Pen tool into the Direct Selection tool. Move your anchor point to a new location. Release the ⌘ [Ctrl] key — your anchor point moves to the new location, just like that!

Figure 7-9:
This path has points placed at the "correct" locations for the best possible curve.

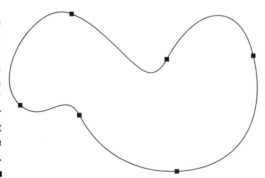

Drawing the tricky anchor points with the Pen tool

A bit of practice with curves and smooth anchor points may get you used to smooth transitions from one line segment to another. Those anchor points are fairly easy to create — just click and drag a new point and *whammo!* you have a smooth anchor point. But both the curved corner anchor point and the combination corner anchor point are a little trickier — they always require two steps. Still, they can't scare a veteran of the draggin' wars. Not a bit.

Curved corner anchor points revisited

Because curved corner anchor points have two curves sticking out of them (one on each side), they need two direction points (one for each curve). But because these points are anchoring independent curves, you have to make those direction points independent of each other. Here's the move: As you're dragging out a smooth anchor point, you can quickly change it into a curved corner anchor point by pressing and releasing the Option [Alt] key. Doing so "breaks" the control-handle lines into independent lines.

Be sure to make your original line segment the proper length and angle before you press the Option [Alt] key. After you press the key, the only way to edit the line is to stop drawing and modify it with the Direct Selection tool. See Chapter 6 for all sorts of great tips on how to get the most out of point adjustment using the Direct Selection tool.

Combination corner anchor points revisited

Using a similar fancy move, you can create combination corner points from smooth or straight corner anchor points — while you're drawing. Here's how:

✔ To go from a straight line into a curved line, as you're drawing a smooth anchor point, press Option [Alt] after you click, but before you release the mouse button. This action lets you drag the direction point for the next line segment without affecting the previous segment as Illustrator normally does. To create the curve, drag the direction point to wherever you need it.

✔ To go from one curved line into another (with a curved corner point instead of a smooth point), click and drag as though you were creating a smooth point. After you have the first curve the way you want it, but before you release the mouse button, press Option [Alt]. As soon as you press Option [Alt], the second direction point moves independently of the first. Use this Option [Alt] technique to move the direction point to wherever you need it.

These two techniques take a little practice because so much depends on the timing of when you press Option [Alt]. Don't worry, though. If you don't get it right the first time, you always have the Convert Anchor Point tool to fall back on.

Drawing Shapes with the Pen Tool

In previous sections, you discover how to draw a triangle and a wavy line. This section walks you through drawing some other basic shapes — because knowing the best ways to do that can make the more complex shapes much easier to draw.

Take, for example, a garden-variety circle — shapes don't get any simpler than that. . . or do they? When you draw one in Illustrator, you can get widely differing results with the Pen tool.

Drawing a sad, lumpy circle with the Pen

You're probably saying to yourself, "Why would anyone be foolish enough to draw a circle using the Pen tool when you can draw a perfect circle in a single step using the Ellipse tool (covered in Chapter 4)?" There are a couple of very good reasons: 1) Practice makes perfect. A circle is an object made entirely of smooth anchor points. Master the circle, and you are the master of smooth curves! 2) The Ellipse tool makes perfect circles *every time*. Sometimes you may want to be a little more creative than that, and drawing the imperfect circle you want with the Pen tool can be a lot faster than modifying a perfect circle created with the Ellipse tool.

So, without further ado, follow these steps, as shown in Figure 7-10:

1. **Hold down the Shift key and click and drag to the right with the Pen tool. Extend the direction point line about ¼ inch.**

2. **Keep the Shift key pressed, click about ½ inch above and to the right of the first anchor point, and then drag up about ¼ inch.**

   You've drawn an eye-pleasing arc — kind of a skateboard-ramp sorta thing.

3. **Keep the Shift key pressed, click about ½ inch above the second anchor point (directly above the first anchor point), and then drag left about ¼ inch.**

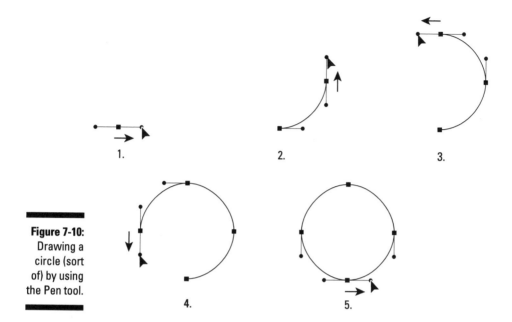

1.   2.   3.

Figure 7-10:
Drawing a
circle (sort
of) by using
the Pen tool.

4.   5.

You've drawn a lovely half circle. And you're actually more than halfway there. (Five steps are listed here, and you've done three — that's *more* than half, for those of you who skipped higher math.)

4. **With your left hand developing a cramp from holding down the Shift key, click about ½ inch to the left of the first anchor point and directly opposite the second anchor point, and then drag down about ¼ inch.**

   (You can probably guess where we're going with this last click. . . .)

5. **Click the first anchor point, drag to the right about ¼ inch, and then (finally) release the Shift key.**

   Your creation is a perfectly *lumpy* circle! If your circle isn't as round as you want, select the Direct Selection tool (the hollow arrow) and tweak the points and direction points until the circle looks less lumpy.

Congratulations — you just drew a circle! Try drawing a second circle using the same steps. And another. You'll find that not only does each circle get easier and better, but you'll have much more control whenever you create a smooth curve anywhere.

Drawing a heart

Ah, a *real* challenge. None of this "circle" stuff for you! Still, similarities to our circle friend abound. You do need four anchor points — two of them smooth points. And most of the anchor points need to be in similar positions to the anchor points you drew for the circle. Hmmm. Figure 7-11 shows the procedure in all its glory. Just complete the following steps:

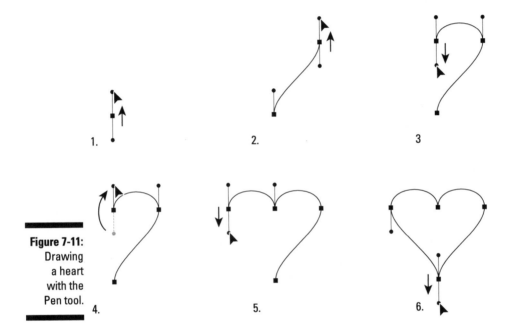

Figure 7-11: Drawing a heart with the Pen tool.

1. **Click and drag up about ¼ inch. Use the Shift key to constrain the angle of the direction point line to a perfectly vertical line.**

2. **Move your cursor about ¾ inch above and ½ inch to the right of the first anchor point and click and drag up about ¼ inch. Use the Shift key to constrain the angle of the direction point.**

3. **Move your cursor about ½ inch to the left (above the first anchor point) and then click and drag down about ¼ inch.**

   This procedure is almost too easy, isn't it? Well, take heart (so to speak). The next step tests your mettle.

4. **Press the Option [Alt] key, click the anchor point you just created, and drag *up* about ¼ inch.**

   This action breaks the two control-handle lines and sets you up for a nice curved corner point at the top of the heart.

5. **Move your cursor about ½ inch to the left of the last anchor point and then click and drag down about ¼ inch.**

   Again, you can press the Shift key to make sure you're dragging a perfectly vertical line.

6. **Move your cursor onto the first point, press the Option [Alt] key and click and drag down about ¼ inch.**

   This completes the heart. With all the practice you have, this shape probably looks a lot better than that circle you drew in the previous exercise.

That was the toughie. After you draw a heart, you can try your drawing prowess on pretty much anything anyone throws at you. If you have the time, you can recreate the ceiling of the Sistine chapel to scale within Illustrator. That is, if you have the time *and* the inclination.

Chapter 8

Wielding the Versatile Pencil Tool

· ·

· ·

*I*n the beginning, there was the Pen. And users said that the Pen was good. But the users also said that the Pen was too hard. And too frustrating. And inefficient for quickly creating paths. And the users griped. And behold! Adobe gave them the Pencil tool — the wondrous, magical Pencil tool that makes creating paths as easy as drawing with a, well, *pencil*. And there was great rejoicing.

In this chapter, you find out all about the Pencil tool. You discover how to create and modify paths, and how to customize the Pencil tool to match your personal drawing style. And then you can join in the rejoicing!

Using the Pencil Tool as a Pencil

Computer mice (mouses?) have never been good drawing tools; often you need a steady hand and more patience than the guy at the mall in the Santa suit needs. That was then. These days, the Illustrator Pencil tool makes even the most hopped-up-on-caffeine, impatient Picasso-wannabe into a computer artist. (Just looking at it makes you feel better about drawing, doesn't it?)

Minimal effort and hefty stress reduction

The whole idea behind the Pencil tool is to let you draw exactly what you want — as quickly or slowly as you want. Regardless of the speed at which you draw, the resulting path appears the same (a nice thought for those of us on a deadline).

The Pencil tool creates smooth lines even when you're jittering around. (Unless you don't want it to — in which case it makes jittery lines.) The Pencil tool is also intuitive. It looks like a pencil, and when you click and drag with it, it creates a line that more or less follows where you dragged, pretty much like a real pencil would. (For contrast, look at the Pen tool. It looks like a pen, and yet it does nothing even remotely penlike!) And it lets you fix your mistakes without ever having to push or pull a point or a handle. The following steps (deftly illustrated in Figure 8-1) show you how to use the Pencil tool:

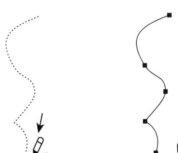

Figure 8-1:
Drawing
with the
Pencil tool.

1. **Choose the Pencil tool from its slot in the Toolbox.**

   Your cursor changes into (surprise!) a Pencil.

2. **Click and drag in the document window. As you drag, a dotted line appears.**

   Think of these dots as breadcrumbs that show you where you've been.

3. **Release the mouse button after you amass a nice little trail of breadcrumbs (dots).**

   A path forms where the breadcrumbs were. (If Hansel and Gretel had used the Pencil tool, that poor witch would be alive today.)

 If you stop drawing with the Pencil tool, you can just start up where you left off — simply by clicking at the end of the path and continuing. Be careful, though. If you don't click close enough to the end of the path, you start a whole new path. Fortunately, the Pencil tool tells you when you are in the right place. When you're creating a new path, a little X appears to the right of the tip of the Pencil. When you're close enough to a selected path to add to it, the X disappears.

A few unexpected exceptions to all this bliss

You're right. Using the Pencil tool *does* sound too easy. Although the Pencil is undeniably wonderful, it can cause frustration (or at least uncertainty) in the unwary. Here are instances to watch out for (and avoid if possible):

- ✔ **You can't continue your path.** You need to select a path in order to add to it. For example, if you stop drawing, do something that deselects the path, and then return to drawing your path, you create a *second* path, instead of extending the first one. To continue the path you were origi-nally working on, you must select it *before* you start drawing again with the Pencil tool. Just hold down the ⌘ [Ctrl] key to temporarily change the Pencil into the Selection tool. Click the path, let go of the ⌘ [Ctrl] key, and start drawing, starting at either end of the newly selected path.

  To get to the selection cursor right away, hold down the ⌘ [Ctrl] key.

- ✔ **You accidentally edit an existing path.** If you start a new Pencil path near a *selected* path, you may edit the selected path instead of creating a new one. In fact, you can do so with *any* path that was created with the Pen, Pencil, Star, or any other tool in Illustrator. You can edit any of them with the Pencil tool. (So is the Pencil versatile or overzealous? Your call.)

- ✔ **You create a path that's too lumpy or too smooth.** You can set up the Pencil tool to be very smooth *or* very accurate (in this case, *accurate* really means that it follows all the skittles and bumps you make as you draw). If someone you love changes the Pencil tool preferences (which you can access by double-clicking the Pencil tool), the Pencil retains those settings. Pencil tool preferences are loyal to the most recent user; they never return to their original settings.

- ✔ **You get a wacky fill or stroke as you draw.** This situation really isn't the Pencil tool's fault, but it's not exactly unknown to habitual Pencil tool users. If, before you start to draw, a nameless *somebody* sets the fill or stroke to something a little odd, *boom!* you get a mess. Fortunately, you can change the fill or stroke back to the default settings by pressing D. Before you know it, you're back to normal. (Well, at least the *path* is....)

- ✔ **You can't close a path.** Often when you use the Pencil tool in an attempt to create a closed path (by ending the path where you started), you wind up with two points that are very close to one another without actu-ally being joined. For some reason, the Pencil tool has a hard time making a closed path if you draw the entire path with one continuous stroke. When you near the end of the path, hold down the Option [Alt] key and release the mouse with Option [Alt] still pressed when the end of the line that you are drawing is near the beginning. The two ends of your path will be joined together.

- ✔ **You can't draw a straight line.** In Illustrator, pressing the Shift key *doesn't* keep the Pencil tool on a horizontal or vertical plane. Just about every other tool in Illustrator draws or moves in straight lines at 45-degree angles. In fact, just about every other tool in every Adobe product moves or draws in straight lines when you hold the Shift key down! But the Pencil tool can't even *think* straight! Fortunately, you can switch over to the Pen tool to draw straight lines and then switch back to the Pencil tool to create the rest of the drawing.

Cherishing the Multipurpose Pencil Tool

If you ever had one of those pocketknives with enough blades to do or fix anything, then you can appreciate how much more the Pencil tool does than a mere pencil! Use the amazing Pencil tool to edit existing paths, create new paths, append one path to another, and close existing paths.

But wait, there's more! You can set the Pencil tool to work in a variety of ways, so that it accurately reflects the way you want to draw, by setting its preferences. You can also use variations on the Pencil tool: the Smooth tool and the Eraser tool. The Pencil tool slot contains these two other Pencil-like tools. Use the Smooth tool (a mummy-wrapped pencil) to make paths less bumpy, with nary a smear. Use the Eraser tool (an upside-down pencil, logically enough) to zap away portions of paths, leaving no rubber crumbs to get into your keyboard.

Making the Pencil tool work just for you

You can set preferences for the Pencil tool by double-clicking the Pencil tool in the Toolbox. Figure 8-2 shows the Pencil Tool Preferences dialog box. Straight out of the box, the Pencil tool works pretty well. But to be honest, it's really set up to work reasonably well for everyone and not set up to work as well as it possibly can for *you*. Use the Pencil tool preferences to make the tool work *just* for you, and don't settle for less than the best!

Figure 8-2: Using the Pencil Tool Preferences dialog box, you can change the attributes of the Pencil tool.

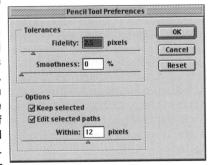

Hi-fi and lo-fi paths

The first slider under Tolerances (at the top of the dialog box) is labeled *Fidelity*. Nope, nothing to do with divorce courts — this kind of Fidelity affects how closely the path follows where you drag the Pencil tool. A high setting (toward the left of the dialog box) means that the path matches precisely what you drew with the Pencil, adding as many points and corners as necessary. A low setting (toward the right of the dialog box) means that the path loosely follows what you drew, making a smoother line with fewer points. So paths created with the Fidelity slider all the way to the left appear more natural and bumpy; paths drawn with the slider all the way to the right appear smoother and more computer-like. Compare the images shown in Figure 8-3. This Fidelity setting isn't just an arbitrary special effect; it's a way to make the Pencil tool match your personal drawing style.

High Fidelity   Low Fidelity

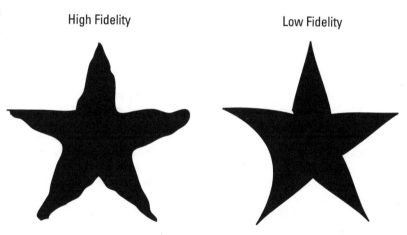

Figure 8-3: The path on the left was drawn with a Fidelity setting of .5 pixels; the path on the right was drawn with a Fidelity setting of 20 pixels.

Fidelity is measured in pixels. A pixel can mean many things as a unit of measurement. In this case, a *pixel* refers to a distance on your screen. (For more information, see the "Just how big IS a pixel?" sidebar.)

Drawing with the mouse is about as easy as drawing with a brick; the lines you make tend to be pretty shaky. The Fidelity slider determines how shaky your hand can be and still produce a smooth line. As you use the Pencil tool, you create a breadcrumb trail (a dotted line). After you release the mouse button, your computer pauses for a split second to create an imaginary line that is the average of all the movement you just made with the mouse. Then Illustrator compares that imaginary line with your breadcrumb trail and creates the actual path based on the Fidelity slider's setting.

Suppose that your Fidelity setting is 20 pixels — the lowest Fidelity setting possible. As you draw your naturally shaky line, you move away from the imaginary average line. With a setting of 20 pixels, Illustrator assumes that everything less than 20 pixels away from that imaginary line is unintentional shaking, induced by the unwieldy nature of the mouse (or by too much caffeine) — so Illustrator just ignores that stuff when it creates the path. Everything more than 20 pixels away is considered intentional, which prompts Illustrator to put in a curve or a corner point.

All of this is just an extended way of saying that if you are at one with yourself and the Universe and are a Zen master of mouse movement, you want to keep your Fidelity settings high. That way, you only move the mouse to exactly where you want the path, and you don't have Illustrator second-guessing what you *really* intended. However, if you have really shaky hands (as most of us do when we get too much caffeine and not enough sleep), you probably want to use a low Fidelity setting. More than likely, you fall somewhere between these two extremes. So just double-click the Pencil tool and set the Fidelity slider to match *your* style!

Now, that is smooth!

The second slider is a little harder for most people to figure out. The slider reads *Smoothness* — but didn't the first slider smooth out the image? As many a good sketcher can tell you, drawing with the mouse tends to be pretty shaky, and this setting helps compensate for the shakiness in a slightly different way from the Fidelity setting. The Fidelity setting helps Illustrator determine whether you drew the path because you meant to — or if it was just because of the shaky mouse. The Smoothness setting helps Illustrator figure out what kind of corner you meant to create when you deliberately changed the direction of the path. When you change the direction of a path, you can do it with a sharp corner point or with a smooth, curving point. When Illustrator converts your breadcrumb trail into a path, it must determine which of these points you truly intended to use. A Smoothness of 0% makes the Pencil tool use a corner point almost everywhere that the path changes direction. A Smoothness of 100% makes the Pencil tool use a smooth point in all but the most extreme path direction changes.

Just how big IS a pixel?

That question has no easy answer, my friend. In the olden days, a pixel was $\frac{1}{72}$ of an inch, because computer screens used a fixed grid of 72 pixels x 72 pixels for every inch of screen. Nowadays, we use multisync monitors that let us change the number of pixels on the screen. How big is a pixel? Take the current resolution of your monitor, divide by its size, and then. . . . Better yet, forget all that and just pay attention to how the Pencil tool works with different Fidelity settings. Choose the one that works best for you, and don't worry about the numbers!

Again, the setting that works best for you is a matter of your personal style. If your lines are as shaky as a balloon vendor at a porcupine convention, set your Smoothness to 100%. If your hands are as steady as a gunslinger's in a Western, leave it set to 0%. Otherwise, experiment until you find the right setting for you. Figure 8-4 shows the same image created with different Smoothness settings. Note how the settings change the way the drawings look.

Low Smoothness   High Smoothness

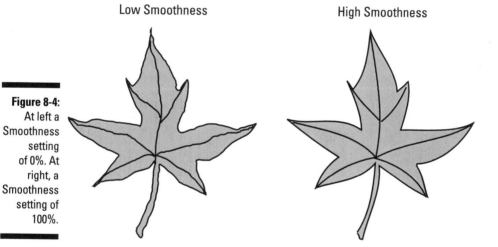

Figure 8-4:
At left a Smoothness setting of 0%. At right, a Smoothness setting of 100%.

At first glance, the differences between the right-hand drawings in Figures 8-3 (low Fidelity) and 8-4 (high Smoothness) appear minimal. However, looks can be deceiving. The Smoothness and Fidelity settings are actually two distinct approaches to making a path: A low Fidelity setting creates a simplified curve by following the path you draw more loosely and using fewer points; a high Smoothness setting creates a smoother curve by using *different types* of points (smooth points as opposed to corner points) to create the path. Which is better? It really depends on your drawing style — and some experimenting!

Tweaking the Pencil tool — It's your option

Under Options in the Pencil Tool Preferences dialog box, you find two options: Keep Selected and Edit Selected Paths. These settings determine what happens to the path after you draw it and how the Pencil tool interacts with that path (or with other selected paths).

- **With Keep Selected checked,** the path you just created with the Pencil tool stays selected after you finish drawing and release the mouse button.

- **With Keep Selected unchecked,** the path you just created doesn't stay selected. (But you knew that.)

The Keep Selected option also determines how the Pencil tool affects selected paths, as follows:

✔ **Edit Selected Paths:** When you use the Pencil tool near any selected path (with the Keep Selected option checked), the path you just drew with the Pencil tool replaces the previous path. You can even adjust how close you need to be to that path to edit it; just tweak the Within setting found just beneath the Edit Selected Paths option.

When the Edit Selected Paths option is *not* checked, the Pencil tool works the same regardless of whether Keep Selected is checked or unchecked. When the Edit Selected Paths option *is* checked, it changes the way the Pencil tool works — instead of moving on to create a new path, when you draw near a selected path, you linger over the old one to modify it.

✔ **With Keep Selected checked,** you can start drawing a path, stop, and then continue where you left off. If you decide to replace the path, you can place the Pencil tool near the path you just drew and start drawing a new one. (*Poof.* The old one disappears.) But beware: You have forbidden the Pencil tool to draw multiple paths that are close together. (You know: No grass, no hair — no heads unless they're bald.)

✔ **With Keep Selected *and* Edit Selected Paths checked,** every stroke you make that is close to another selected stroke replaces the old stroke with the new stroke. (All together, now: *Stroke! Stroke!*)

✔ **With Keep Selected unchecked,** the Pencil tool can change only the paths you tell it to change (by first using a Selection tool). By removing the check mark from Keep Selected, you enable the Pencil to draw hair or grass (for instance) with utter abandon. With Keep Selected unchecked you can also *edit* hair or grass, but don't forget to select the part you want to edit (by first using a Selection tool).

Changing the path not Penciled

A really amazing attribute of the Pencil tool is that it can edit *any* path, and not just the paths created with it. For example, you can edit a circle, a star, or a path drawn with the Pen tool. You can replace any portion of any path with the Pencil tool, provided that the path is selected and the Edit Selected Path option is checked in the Pencil Tool Preferences dialog box (see "Making the Pencil tool work just for you," in this chapter). Just make sure that the path is selected — and then click and drag near the path to reshape it. The following steps walk you through the process of editing an existing path:

1. **Using any Selection tool, select the path you want to modify.**

   The path need not have been created with the Pencil tool.

2. **Select the Pencil tool.**

3. **Click near the part of the path you want to modify.**

   When the little X at the bottom right of the Pencil tool disappears, you know you're close enough to click.

4. **Click and drag a new shape for the part of the path.**

   You can create any shape you want, but it must start and end near the existing path; otherwise the new path won't reconnect with the old path.

5. **Release the mouse button.**

   The path reshapes itself into the new path you just drew.

Working with the all-natural "Smoothie" tool

Illustrator's Smooth tool makes your paths, well, *smoother*. (Not that you need us to tell you that, huh?) The Smooth tool lets you change the way a path looks *after* it's drawn, in the same way that the Pencil tool lets you change the way a path looks as it's being drawn.

Drag the Smooth tool over any selected path to "smooth" it. You aren't limited to smoothing paths drawn with the Pencil tool; you can smooth any path in Illustrator. Your results, however, depend on the path that you're smoothing (if you try smoothing a path that is already smooth, you aren't going to see much difference) and upon the Smooth Tool Preferences.

You access the Smooth Tool Preferences by double-clicking the Smooth tool. There are only two settings, and they should seem hauntingly familiar from the discussion of the Pencil tool: Fidelity and Smoothness. In fact, these settings function identically to the settings in the Pencil Tool Preferences dialog box (see the "Making the Pencil tool work just for you" section earlier in this chapter for more details); the only difference is that you apply them to lines that have already been drawn. Just sweep over them with the Smooth tool, and the result is as if you drew those paths using different Pencil Tool Preferences settings.

As you may expect, using the Smooth tool is pretty smooth. Here's the drill (or is it a sander?), as shown in Figure 8-5:

1. **Using any Selection tool, select the path that you want to smooth.**

2. **Drag the Smooth tool on or near the path that you want to smooth.**

   Et voilá! The path is smooth!

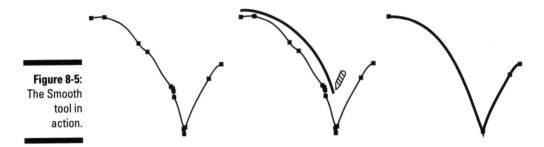

Figure 8-5:
The Smooth tool in action.

Using the Pen with the Pencil

The Pen and Pencil tools are the primary tools for drawing in Illustrator, and they happen to work really well together. As you gain a knack for knowing which tool to use when, your work flows more smoothly — and your illustrations look more and more the way you want them to.

Swapping one tool for another

A common technique that is useful for combining the Pen and Pencil tools is to switch between them while drawing. You *can* click each tool whenever you decide to change from one to the other, but the really zippy way to do this is to press the key that corresponds to each tool. Press **P** to switch to the Pen tool and **N** to switch to the Pencil tool.

As your drawing changes from free-flowing curves to precise straight lines and back, you want to change between the two tools. When you change between them, click the endpoint of the path you were previously drawing with the other tool and then continue drawing.

Watch those icons! Working with the Pen and Pencil tools together is much easier if you pay attention to what the icons are doing. When the Pen tool is over an endpoint, a little slash (/) appears to the lower right of the pen icon. When you are about to close a path, a hollow circle appears beside the tool. When you have the Pencil tool in position to edit a path, its icon doesn't have anything beside it. Both tools, however, get Xs beside them when they are about to create a new path.

Precision versus speed: You make the call

You want to keep in mind the types of shapes and paths that are best drawn with each tool. Here's a breakdown of the shapes and paths each tool draws best:

Shapes and paths best drawn with the Pen tool

To draw anything with straight lines, you choose the Pen tool, because the Pencil tool really can't draw a straight line. To create a path or shape that has a specific smooth curve, you choose the Pen tool, because the line the Pencil tool creates is just an average of the total strokes you make, which means absolute precision is impossible. Finally, to trace a logo or other scanned art that requires precision and accuracy, you're better off choosing the Pen tool, because it offers you precision down to the thousandth of a millimeter.

Shapes and paths best drawn with the Pencil tool

When speed is more important than accuracy in your drawing — such as when you need to put a lot of hairs onto your lovely kiwi-fruit illustration, and the precise length and position of each and every hair doesn't matter — you choose the Pencil tool. For quick sketching, such as doodling an insulting picture of your favorite coworker, you choose the Pencil tool because it is more efficient than the Pen tool. With the Pencil tool, you don't have to worry about each and every point and handle the way you do with the Pen tool. The Pencil tool lets you focus on creating the lines where they should be — and lets Illustrator do the rest of the work for you. (Ah, progress.)

Chapter 9

Creating Magnificent Brushstrokes

· ·

In This Chapter

▶ Getting a line on why the Paintbrush is so unlike the Pen and Pencil tools

▶ Creating brushes from Illustrator artwork

▶ Looking at the four brush types

· ·

*H*ardcore users of Illustrator would never call it a *painting* program. So you can mix colors and use a paintbrush tool. They don't care; Illustrator uses vectors. To them, all painting programs are pixel-based and only drawing programs are vector-based. Very neat . . . if it were true. As usual, reality is fuzzier.

Regardless of what the hardcore users think, Illustrator *is* a painting program. It happens to have some of the most powerful painting capabilities ever seen in *any* graphics program, vector- or pixel-based.

 What, for example, would you call this? Illustrator calls it the Paintbrush tool; it's also at least one-third magic wand. In this chapter, you discover the magic of the Paintbrush and the wonders of vector-based brush strokes. You get to push the definitions of "brush" by creating brushstrokes of every conceivable size and shape, from brushes that make simple calligraphic strokes, to brushes that make strokes using other Illustrator artwork.

Brushing Where No Stroke Has Gone Before

Brushes are wildly creative strokes that you can apply to paths. If you think of them this way, brushes become much easier to get a handle on (especially if they sometimes make you bristle with frustration).

Brushes, as shown in Figure 9-1, can be any of four different types: Art brushes, Scatter brushes, Calligraphic brushes, and Pattern brushes.

Here are the four types of Illustrator brushes and their functions:

- ✔ **Art brushes.** These brushes stretch a single piece of artwork along an entire path.

- ✔ **Scatter brushes.** These brushes scatter artwork around a path. The artwork is repeated, scaled, and rotated randomly.

- ✔ **Calligraphic brushes.** These brushes emulate drawing or writing with a calligraphy pen.

- ✔ **Pattern brushes.** These brushes repeat artwork along a path that you draw with the Paintbrush tool. Unlike the random Scatter brush, the Pattern brush repeats the artwork in a precise pattern.

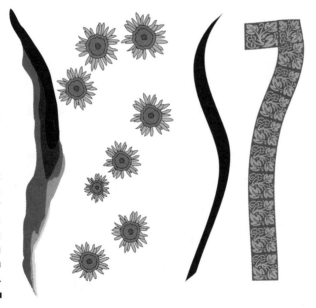

Figure 9-1:
From left to right, examples of painting with an Art brush, a Scatter brush, a Calligraphic brush, and a Pattern brush.

Illustrator's Brushes palette, shown in Figure 9-2, contains samples of each of the four brush types. (Choose Window➪Show Brushes to display the Brushes palette.) In addition, the "Creating a New Brush" section of this chapter enables you to take virtually anything you create in Illustrator and turn it into a brush.

Calligraphic brushes

Scatter brushes

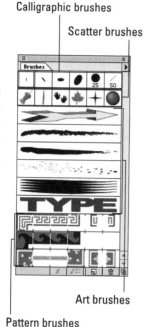

Figure 9-2:
The default
Brushes
palette in
Illustrator
contains a
smattering
of the four
different
types of
brushes.

Art brushes

Pattern brushes

Embracing your inner artist

Regardless of your artistic background or intentions, you can make astounding artwork by using the Paintbrush tool in combination with the different types of brushes. Of course, someone with an utter vacuum of talent (or more than the legally allowed measure of bad taste) may have an uphill battle to create something that looks good. Even so, you may be surprised at how quickly you can tool up some snazzy images, as shown in Figure 9-3, by using the Paintbrush — even if you're new to computer graphics (your secret is safe with us). Just follow these steps:

1. **Choose the Paintbrush tool from the Toolbox.**

   Your cursor changes into a little paintbrush.

2. **Choose Window⇨Brush Libraries⇨Artistic Sample.**

   After you release the mouse button, the Artistic Sample brush palette appears before you can say, "Jackson Pollock."

3. Click the Chalk Art brush.

Topmost in the palette, this brush looks like what you get by rubbing a stick of black pastel sideways against rough construction paper.

4. Click and drag with the Paintbrush tool to draw a path where you want your new stroke to be.

5. Release the mouse button.

The path you drew becomes the stroke of the brush that you chose. In this case, the Chalk Art brush's rough pastel stroke stretches along the entire length of the path. With the path still selected, try clicking and dragging with the other brushes to get a feel for what the different brushes can do.

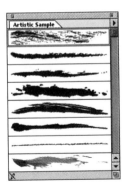

Figure 9-3:
Creating
wild and
wacky
strokes.

Because brushes reside on paths, you can change the position and dimensions of any brushstroke just as you modify any path. You can use the Pencil tool to reshape an existing path, or if you're really brave, you can use the Direct Selection tool to push and pull points and handles around until the brushstroke looks the way you want it to.

The Paintbrush tool options

The Paintbrush tool offers several options that you can use to customize the way it draws. All these options are found in the Paintbrush Tool Preferences dialog box, shown in Figure 9-4, which appears after you double-click the Paintbrush tool. These preferences function almost identically to the Pencil tool's preferences, with one exception: the Fill New Brush strokes option. When you leave the checkbox for this option unchecked (which we recommend), Illustrator automatically sets the Fill color to None. For a more exhaustive and exhausting explanation of the other settings, refer to Chapter 8.

Figure 9-4:
The
Paintbrush
Tool
Preferences
dialog box.

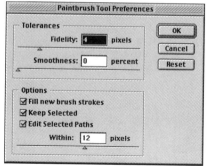

Why set the Fill to None? Well, the path you make with the Paintbrush tool can contain a fill color, but brushstrokes can also be randomly placed pieces of artwork or have unique shapes. The stroke can appear partly inside and partly outside the fill color, which makes the fill seem random and unrelated to your stroke. So brushes work better when you don't use a fill color with them.

Creating a New Brush

Although Illustrator ships with several hundred brushes, obsessively creative folks (no, don't raise your hand; keep it our secret) can't stand to be limited to so few. If you want to create your own brushes, go right ahead. You can create a brush using darn near any set of paths in Illustrator, as shown in Figure 9-5. Furthermore, the process works to create a new Art, Pattern, or Scatter brush.

The Calligraphic brush is the only brush for which you can't create a new brush because the Calligraphic brush doesn't create its stroke from another graphic.

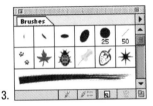

1.

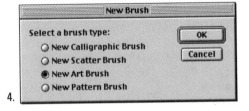

2.

3.

4.

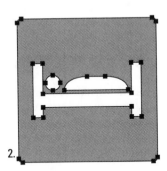

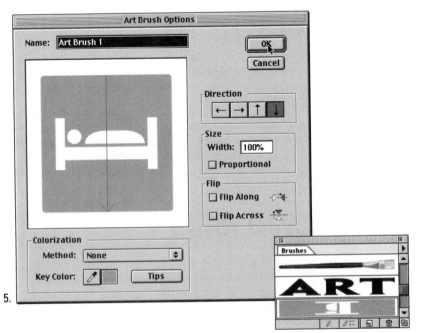

Figure 9-5:
Creating a
new brush.

5.

1. **Create (or open a document with) artwork that you want to use as a brush.**

2. **Using any Selection tool, select all the paths in the artwork.**

3. **Click the New Brush button in the Brushes palette.**

   After you release the mouse button, a New Brush dialog box appears and asks what type of brush you want to create.

4. **Select New Art Brush, New Scatter Brush, or New Pattern Brush; then click OK.**

   For the purpose of this example, we selected the New Art Brush option. The Art Brush Options dialog box appears.

5. **Just click OK to accept the default settings.**

   If you're concerned about accepting the default settings in the Art Brush Options dialog box, keep in mind that you can always make changes to the Art Brush options by double-clicking the Art brush itself in the Brushes palette. We talk about all those different options in the "Working with the Different Brush Types" section later in this chapter. These options have the same effect whether you're creating a new brush or modifying an existing one.

   The new Art brush appears in the Brushes palette, ready for you to use.

 You can create all sorts of interesting effects by using text as Art brushes. Because brushes can contain only paths (not text objects), you must first change the text into paths before you can make it into a brush. You do this by selecting the text object with a Selection tool and then choosing Type⇨Create Outlines.

Working with the Different Brush Types

The following sections talk about the four brush types and some options that you can use when painting with them.

Art brushes for when you're feeling a bit wacky

Art brushes take any Illustrator paths and stretch them along a path. Figure 9-6 shows several examples of Art brushes.

You can use several Art Brush Options to make Art brushes look exactly the way you want. Figure 9-7 shows the Art Brush Options dialog box, accessed by double-clicking any Art brush in the Brushes palette.

Figure 9-6:
All these objects are (believe it or not) Art brushes.

Figure 9-7:
The Art Brush Options dialog box.

In the Art Brush Options dialog box, you find a variety of options to affect the way the brush makes a stroke. The following list describes how you use some of those options:

- ✔ **Name.** Give the brush a descriptive name here. This name appears when you choose View By Name from the Brushes palette's pop-up menu.

- ✔ **Preview.** Select the Preview option to get a look at any stroke in your artwork that uses the brush stroke you're changing. What you see is what you'll get — the stroke as it will look *if* you apply the new changes. This doesn't alter your actual artwork. This feature is extremely handy because you don't have to remember what all the different settings do — you can just watch what happens after you change them!

✔ **Direction.** This option determines whether the graphic rotates clockwise or counterclockwise (relative to the path) as you stretch it.

✔ **Proportional.** Should the artwork stay exactly as wide as it is and just get stretched out along the length of the path, or should it get bigger or smaller so the width of the artwork matches its length? With the Proportional option selected, the artwork grows wider as the path gets longer. With Proportional option deselected, the artwork stretches.

✔ **Flip.** This option resembles the Direction option, except that it flips the artwork upside down instead of rotating it.

✔ **Colorization.** Brushes have fill and stroke colors of their own. They are ordinary Illustrator artwork endowed with the power to be brushes, so distinct fill and stroke values are part of the deal. The Colorization setting determines whether the brush keeps the colors of the original artwork or replaces them with Fill and Stroke colors from the Toolbar. A Method setting of None preserves the original artwork's colors. Other settings blend the Fill and Stroke colors with the artwork. How they perform this miracle depends on the colors in the original artwork for the brush and on the specific options you choose.

Figure 9-8 shows the same brush with three different sets of options applied to it.

Figure 9-8:
The same brush changed by only one setting produces variations like these.

Default settings   Different Direction setting   Size Proportional setting   Flip Along setting

Scatter brushes for when you are a bit wacky

Scatter brushes are similar to Art brushes; they're made up of Illustrator paths. However, the similarities end there. Instead of stretching art along a path, Scatter brushes toss, fling, and *scatter* art along a path. Figure 9-9 shows the result of using a Scatter brush.

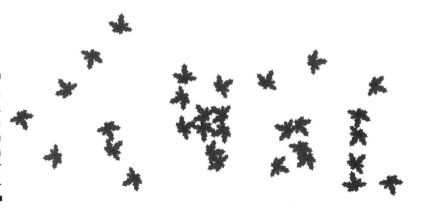

Figure 9-9:
This artwork
is actually a
single path
used as a
Scatter
brush.

Scatter brushes have even more options than Art brushes, but as much as it pains us to say this, Scatter brushes *need* more options. Imagine a brush of randomly scattered ladybugs becoming a brush of *organized* ladybugs that follow the path you create with the brush. Ten-hut, you bugs!

Two versions of the Scatter Brush Options dialog box appear in Figure 9-10. Next to each version is a brushstroke created with the option settings shown in the dialog box.

The Scatter brushes repeat and randomize artwork based on four variables: Size, Spacing, Scatter, and Rotation. You set the specific amounts for these options by dragging their respective sliders to the left or right. How the brush uses these values is determined by the method (Fixed, Random, or Pressure) that you select in the pop-up menu to the right of each slider. The following list describes how each method works:

- **Fixed.** This method uses the exact value in the associated text box, which you previously specified using the slider.

- **Random.** This method gives you two sliders instead of one, so you can specify Minimum and Maximum amounts of variance in the associated option. For example, after you set the Size to a Minimum value of 50% and a Maximum value to 200%, the Scatter brush varies the artwork randomly between half its original size and twice its original size. (Well, okay, it isn't *truly* random, just random within a specified range. So what do you want from a computer anyway?)

- **Pressure.** As with Random, Pressure uses Minimum and Maximum amounts of variance in the associated option. This method only works when you have a pressure-sensitive tablet hooked to your computer. If you don't have a pressure-sensitive tablet, this feature is so cool that you may want to run out and buy one! A *pressure-sensitive tablet* is sort of like a mouse, except that you draw with a pen-like stylus instead of a bar of soap on a string. Instead of just painting or not painting (your only options with a mouse), the stylus recognizes just how hard you press. The Minimum and Maximum settings correspond to the amount of pressure. The lightest pressure uses the Minimum value; the hardest pressure uses the Maximum value. The values you get vary according to just how hard you press.

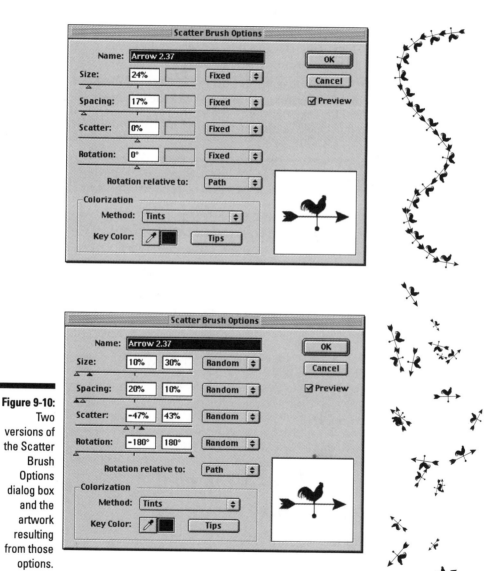

Figure 9-10: Two versions of the Scatter Brush Options dialog box and the artwork resulting from those options.

After you determine which Method to use, you can set the sliders on the left side of the dialog box to specify how you want the artwork repeated along the path. Here are the options:

- **Size:** This option controls the size of the scattered objects relative to the original.

- **Spacing:** This option controls the amount of space that appears between the scattered objects.

- **Scatter:** This option controls how far away objects can scatter on either side of the path.

- **Rotation:** This option controls how the objects are rotated and whether they're rotated in relation to the path or to the document. Figure 9-11 shows the difference between a Scatter brush rotation based on the path (left) and one based on the page (right).

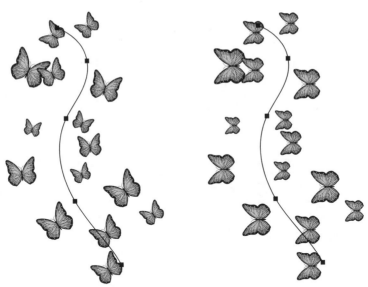

Figure 9-11: The Scatter brush on the left is set to rotate at 90 degrees relative to the path; the one on the right is set to rotate at 90 degrees relative to the page.

Pattern brushes — too cool and utterly wacko

Pattern brushes (see Figure 9-12) are too cool for words, so we can just move on.

Seriously, even though Pattern brushes *are* that cool, we still have to talk about what *makes* them so cool. For openers, you can use five different pieces of art for Pattern brushes, rather than just one! Of course, that fact can also make them difficult to create. You need a graphic for straight lines and curves, one for inside corners, one for outside corners, one for the start of a line, and one for the end of a line. Making sure that these five graphics work together can be time-consuming and difficult. But oh, the feeling of satisfaction you get after you succeed!

Figure 9-12:
A sampling of the Pattern brushes that come with Adobe Illustrator.

Well, okay, if making five pieces of art is too time-intensive, you *can* get away with using just one. The Side pattern is the key pattern. If you don't create five different graphics, the Pattern brush just repeats the Side pattern for any missing pattern. But come on, now, that's cheating. If you want eye-popping results, make those five graphics and take full advantage of what this wonderful brush can do.

Making the artwork for a Pattern brush

If you find that creating a Pattern brush is pretty tricky and counterintuitive, you're not alone; a lot of trial and error is par for the course, especially at first. The first step in building a Pattern brush is to create the five pieces of artwork. Before you can do that, however, you need to know just what these pieces of artwork are for. Double-click the Brushes palette to open the Pattern Brush Options dialog box for a peek at the possibilities. Figure 9-13 shows the Pattern Brush Options dialog box, in which you tell Illustrator just where to put the artwork on a path. Pattern brushes are *context-sensitive;* they know what the specific part of the path they are on is supposed to look like — so they use the graphic that corresponds to that part of the path.

You may find it helpful to examine existing Pattern brushes. The Tile Options list in the Pattern Brush Options dialog box offers a sampling.

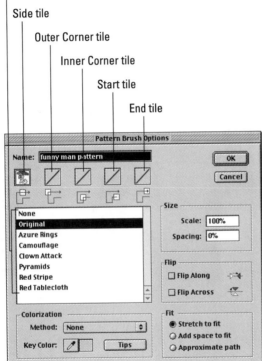

Figure 9-13: The Pattern Brush Options dialog box. Each Pattern brush tile knows where it is on a path and uses the corresponding artwork.

Setting Pattern Brush Options

The Pattern Brush Options dialog box looks more complicated than it really is. Double-click any brush in the Brushes palette and the Pattern Brush Options dialog box appears, displaying the following features:

- **Tiles.** These squares are thumbnail representations of each piece of art-work. Beneath each tile, a graphic shows the artwork's position on the path. Click a thumbnail to modify it using the Tile Options list.

- **Tile Options.** Click these options to change your pattern tiles. Click None to remove the selected tile's graphic. (The Original option is already selected if you added your own graphics.) The remaining options correspond to the Pattern swatches in the Swatches palette. This arrangement enables you to use Pattern swatches as an alternative to creating your own tiles. (See Chapter 5 for more details on Pattern swatches.)

- ✔ **Colorization and Flip.** See the "Art Brushes for when you're feeling a bit wacky" section of this chapter for details on these options.

- ✔ **Size.** The Scale option enlarges or shrinks the tiles as they run along the path. If they get too big, the Spacing option enables you to increase the distance between tiles.

- ✔ **Fit.** This option determines how the tiles get distorted to fit around spaces that don't quite match the five different Tile types. Stretch to Fit distorts artwork the most, mashing it into whatever shape it needs to be to fit the path. Add Space to Fit adds space between tiles to distort them as little as possible. Approximate Path only works when the path is rectangular. This option doesn't distort the tiles at all; instead, the tiles "approximately" follow the path.

Positioning the artwork in the Pattern brush

After you create your graphics, think about what position each graphic is going to play. You may find it helpful to create a single guide that actually contains all five positions, as shown in Figure 9-14. Use this graphic as a way of visualizing how each graphic element is going to work at the different points.

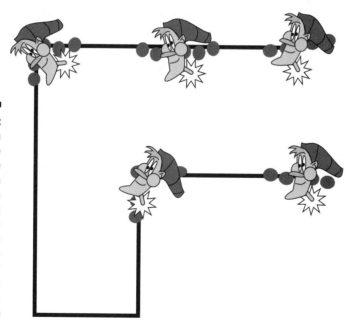

Figure 9-14: Creating a guideline with all five pattern positions can be a big help when you're creating the artwork for the Pattern brush.

Using the guideline, create five pieces of artwork to correspond to the positions on the path. Knowing exactly how each piece of the artwork needs to change in response to its position takes practice. Some differences can be subtle (such as between the starting art and ending art) or obvious (such as between the side piece and corner pieces), as shown in Figure 9-15.

Figure 9-15:
Left to right:
The start,
side, outside
corner,
inside
corner, and
end pieces.

Once you have all the artwork, you're ready to create the Pattern brush. Forward, intrepid artist! Just follow these steps:

1. **Select the Side tile and click the New Brush button in the Brushes palette.**

   The New Brush dialog box appears.

2. **Click the New Pattern Brush option and click OK.**

   The Pattern Brush Options dialog box appears, with the Side piece in the proper position. (For a refresher on how that looks, refer to Figure 9-13.)

3. **Give the new brush a name and click OK.**

   The new Pattern brush shows up in the Brushes palette. (Don't worry about the other options right now. We come back to those!)

Technically, the new brush is ready to use right now (the side artwork would fill in the other positions). But we true artists (no slackers here!) want to add the rest of the artwork to the brush. Naturally, this part of the process gets tricky. Notice that the brush, as it currently appears in Figure 9-16, has six slots, two of which are filled by the side artwork. The remaining four slots are for the remaining four pieces. The next set of steps creates them.

Figure 9-16:
The new
Pattern
brush,
awaiting the
four remain-
ing pieces.

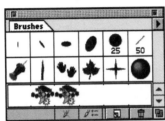

Here's how true artists (the aesthetically dedicated) add the rest of the art-work to the brush, one piece at a time:

1. **Click the artwork and press and hold down the Option [Alt] key.**

2. **While holding down the Option [Alt] key, drag the artwork onto the Pattern brush, over the appropriate slot.**

You're over a slot when a bold, dark line appears around the slot. Ah, but how do you know what the *appropriate* slot is? The brush has no label to tell you what's what. The Pattern Brush Options dialog box obligingly labels the slots, but tragically the order of the Pattern bushes in that dialog box does not correspond to the order in the Brushes palette. The only way to add a new brush to the Pattern brush is to hold down the Option [Alt] key and drag it (kicking and screaming) onto the slot in the Brushes palette. But you're in luck! We labeled the slots in the brush for you in Figure 9-17.

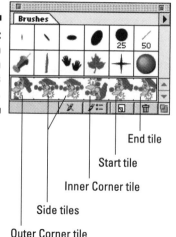

Figure 9-17:
The Pattern brush with its slots labeled.

End tile

Start tile

Inner Corner tile

Side tiles

Outer Corner tile

3. **Using the figure as a map, hold down the Option [Alt] key and drag your graphic onto the Brushes palette, over the slot you want it to occupy; then release the mouse button.**

The Pattern Brush Options dialog box appears, displaying the new artwork in its appropriate place.

4. **Click OK.**

Don't worry about the other options for now.

5. **Drag all the remaining graphics to their appointed places.**

Each time you add a graphic, the Pattern Brush Options dialog box appears again. Just click OK and keep going.

Testing your new Pattern brush

When you finally have all your graphics in place, you can test the new brush by applying it to open and closed paths: After making sure the new brush is selected in the Brushes palette, you create two simple graphics. Anything you create when a brush is selected will use that brush as its stroke, even when you aren't using the Paintbrush tool! Any path will work, but since the Pattern brush uses different artwork at corners, testing the shape on an object that has corners (such as a rectangle) is helpful. In this example, we use the Rectangle tool to create a square. With the new brush still selected, we choose the Brush tool and paint a squiggly line. This procedure shows us how our corner, side, and end tiles look on both curved and straight lines. Testing this way (as we did in Figure 9-18) gives you a good idea of whether all your artwork is working well in the new brush.

Figure 9-18:
The new
Pattern
brush tested
on a square
and a
squiggle.

If any of your tiles aren't working, tweak the original artwork, select it, and drag it back to the appropriate slot.

If you're suddenly inspired to create more Pattern brushes, a good way to start is by examining the Pattern brushes (nearly a hundred of them) that come with Illustrator. Tinker with them to figure out how they work and how to create them.

Calligraphic brushes for formal occasions

Calligraphic brushes create strokes that emulate the kind of strokes you might make with real calligraphic pens; the strokes they make vary in width depending on the direction of the stroke. As the only brushes that *aren't* created by paths that you can drag into the Brushes palette, Calligraphic brushes are the nonconformist brushes in Illustrator. You set them up by using controls in the Calligraphic Brush Options dialog box, as shown in Figure 9-19.

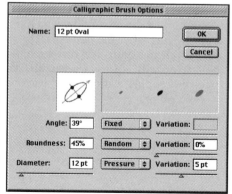

Figure 9-19:
The
Calligraphic
Brush
Options
dialog box.

Calligraphic brushes are deceptively simple. Don't let the name fool you; you can use them to create any type of artwork, not just calligraphy (although they're especially good for emulating traditional pen-and-ink type drawings).

Yep, the Calligraphic Brush tool seems a lot more like a real pen than the powerful-but-weird Pen tool. A tidbit of international art lore may help you keep them straight: In Japan, calligraphy is an art practiced with brushes.

To create a Calligraphic brush, just follow these steps:

1. **Click the New Brush icon in the Brushes palette.**

   The New Brush dialog box appears.

2. **Select the New Calligraphic Brush option and click OK.**

   The Calligraphic Brush Options dialog box appears — and though it may look intimidating, you have only the following three options to set (after you name the brush):

   • **Angle.** If you were using a real-world brush (or pen, as the case may be), this setting would be the angle at which you're tilting the brush.

   • **Roundness.** This setting enables you to change just how round the brush is — from a narrow ellipse to a circle.

   • **Diameter.** This setting determines how large the brush is.

   The boxes in the middle column determine how (and by how much) those first three options may vary, if at all. Select one of three options in these drop-down list boxes to determine whether the preceding three options may vary not at all (Fixed), randomly (Random), or according to the amount of pressure you apply using a pressure-sensitive stylus (Pressure).

The boxes in the third column enable you to set the amount by which those first three options may vary (if the method by which they may vary is either Random or Pressure). The higher the numbers, the greater the range of sizes the brush will produce. Figure 9-20 offers a hint of what the Calligraphic Brush tool can do with a pressure-sensitive tablet — the variable width of the stroke adds sophistication to the cartoon.

Figure 9-20:
Artwork created on a pressure-sensitive tablet using Calligraphic brushes.

3. **After you set your options, click OK.**

    The new Calligraphic brush appears in the Brushes palette for you to use.

As you begin creating artwork with brushes, you discover that it's just like painting with real paint brushes — the best artwork requires a combination of several different brushes. Fortunately, you have an astonishing variety of brushes to choose from! The most well-stocked art supply store pales in comparison to the Brushes palette. Best of all, you don't have to pay extra whenever you need a new brush. You can just build your own!

Chapter 10

Extreme Fills and Strokes

. . . .

. . . .

To say that in Illustrator you can create just about anything you can imagine isn't an overstatement. The trick is knowing what buttons to push to make your artistic vision become an Illustrator document. This chapter pushes fills and strokes to their limits, so you can create *the cool stuff*. You know — the stuff you look at, scratch your head, and say, "How did they do *that?*" And then you wonder whether you'll ever be able to create anything so artistic.

Well, it isn't so hard. You just need to use some of Illustrator's more arcane tools (the Gradient Mesh tool, for example) and a few cantankerous menu commands that don't seem to want to do anything unless you apply them *just right.* This chapter shows you how to use them to get good results. In this chapter, the tools and commands that do the really cool stuff take center stage. Like temperamental sports cars, they're a little tricky to use but worth the effort!

Messing Around with Meshes

Illustrator is really great at filling areas with solid colors or continuous patterns or even gradients. Illustrator really gets testy, though, when you try to create a continuous tone — such as the many skin tones that define a human face, the way colors fade into one another in a piece of folded fabric, the way shining a light on an orange creates a bright reflection of light that blends into darker and darker shades of orange until it is almost black on the side away from the light. . . . Where was I? Oh yeah. Illustrator is great at many things, but most artists use paint programs such as Corel Painter whenever they need to do anything with continuous tones. However, the Illustrator Gradient Mesh tool is like a crotchety magician: If you talk nicely to it, it can help you bend the rules a bit.

Using a Gradient Mesh, you can create the shading and tonal effects you expect to find in a paint program. Even so, Gradient Meshes don't replace the need for a paint program. Gradient Meshes can't quite give you the total control over tones that a paint program can. They *can* give you cool, painterly effects.

Gradient Meshes overcome the limitations of Gradients, the other Illustrator feature that enables you to blend colors together. (For more information on Gradients, see Chapter 5.) Simple Gradients fill areas with linear and radial color shifts. Period. Gradient *Meshes* have no such limitation. You can use them to assign colors to the specific points and paths that make up an object. Where the mesh lines cross, you can assign a different color to every line and every point. These colors blend with the colors of the other points. Take a look at Figure 10-1 for a sample of what you can do with a Gradient Mesh. (Retro '70s-style record jackets, anyone?)

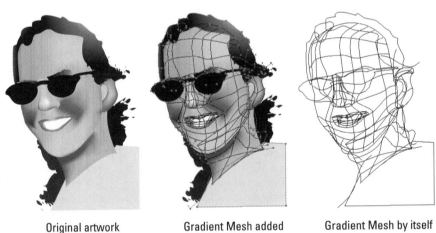

Figure 10-1:
This healthy youngster was colored entirely using the Gradient Mesh tool.

Original artwork   Gradient Mesh added   Gradient Mesh by itself

Figure 10-1 may seem complex, but it really is just the same simple steps repeated over and over. The tool seems daunting at first, but you can tackle it if you begin by adding a highlight to a simple shape, as shown in Figure 10-2.

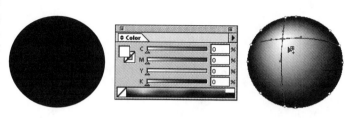

Figure 10-2:
Using the
Gradient
Mesh tool to
create a
highlight in
a path.

To add a Gradient Mesh to a simple shape, just follow these steps:

1. **Create a shape by clicking and dragging with any of the basic object tools (see Chapter 4 for more on basic objects) and fill the shape with a dark color. You can use any shape at all.**

   For this example, we create a circle and color it black.

2. **Deselect the path (you can deselect everything by choosing Edit➪ Deselect All).**

   Deselecting the path enables you to pick a different color for the Gradient Mesh tool. If you choose a different color with the path selected, you change the color of the object.

3. **Set the Fill color to any light color.**

   Choose Window➪Show Color to open the Color palette. Click the Fill box and choose a light color to use as a highlight. (Gradient meshes use only Fill colors and ignore Stroke colors.)

4. **Choose the Gradient Mesh tool from the Toolbox, and then click the object where you want to add a highlight.**

   As if by magic, two intersecting paths appear on the object, crossing at the spot where you clicked. This intersection is called the mesh point. These paths are the Gradient Mesh. The highlight appears where the paths intersect.

5. **Click other areas within the path to add more highlights — as many as you want.**

The paths that make up the Gradient Mesh can be edited the same as any other path. You can click the mesh points in the path with the Direct Selection tool and move them to create different effects. Mesh points also have direction points, just like curved paths (see Chapter 6). These direction points can be moved to change the shape of the gradient. You can also change the color of any point or path segment by clicking it and choosing a different color in the Color or Swatches palette. Figure 10-3 shows different effects made by mashing the mesh around.

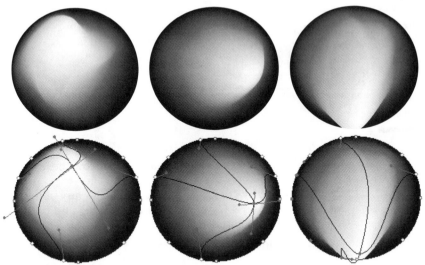

Figure 10-3:
These
objects use
the same
Gradient
Mesh, but
the mesh
points have
been moved
using the
Direct
Selection
tool.

That's really all there is to this tool! Figure 10-3 is just a whole bunch of clicks with the Mesh tool. We moved those points using the Direct Select tool and then tweaked the colors by selecting a point or a path and choosing a new color in the Color or Swatches palette.

You can automate the process by clicking the object you want and choosing Object➪Create Gradient Mesh. This method adds a Gradient Mesh to the object automatically. Illustrator does its best to estimate where the mesh paths should go. It does this by looking at the shape of the object and figuring out where the mesh paths should go to shade the object so it looks three-dimensional. You can even have the Gradient Mesh create the shading for you. Figure 10-4 shows the Create Gradient Mesh dialog box.

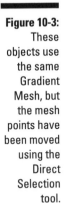

Figure 10-4:
The Create
Gradient
Mesh
dialog box.

After you select the Gradient Mesh command, the Create Gradient Mesh dialog box opens. Set your options, click OK, and the command does the meshy work for you. Here's the all-star lineup of options:

✔ **Rows and Columns.** These options set the number of mesh paths the command creates. The higher the number, the more control you have over the colors in your object but the more complex the graphic becomes to work with.

✔ **Appearance.** You can select one of three Appearance options: To Center, To Edge, and Flat. To Center lightens colors to place a highlight in the center of the object, creating the appearance that the graphic is being pulled outward. To Edge places a highlight at the edges of the object, creating the appearance that the graphic is being pulled inward. Flat doesn't change any colors at all but still creates the mesh for you, so you can change colors on your own. See Figure 10-5 for a look at the differences between options.

✔ **Highlight.** When you select an Appearance option of To Edge or To Center, the Highlight setting is the maximum amount that the colors lighten to create the 3D effect.

Figure 10-5 shows an object with a highlight applied to it using Illustrator's "automatic" highlighting process.

Figure 10-5:
Three versions of the same Gradient Mesh, with Appearance settings of Flat, To Center, and To Edge.

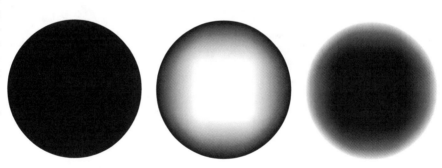

Making Objects Partially Transparent and Blending Colors

By default, Illustrator creates objects that hide whatever is behind them. However, the Transparency palette enables you to change this situation. Using the Opacity option, you can fade objects so that the underlying objects show through them. You can also blend the colors in the top graphics with the underlying graphics (in an astonishing variety of ways) by using Blend Modes.

One of the powerful features of the Transparency palette is that everything you do in it is *live*. That means your paths suffer no permanent changes after you make them transparent. You can change opacity again and again — or remove it altogether if you want — without changing your path data. This capability gives you tremendous room to play and experiment with different opacities.

Fade away with opacity

In Figure 10-6, a solid black oval faded out to 40% opacity partly reveals an angry writer behind it (nobody *we* know, of course).

Figure 10-6:
The oval at its original opacity (left) and faded to 40% (right) to reveal a disgruntled writer.

To make something partially transparent, just follow these steps:

1. **Select the object (or objects) you want to fade.**

   When you select multiple objects, they all get the same Opacity setting.

2. **Choose Window⇨Show Transparency.**

   The Transparency palette appears, as shown in Figure 10-7.

Figure 10-7:
The Transparency palette.

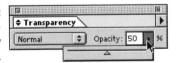

3. **In the Transparency palette, drag the Opacity slider until it shows the percentage of opacity you want to give to the selected object(s).**

    After you release the mouse button, the selected objects become partially transparent.

By default, transparency applies evenly to both the fill and stroke. If you want to give the fill and the stroke independent Opacity values, you can do so by using the Appearance palette. See Chapter 11 for full details.

Big fun with math! Blending graphics with Blend Modes

Pssst! Listen very, very carefully while we tell you what's *really* going on with Blend Modes (we're whispering because you never know who's listening in on these deep, dark secrets). Here's the scoop: Forget the math and pay attention to what the resulting artwork *looks* like.

Illustrator defines every color mathematically. You see that math when you drag sliders in the Color palette. A bright red color may be defined as R:216, G:20, and B:7 (in RGB) or C:20%, M:95%, Y:95%, and K:5% (in CMYK). Each of these numbers reflects a different amount of a component color; every different color has its own color value.

The Blend Modes take the colors in an object and mix them with the colors in underlying objects, performing a mathematical calculation using numbers that identify the colors of the objects. So if the top object is red, the underlying object is blue, and you have the Blend Mode set to Multiply, red's number gets multiplied by blue's number. The resulting color is what you see. Other modes do more complex calculations. What does that mean? It's Zen. What is blue times red? What is the difference between yellow and mauve? What is the sound of one hand clapping?

In short, it doesn't matter. What the result looks like is what matters! Try this approach for yourself: Select the top object and choose a different Blend Mode. The Blend Modes hang out in the Transparency palette's Blend Mode menu, as shown in Figure 10-8.

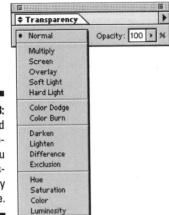

Figure 10-8:
The Blend
Mode pop-
up menu
in the Trans-
parency
palette.

Figure 10-9 shows three different Blend Modes at work on the same image — and they're completely changeable. If you try one and don't like it, just choose another from the menu.

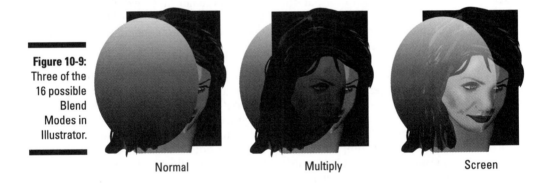

Figure 10-9:
Three of the
16 possible
Blend
Modes in
Illustrator.

Normal   Multiply   Screen

Discovering How Strokes Work

Any path in Illustrator can pick up a stroke (. . . stroke . . . *stroke!* Sorry. Just daydreaming about going for a nice row on a lake). In Illustrator, a *stroke* is a line placed on a path. A stroke can be of any thickness, which Illustrator calls its *weight.* Strokes can be any color or pattern.

Chapter 9 discusses the specialized strokes that you can make with the Paintbrush tool. The Pen tool and Pencil tool also provide distinctive strokes of their own.

In addition to color and weight, you can give strokes special attributes. These attributes include the specific look of corners (called *bends*) and endings (called *caps*), as well as whether the stroke has a pattern of dashes applied to it. To investigate all the advanced ways you can modify strokes, have a look at the Stroke palette shown in Figure 10-10. (Choose Window➪Show Stroke and select Show Options from the Stroke palette's pop-up menu.) To change the way a stroke appears, select a path and play around in the Stroke palette to see what happens. We won't tell a soul.

Strokes are always applied to the *center* of a path, which means the strokes, especially those of larger weight, can ooze beyond the path. The path runs right along the exact middle of the stroke. For more information on the relationship between strokes and paths, see Chapter 5.

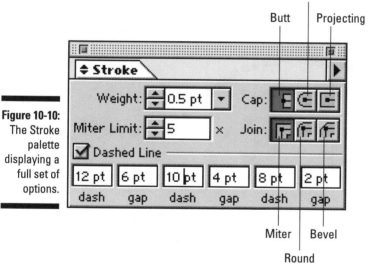

Figure 10-10:
The Stroke palette displaying a full set of options.

Joins, Bends, and Dashes

A stroke can be (and often is) a continuous line of color that follows a path, even if the path is as convoluted as a strand of spaghetti. But paths can also appear chopped up into dashes. You can tweak the shape of the dashes all at once, without having to fuss over every single one. You can set the shape that an individual dash (the basic unit of such an *open path*) begins or ends with — its *Cap* — and the shape of its corner points (its *Join*).

Strokes can have any of three different caps and any of three different joins applied to them. Combine these with the almost-limitless combinations possible for dash patterns and weights, and you can see the incredible versatility of strokes. To access these additional options, choose Window⇨Show Stroke. In the Stroke palette that appears, select Show Options from the palette's pop-up menu. (Refer to Figure 10-10.)

Caps

Shaping the ends of the dashes that make up an open path can change the entire look of the path. For example, imagine a dashed line that is 500 dashes long. Then imagine that all 500 dashes have identical ends, shaped like one of the three shapes in Figure 10-11.

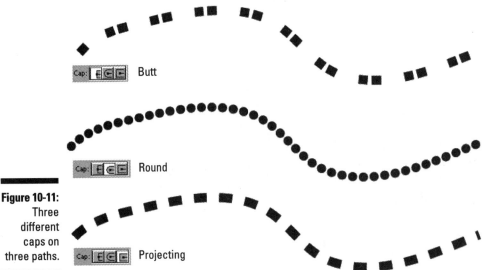

Figure 10-11: Three different caps on three paths.

Depending on which Cap shape you choose, you get three noticeably different capped lines. Here are the options:

- ✔ **Butt Cap** chops off the stroke at the ends.

- ✔ **Round Cap** extends the stroke past the ends (or around the dash location) with semicircular ends; the radius of each semicircle equals half the stroke weight.

- ✔ **Projecting Cap** extends the stroke past the ends (or around the dash location) with squared ends; the amount of each extension equals half the stroke weight.

To change the way a line is capped, select it with any Selection tool, then click the desired cap in the Stroke palette.

Joins

The Stroke palette offers three different joins. Figure 10-12 shows how they appear on paths. Joins only affect corner points (not smooth points. See Chapter 6 for more info on corner points). They make corners appear sharp and pointy, blunt and rounded, or squared-off.

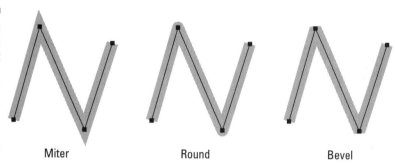

Figure 10-12:
Three different joins on a path (left to right): Miter, Round, and Bevel.

Miter   Round   Bevel

Depending on which Join shape you choose, you get three noticeably different corners. Here are the options:

- ✔ **Miter Join** causes the outside corner of the stroke to come to a sharp point.
- ✔ **Round Join** causes the outside corner of a stroke to come to a rounded or smooth curve.
- ✔ **Bevel Join** cuts off the corner so the width of the stroke is the same at the bevel as on the rest of the stroke.

If these terms look familiar, then you're probably familiar with woodworking — or you actually paid attention in industrial-arts class.

Dashes

Dashes break up the stroke into repeating segments of any length, with gaps between them, also of any length. You can set up to three different dash sizes — and three different gap sizes — in any stroke, as shown in Figure 10-13).

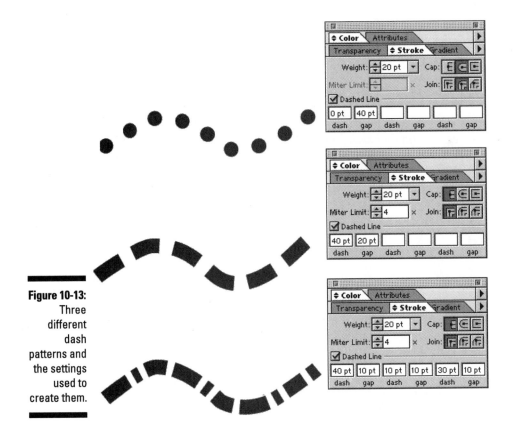

Figure 10-13:
Three different dash patterns and the settings used to create them.

Dashes work with the Cap settings. (What the heck, call it a labor-saving device.) Whatever Cap setting you use applies to the ends of all the dashes, not just to the ends of the path.

To create a dashed line, follow these steps:

1. **Select the Dashed Line option in the Stroke palette.**

2. **Set a Dash size.**

   Remember that the Round and Projecting Cap settings extend the dash from its center by half the width of the stroke. So if you use the Projecting Cap, and your Dash setting is 10 points, on a line with a 20-point stroke, the dash will be 30 points long.

    Choose a Butt Cap when you want your dashes to be an exact length that does not vary with the width of the stroke. If you want an exact circle for a Dash (or, in effect, a Dot) you use a 0 point dash. That creates a dot the width of the stroke.

3. **Set the Gap size (the distance between the ends of the dashes).**

This setting can be a little confusing if you're using the Round or Projecting Cap settings, since these extend the length of the dash past the end of the dash and into the gap, based on the width of the stroke, creating a gap that looks smaller than what you specified. The width of the stroke also affects the Gap size. If you want a gap of 20 points, and you are using a 10-point stroke, set the gap size to 30 points.

The Effect Menu

The Effect menu contains more amazing things than Area 51 (you know, the place where the government supposedly keeps a crashed alien spacecraft). Everything that you apply remains *live* — that is, changeable until you tell it to stop changing. Effects change the way an object *looks* but not the way the object *is*. Applying effects is something like telling the object to put on a specific costume and makeup, or changing the appearance of the world when you look through rose-colored glasses. No permanent change takes place.

To put this information technically, instead of rewriting the code for an object (which is what you tell Illustrator to do when you move a point), Effects just tack on extra code, leaving the original code untouched. That extra code can be changed or removed, without affecting the original in any way whatsoever.

Ah, yes, all things must change — and sometimes *you* get to change them. Contemplate the concept of *infinite editability* for a moment. An object in Illustrator is saying, in effect, *Turn me into anything.* Although Illustrator has always provided the capability of manipulating points, the current version is the first to make such extreme changes *possible but not permanent.* You can simply get rid of them at any time, without putting a scratch on your original artwork, without having to redo it, without having to resort to Edit⇨Undo, and without having to growl at the dog. Now, *that's* progress.

Applying "live" effects to objects

Figure 10-14 shows the difference between applying Roughen as a permanent change versus as a live effect. The biggest difference is that the path on the "dead" object shows the additional points generated by the permanent Roughen command, found under the Filter menu, and the live Roughen command, found under the Effect menu. The first command adds and moves points in the path, while the second command leaves the path untouched.

The trickiest part of the Effect menu is that many of its commands share identical names with commands found under other menus, such as Roughen under the Filter menu. The dialog boxes are even identical! And the results *look* the same, but the way the commands produce those results are different. Just keep in mind that if you don't select the command from the Effect menu, you're probably permanently changing the artwork in some way. So pay attention to whether your paths change. That way, if you see a difference, you can use Edit⇨Undo and select the same command from the Effect menu.

Figure 10-14:
Filters versus Effects — a path (left) roughened with the Roughen filter and the same path (right) roughed with the Roughen effect. (Who would do such a thing to an innocent doughnut?)

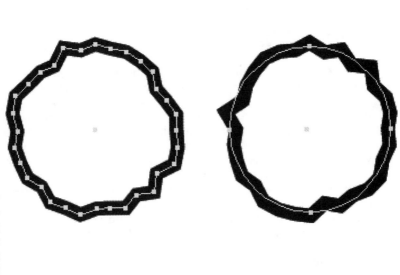

To apply an effect to a path, follow these steps:

1. **Select a path.**

2. **Choose an effect from the Effect menu.**

   For example, you can choose Effect⇨Distort and Transform⇨Punk & Bloat. A dialog box opens for that effect, and you can enter the specific settings.

   You can always go back and change the settings if you don't like the result. (If only we could do that in real life.)

3. **Click OK to apply the effect to the path.**

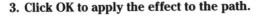

Many effects only work when the document is in the RGB Document Color Mode (see Chapter 1). If an effect is grayed out (unavailable) after you select an object, your document is probably in CMYK mode. You can, however, create your graphics in RGB Document Color Mode and *change* to CMYK later on. The only catch to this magic trick is that you must first rasterize (hang on, we're getting to that) any RGB-specific effects before you convert the document.

Rasterizing is the process whereby vectors are transformed into pixels. See Chapter 2 for the lowdown on pixels and vectors, and see "Here's the catch . . . rasterization," later in this chapter, to find out how to rasterize vectors.

Removing and changing effects

To change or remove effects, you use the Appearance palette, as shown in Figure 10-15. The Appearance palette is such an amazing palette that an entire chapter (Chapter 11 to be precise) of this book is devoted to it. For right now, though, you want to use the Appearance palette to remove and change effects.

Figure 10-15:
The
Gaussian
Blur Effect
in the
Appearance
palette.

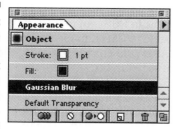

Appearances aside (so to speak), removing an effect is as simple as following these steps:

1. **Select the object that has the effect you want to get rid of.**

2. **Choose Window⇨Show Appearance.**

   In the Appearance palette, the selected object is listed as Object. Beneath the object is a list that includes the Stroke and Fill of the object, and all the effects applied to it.

3. **In the list, click the effect that you want to discard.**

4. **Click the trash can at the lower right of the Appearance palette.**

   The effect disappears, and the object returns to its former appearance (before you applied the effect).

To change an effect, follow the steps above, except instead of clicking the trash can, double-click the effect in the Appearance palette. Doing so opens the particular effect's dialog box, where you can enter new settings. Click OK to apply the effect with the new settings.

Here's the catch . . . rasterization!

All this power comes with a terrible price. By using these effects, you agree to give Adobe your firstborn child (or at least your favorite pet gecko) . . . unless you can spin a pile of straw into gold. (Whoa. Guess the princess should have read that shrink-wrap licensing agreement *before* she broke the seal on the software! But hey, it was long ago in a land far away. Who knew?)

Fortunately, you can escape this predicament by naming Illustrator's product manager in three guesses when he comes to collect his fee — or by figuring out *rasterization*. (No, that isn't his name.)

Unfortunately, live effects can't always remain live indefinitely. Effects like Colored Pencil and Neon Glow only work when the image is in RGB Document Color Mode. You can create your artwork in RGB, but many times when you're ready to print, you need to change to CMYK mode (For more information on color modes, see Chapter 1). After you change to CMYK, though, all those effects disappear! What's a poor artist to do?

Here's where rasterization comes in. Rasterization converts the information into pixels, just like the pixels Photoshop uses (see Chapter 2 for more information on Pixels). You're no longer able to edit individual points, but you are able to convert to CMYK without loosing your artwork. After you rasterize an Illustrator graphic, the graphic has all the limitations of any other pixel-based graphic, even though it's in Illustrator.

To rasterize a graphic, choose Effect⇨Rasterize⇨Raster Effects Settings. The Raster Effects Settings dialog box appears, as shown in Figure 10-16.

Figure 10-16:
The famous Raster Effects Settings dialog box takes a bow.

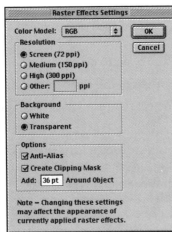

In the Raster Effects Settings dialog box, you can set the following options:

✔ **Color Model.** This setting determines the color model used by the resulting graphic. You should try to use the color model of your target output as much as possible. If you're creating a graphic print in grayscale, choose Grayscale. If you're bound for the Web, choose RGB.

✔ **Resolution.** This setting determines how much information the resulting image contains. You should try to match this setting with the graphic's purpose. For the Web, select 72 ppi (pixels per inch). For most ink jet printers, 150 ppi is sufficient. For high-resolution printing, 300 ppi is a good, all-purpose size.

✔ **Background.** Pixel-based images are always rectangular. If the graphic you're rasterizing is anything but rectangular, you have to add a background to it to make it rectangular. That space can be White or Transparent. White is fine for a stand-alone graphic, but if that graphic is in front of other objects, the white background will obscure them. When this is the case, choose Transparent.

✔ **Options.** The Anti-Alias option adds a slight blurring wherever different colors meet. Believe it or not, this setting usually makes the resulting graphic look better. Results vary from graphic to graphic, of course, so try rasterizing with and without the Anti-Alias option selected. The Create Clipping Mask option only matters if you selected White for the Background setting. In Illustrator, a *Clipping Mask* is a special graphic that serves to hide parts of other graphics. If you select the Create Clipping Mask option, a Clipping Mask is added to hide the white parts added to make the graphic rectangular.

✔ **Add.** Selecting this option adds extra pixels around the graphic, just in case you need them. Hey, you never know! Nobody wants to run short of pixels. (Okay, just kidding. This option actually helps prevent circles from getting clipped on the edges. Nothing grouchier than a circle that's having a bad hair day.)

After you choose your settings, click OK to convert your graphic to pixels.

Clipping Masks

No, they're not some special headgear the barber wears to entertain younger customers. Clipping Masks are a simple, yet incredibly handy, Illustrator feature. Simply put, they hide things. Like Effects and Transparency settings, Clipping Masks are live functions in that they make no permanent change to path data. They make things look different, but you can take them away with a single command, and your paths remain exactly as they were before.

Clipping Masks use objects to hide other objects, as shown in Figure 10-17. The top object (the masking object) becomes completely transparent. The underlying objects become invisible except for where the mask object is. The number of objects beneath the mask doesn't matter. Only the topmost object functions as the masking object. The top object's fill and stroke also don't matter, because the top object becomes invisible.

Figure 10-17:
The original artwork, the masking object in front of the artwork, and the masked artwork. (Maybe that poor, stressed writer gets to be a star after all.)

To create a clipping mask, here's the drill:

1. **Create an object to be used as a mask.**

   Masks can be any shape or color. You can even use text as a mask.

2. **Position the object in front of whatever you want to mask out.**

3. **Select the object, and all the objects behind it that you want to mask out.**

   Shift+click with the Selection tool to select multiple objects.

4. **Choose Object⇨Clipping Mask⇨Make.**

   The masking object and anything outside the mask disappear, leaving just what is inside and behind the masking object.

The things that seem to disappear after you apply the mask aren't really gone. They're just hidden. You can bring them back by choosing Object⇨Clipping Mask⇨Release. Sometimes that's more impressive than pulling a rabbit out of your hat.

Chapter 11

Keeping Up Appearances, with Style(s)

. . . .

In This Chapter

▶ Looking at the Appearance palette

▶ Adding additional fills and strokes

▶ Combining Effect settings to create different effects

▶ Creating a style

▶ Manipulating existing styles

. . . .

*L*ong ago (well, okay, in the not-too-distant past), Illustrator was a straight-forward program that offered relatively few (and relatively obvious) choices. You knew when you looked at a pink rectangle that it was made with four corner points joined by four paths and was filled with a single, solid pink color. But those days of blissful innocence are past. Now that pink rectangle may really be a *red* rectangle that some fiend faded to 50% opacity by using the Transparency palette. And that rectangle may not be a rectangle at all, but a graphic of an old shoe that has been *disguised* as a rectangle using the Effect⇨Convert to Shape⇨Rectangle command. In this world of illusions, where anything can appear to be anything else and nothing is as it seems, what's an artist to do?

In this chapter, you discover a wonderful tool for cutting through (and taking control of) the illusions of Illustrator: the Appearance palette. The Appearance palette enables you to see exactly what secrets your artwork is hiding. If that were all it did, it'd be worth its weight in gold. But it does so much more! Beyond just seeing what's been done to an illustration, you also find out how to change the attributes of the illustration. For example, you can alter applied effects — or delete them altogether.

You also discover how to use the Appearance palette to target just the fill of an object (or just the stroke) when you apply Transparency or Effects settings. (If you don't use the Appearance palette, Illustrator applies the same settings to both the fill and stroke simultaneously.) You also use the Appearance palette to perform casual miracles that were impossible in any previous version of Illustrator, such as assigning multiple fills and strokes to a single object.

To make matters even better, you find out how to save all the Appearance settings as a Style. Styles are saved in the Style palette. You can apply a style to any object you create in the future. In addition to being a quick way to apply all these attributes to objects, styles can be updated in a way that also updates all objects with those styles applied.

The Appearance Palette

The Appearance palette, shown in Figure 11-1, is where you go to see why your artwork looks the way it does (though the palette can't explain why *anybody* would put neon-pink paisleys all over the place). You can view the Appearance palette by choosing Window⇨Show Appearance. When the Appearance palette wafts into view, it bears a vast treasure of option information. In its basic state, the palette displays Fill, Stroke, and Transparency settings. In its more complex state, the palette displays additional fills and strokes, and effects applied to those fills and strokes (as well as to the object itself).

Figure 11-1:
The
Appearance
palette.

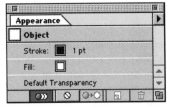

Not to worry: This welter of information isn't *nearly* as confusing as, say, your income tax form. Here's why: All along, in the course of creating your artwork, you've been putting all these information tidbits into the Appearance palette. You tell Illustrator to add info to this palette every time you set an option that changes the way your object looks (such as Stroke, Fill, and Transparency).

The Appearance palette faithfully records all this information all the time, even if you don't look at it. (It doesn't tap your TV cable, so you won't find a copy of that movie you missed last night.)

Reading the Appearance palette

The Appearance palette, shown in Figure 11-2, displays accumulated information about a particular object. Now, about this silly matter of *reading* all that balderdash. . . .

Figure 11-2:
The
Appearance
palette (left)
displays an
array of
information
about the
object
(right) (non-
restrictive
usage),
such as the
stroke and
fill data
shown here.

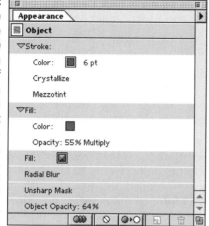

To make sense of all the Appearance palette's information, we compiled the following list of its features:

✔ **Target:** This feature identifies the *type* of graphic that the information in the Appearance palette refers to. Typically this feature says Object, meaning the information in the palette refers to (or will be applied to) appearance that is or will be applied to a single selected object. When you select a group or a layer, the target says Group or Layer. If text is selected, the target says Text. The target section is always at the top. A tiny thumbnail image emulates the appearance of the graphic.

✔ **Global effects:** These effects apply equally to, and affect all aspects of, the entire object. Whenever you apply Effects or Transparency settings (as described in Chapter 10) without using the Appearance palette, you apply the effects as global effects. Although they are usually the first attribute you apply, they always appear near the bottom of the list in the Appearance palette.

Another way to differentiate global effects from other effects is the way they line up with other items listed in the palette. Global effects appear in alignment with the Stroke and the Fill listings. Effects applied to a specific stroke are indented beneath the listing for that specific stroke. In Figure 11-2, Radial Blur and Unsharp Mask are the global effects.

✔ **Strokes:** Because objects can have more than one stroke (but only when you add them through the Appearance palette, as described in the "Adding Fills and Strokes" section of this chapter), the first one (listed at the top) is typically the one also shown in the Toolbox. The target may have additional strokes listed here as well. Strokes can have effects applied to them specifically. Here we see a single stroke with a weight of 6 points. See Chapter 5 for more information on strokes.

✔ **Stroke and Fill effects:** Effects can be applied directly to strokes and fills, instead of to the entire object, group, or layer. In this figure, the stroke has both a Crystallize and a Mezzotint effect applied to it.

✔ **Stroke and Fill Transparency:** Each stroke and fill can have various Transparency settings applied to it. Here, the first fill has an opacity of 55% and a blend mode of Multiply.

✔ **Fill:** Each object (group or layer) can have multiple fills (as it can have multiple strokes). Each fill can also have any number of effects applied to it. This object has both a solid color fill and a pattern fill applied to it.

✔ **Transparency:** This feature is the transparency appearance for the entire object, group, or layer. Here the transparency is set to Object Opacity: 64%, meaning the entire object has been faded to 64%. If no special Transparency settings were applied, this would simply read Default Transparency. See Chapter 10 for more information on Transparency.

The top-to-bottom order of the fills and strokes in the Appearance palette reflect a front-to-back order in the graphic. Strokes and fills on top in the palette appear in front of the strokes and fills that are lower in the palette. Effects run from top to bottom in terms of which effect is applied to the graphic first.

Most of the items in the Appearance palette can be moved up and down through the list into different positions, and this change is reflected in the actual graphic. For instance, you can take the Feather effect applied to a stroke and move it so that it is applied to a fill. You can also take that effect and move it so it applies to the entire object. To move something in the Appearance palette, drag it up and down through the palette, just as you move things in the Layers palette.

If a fill or stroke has an effect applied to it, the little disclosure triangle automatically appears on the left and points down, listing the attributes of that fill or stroke. When you have a whole lot of different effects applied to a fill or stroke, the palette can get cumbersome. Clicking the disclosure triangle hides the list of effects. You can access the list at any time by clicking the disclosure triangle again.

Adding fills and strokes

Chapter 5 explores fills and strokes in greater detail (and if you want to nip back there for more information, we can wait). When you apply a different stroke or fill to an object without using the Appearance palette, the fill or stroke replaces any existing fill or stroke. You don't have to settle for just one of each, though! Using the Appearance palette, as shown in Figure 11-3, you can add as many fills and strokes as you want. This feature offers some interesting possibilities. For example, you can give a path three different colored strokes of different sizes, to create a striped path. Or you can apply a pattern fill over a solid-color fill.

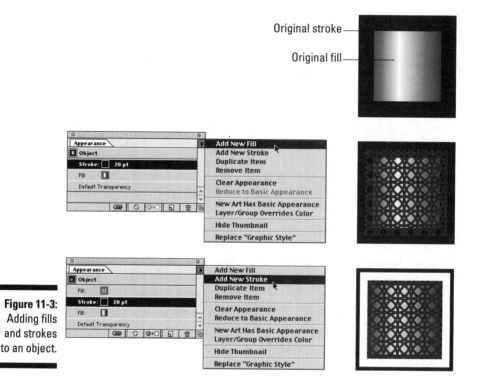

Original stroke

Original fill

Figure 11-3:
Adding fills
and strokes
to an object.

Just follow these steps to apply an additional fill and stroke to an object:

1. **Create an object with a fill color and a thick stroke.**

   In this example we made a rectangle by clicking and dragging with the Rectangle tool (see Chapter 4 for more information on the rectangle tool). We filled it with a gradient by clicking the Fill box in the Toolbox, then clicking a gradient swatch in the Swatches palette. We then added a 20-point black stroke to the square by clicking the Stroke box in the Toolbox, then clicking a black swatch in the Swatches palette, and finally choosing 20 points from the Stroke palette. For more info on fills and strokes, see Chapter 5.

2. **Select Add New Fill from the pop-up menu in the Appearance palette.**

   Illustrator adds a fill, but you don't see any difference, because the new fill is identical to the fill already there. The new fill is highlighted in the Appearance palette, however, and as soon as you select a new fill color from the Color palette or the Swatches palette, you see the new fill over the old one.

3. **With the new fill still highlighted in the Appearance palette change the fill to a pattern fill from the Swatches palette**

   For this example, change the fill to the pattern Azure Rings by clicking it in the Swatches palette.

   If you don't know which pattern is the Azure Rings palette, pause your cursor for a moment above each swatch. Its name pops up.

4. **Choose Add New Stroke from the pop-up menu in the Appearance palette.**

   A stroke appears on top of the original stroke. As with the added fill color, the new stroke uses the same settings as the previous stroke, so you don't see an immediate difference.

5. **In the Color palette, change the color of the stroke to White and change its stroke width to 10 points.**

After you add strokes and fills, you can move them around. Simply click them in the Appearance palette and drag up or down. As you drag, a black line appears in the palette, indicating where that fill or stroke will go after you release it.

Multiple fills and strokes work great with the Transparency palette. Each fill and stroke can have its own Transparency settings. This approach is a great way to blend fills and strokes together to achieve unique appearances. For example, if you apply a solid color fill over a Pattern fill, then change the Blend mode of the color fill to "hue," you replace the color(s) in the pattern with the color of the solid color but still maintain all the detail of the pattern. See Chapter 10 for more information on Transparency and Blend modes.

Changing the appearance of groups and layers

You can change the appearance of groups or layers as well as objects. Groups are collections of separate objects that have been grouped together, using the Object⇨Group command, so that they act like a single object when you select them with the Selection tool (see Chapter 3 for more information on the Group command). Similar to grouping, layers are a method of organizing multiple elements of your graphic into separate areas. Chapter 13 discusses layers in depth.

To change the appearance, you need to *target* those groups or layers first. Targeting is a method of selecting a group or layer so that any changes made to the appearance affect all the objects in the group or layer. Changing the appearance of groups or layers creates a *global* appearance for all objects in the group or on the layer. Objects still maintain their individual appearance settings, but any group or layer changes are added to all the objects.

To change the appearance of a group by adding an effect, just follow these steps:

1. **Select a group by clicking it with the regular Selection tool.**

2. **Add an effect to the group.**

   For this example, add a Gaussian Blur by choosing Effect⇨Blur⇨Gaussian Blur. In the Gaussian Blur dialog box that opens when you choose the effect, set the Radius to 5 and click OK.

   All the objects in the group become blurred. *Just like that.* Wow.

On the other hand, targeting a layer to apply an effect is a little more unusual, as shown in Figure 11-4.

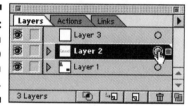

Figure 11-4:
Targeting a
layer to
apply an
effect.

Layers are a way to organize and arrange objects in your document. (Chapter 13 talks about layers in depth.) Every time you add an object to a layer, the appearance of that object changes to match the settings of the layer. When that object goes to another layer, with different Layer Appearance settings, the object's appearance changes again.

To target and apply an effect to a layer, just follow these steps:

1. **Choose Window⇨Show Layers.**

   The Layers palette opens.

2. **In the Layers palette, click the Target Layer Appearance button beside the layer that has the appearance you want to change.**

   The Target Layer Appearance button is the circle to the right of the name of the layer in the Layers palette. Clicking this circle targets the layer, so your changes affect that layer.

3. **Add an effect to the layer.**

   For this example, choose Effect⇨Stylize⇨Feather. The Feather dialog box opens. Set the Feather Radius to 5 and click OK. All the objects in the layer are feathered. (Lay in a large supply of birdseed. Just kidding.)

Applying effects to strokes and fills

Normally, whenever you apply an effect, it's applied to the entire object. However, to keep matters interesting (or confusing), you can also apply any effect to either a stroke *or* a fill. Whichever one you change, the other remains unaffected, as shown in Figure 11-5.

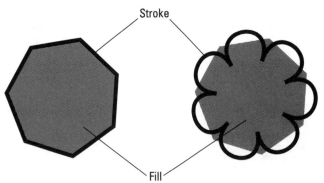

Figure 11-5: The Punk & Bloat effect applied to the stroke, but not the fill.

To apply an effect to a stroke *only* or to a fill *only*, just follow these steps:

1. **Select an object by clicking it with the Selection tool.**

2. **Choose Window⇨Show Appearance to open the Appearance palette.**

3. **In the Appearance palette, select the Stroke or the Fill that you wish to apply the effect to.**

   For this example, select the Stroke.

4. **Choose an effect from the Effect menu.**

   For this example, choose Effect⇨Distort & Transform⇨Punk & Bloat. The Punk & Bloat dialog box opens. Drag the slider towards Punk (to the left) or towards Bloat (to the right). The effect applies to the path and takes an appropriate place in the Appearance palette.

When you look at your artwork, you see that only the stroke has been Punked (or Bloated, depending on what you chose). If you want to apply an effect just to a fill, follow the preceding steps, but select a fill instead of a stroke.

Going back to adjust settings

Any effect previously applied to an object, group, or layer can be modified. You can edit the effect by double-clicking it in the Appearance palette. After you do, the effect's dialog box appears, enabling you to edit the current values for that effect. If the effect dialog box has a preview checkbox, place a check in it and watch your changes in real time!

Don't try to edit an effect you just applied by selecting that effect again in the Effect menu. Doing so applies the same effect a second time over the same path. Instead, double-click the effect in the Appearance palette.

Removing appearances

If you're tired of keeping up appearances (for example, you feel your artwork is too complex and want it to be cleaner and simpler, or you've added so many effects that printing or drawing on screen takes too long), Illustrator gives you three ways to remove them (from on-screen artwork, that is). You can take an appearance apart (one attribute at a time), trash all the appearance except the basics, or zap everything at once. Here's how you accomplish each of these tasks:

✔ **To get rid of a single effect, transparency setting, stroke, or fill,** select what you want to remove in the Appearance palette and then click the little trash-can icon at the bottom right of the palette.

✔ **To get rid of all effects, extra fills and strokes, and transparencies,** click the Reduce to Basic Appearance button (the button with two circles at the bottom center of the palette). This action strips away everything except one stroke and one fill color and resets the Default Transparency to a Blend mode of Normal and an Opacity setting of 100% (see Chapter 10 for more details on Blend modes and Opacity settings).

✔ **To clear everything away,** leaving a path with no strokes or fills whatsoever, click the Clear Appearance button (the circle with a line through it at the bottom left of the palette).

Note that the Appearance palette always shows a Fill, Stroke, and Default Transparency for an object, even after you throw them away. Throwing away a fill or stroke automatically sets it to None; throwing away a transparency sets it to the Default Transparency setting which is a blend mode of Normal and an Opacity setting of 100%.

Killing live effects until they're dead

Sometimes, you want to preserve the way an object looks, but get rid of all the things in the Appearance palette. One reason to do this is that all these multiple fills, strokes, and effects can take tremendous processing power when they are live. This situation can result in long print times, or long times redrawing whenever you make a change to your graphic. The drawback to live effects is that they are previews and need to be recalculated every time you make a change. You can "kill" these live effects so that they permanently change your graphic. You can no longer make individual adjustments to them or remove them, but all the calculations have been made and the graphic has been permanently changed. This results in a much simpler, if limited, graphic.

To permanently set all the live effects, choose Object⇨Expand Appearance. The object "expands" which is a completely counterintuitive way of saying the object gets simpler. All the settings made in the Appearance palette are really just previews. They haven't been applied to the graphic. Every time you make a change, that appearance needs to be completely recalculated. Expanding the object applies all those changes to it permanently, so the calculations do not have to be made again. The graphic is simpler, if less editable. Figure 11-6 shows the difference between live and, um, dead objects.

Figure 11-6:
A live effect on a path (left) and after the Expand Appearance command is applied.

Figuring Out Styles

Styles are collections of colors, transparency settings, effects, and additional fills and strokes that can be applied to any path, group, or layer. Think of all that information in the Appearance palette. Saving it and applying it to different objects (without having to recreate all those settings), can significantly reduce the time and effort you spend. That's the advantage of using styles.

Another advantage is that any update in the style changes all the objects to which you apply that style. For instance, if you apply a style with a red fill and black stroke to a path, and later you update the style to an orange fill, the object you previously applied that style to changes to an orange fill and black stroke.

Applying styles to objects

Illustrator comes with a whole slew of premade styles that are stored in the Styles palette (see Figure 11-7), ready for you to use with just a click.

To apply a style to an object, follow these steps:

1. **Select an object.**

2. **Open the Styles palette by choosing Window⇨Show Styles.**

   The Styles palette appears.

3. **Click a thumbnail style in the Styles palette.**

   Doing so automatically applies all the settings to the selected object.

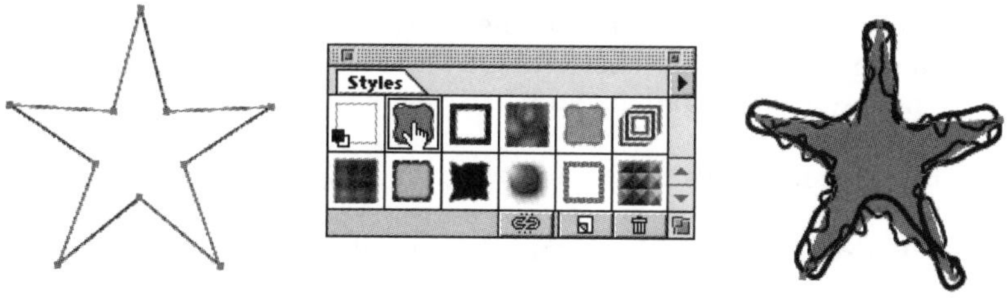

Figure 11-7:
Applying a
style to a
path.

Creating and editing styles

You can create a style from any selected object in the document, as shown in Figure 11-8. You can also create a style based on the current Appearance palette settings. (The Appearance palette contains the settings for the last object selected, even if that object is not currently selected.)

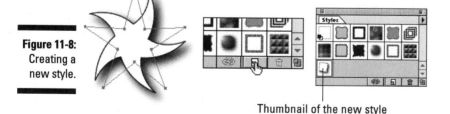

Figure 11-8:
Creating a
new style.

Thumbnail of the new style

1. **Select an object (or not, as the case may be).**

   If you don't select a path, the style you create adopts the current settings in the Appearance palette.

2. **Open the Styles palette by choosing Window➪Show Styles.**

   The Styles palette appears.

3. **Click the New Style button (the middle button at the bottom right of the Styles palette).**

   A thumbnail representation of the new style appears in the Styles palette.

You have more than one method available to edit an existing style. Regardless of the method you use, Illustrator automatically updates all the objects that have that style applied to them, to match the new style. The basic way to edit an existing style is to redefine it.

After you apply a style to an object, you can click the Break Link to Style button on the Styles palette to prevent Illustrator from updating the object to a new style if you redefine the existing one.

To redefine an existing style, as shown in Figure 11–9, just follow these steps:

1. **Create a basic shape and then apply a style to it.**

   In this instance, we created a triangle using the Basic Shapes tool. Then we chose Window➪Show Styles and applied the style Bizzaro to the triangle by clicking that style in the Styles palette.

2. **Edit the selected object as you normally would to create the new appearance that you want.**

   Change the fill and stroke, and/or add effects. In this case, we chose a darker fill color and added two strokes of different colors to the triangle using the Add New Stroke command in the Appearance palette (described in the Adding Fills and Strokes section of this chapter).

3. **After you're satisfied with the changes, open the Appearance palette by choosing Window➪Show Appearance. With the altered object still selected, choose Replace "*Style Name*" from the Appearance palette's pop-up menu, accessed by clicking the triangle in the upper-right corner of the Appearance palette.**

   You are replacing a style, but you have to do it through the Appearance palette. Go figure! Because the name of the style we edited in this example was *Bizzaro*, the menu reads *Replace " Bizzaro."* The menu changes to whatever name the style has been given.

   Illustrator updates the style in the Styles palette with the changes — and updates any object in the document that has that same style applied to it.

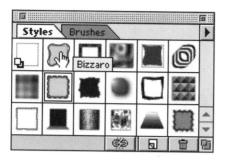

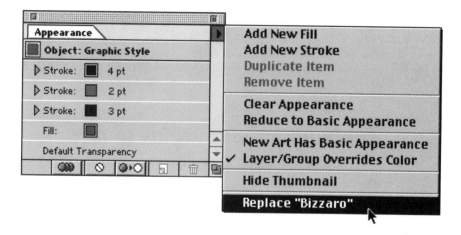

Figure 11-9:
Redefining
an existing
style.

Another way to edit an existing style is to replace it with another set of
Appearance settings. Set the fill, stroke, and effects for an object to make it
look the way you want it to. Then hold down the Option [Alt] key and drag
the object over the thumbnail of the style that you want to replace in the
Styles palette. It may look as if you are dragging that entire object into the
Styles palette, but really, you are just dragging its fill, stroke, and effects settings (in other words, its appearance). To let you know that the object is in
the proper position to replace the existing style, a black border appears

around the style. Release the mouse to update the style to the Appearance settings of the selected object. Illustrator also updates all objects that share the style.

Spotting the difference between graphic and text styles

Illustrator has graphic styles but not text styles. *Graphic styles* specify attributes such as fill color, stroke color, transparency, additional strokes and fills, and any applied effects. *Text styles* specify attributes such as font, size, leading, alignment, and other Character palette and Paragraph palette settings.

Because Illustrator has only graphic styles, you can't save attributes such as font and alignment with your styles. However, you *can* apply graphic styles to text and text objects; the graphic styles just don't apply any text-specific attributes.

Applying graphic styles to text

In effect, Illustrator looks at text as a *picture* of letters and numbers — not as letters and numbers as such — and then applies a graphic style to that picture, as shown in Figure 11-10.

To apply a graphic style to text, just follow these steps:

1. **Select text using the Selection tool.**

2. **Display the Styles palette by choosing Window⇨Show Styles.**

3. **Click a thumbnail in the Styles palette to apply that style to the text.**

   Illustrator applies the graphic style you select to the text object.

You can quickly apply a style to text or other objects by selecting the style you want and then clicking with the Paint Bucket (which is located in the same slot as the Eyedropper tool) on anything you want to change to that style. (It's so much easier than dragging a real paint bucket. And you don't have to worry about the carpet. Is Illustrator great, or what?)

jeepers

Part III

Taking Your Paths to Obedience School

The 5th Wave   By Rich Tennant

"Are you sure that's the best way to apply a stroke to a path?"

In this part . . .

*H*alf the battle in Illustrator is creating stuff. The other half is modifying and organizing the stuff you've created (preferably into something manageable). This section is all about manipulating your creations into exactly what you want them to be. You start by selecting and moving pieces of artwork (and the individual parts that make up the artwork) — you can rotate, scale, skew, or mash your art around in a variety of ways. For a really exciting time (adventures in unbridled mutation), you get to transform one piece of artwork into another by using the Blend tool. Finally, Illustrator reveals a secret of the ages: Organizing can be a fun and exciting activity (instead of a horrible, tedious chore that devours time like a slo-mo shark) when you use delightful innovations like Layers, the Align palette, grids, and guides.

Chapter 12

Pushing, Pulling, Poking, and Prodding

- -

In This Chapter

▶ Understanding how transformations work

▶ Moving and shaking (even stirring) objects and portions of objects

▶ Using the Scale, Rotate, Reflect, and Shear tools

▶ Applying unusual distortions to artwork

▶ Blending paths until they're confused and happy

- -

Art that you create in Illustrator can be modified in a number of ways. Perhaps the most powerful of these ways are transformations and distortions. These enable you to bend, move, and manipulate paths and other Illustrator objects like silly putty, shaping them to your every whim. (Powermongers, rejoice!)

In this chapter, you find out how to use Illustrator's many transformation and distortion tools to alter the shape of your artwork in any way you desire.

Understanding the Five Transformation Sisters

You can do five fundamental things to paths: move, scale, rotate, reflect, and shear. Each of these transformations has both a tool and a dialog box associated with it. Move actually has five tools, if you count all five selection tools (which also are used to move selections).

The key to using all these tools (and their control-freak dialog boxes) is to select what you want to change first and then to apply the transformation. Use the Selection tool when you want to transform an entire object (Shift-click with the Selection tool to transform multiple objects simultaneously) or use the Direct Selection tool to transform just a few points at a time.

Move

Moving objects is probably the most common thing you do to them. In light of this fact, Illustrator lets you move objects simply by clicking and dragging them with any of the selection tools. Figure 12-1, for example, shows an elaborate object moved from one spot to another.

Sometimes, you need to move a selection a specific amount. Suppose you draw a flower (or a weed, if your drawing skills aren't quite up to par yet), and you want to move this flower exactly one inch to the right. The easiest way to do so is to enter **1 in** (for *one inch*) in the Move dialog box. The Move dialog box appears after you choose Object⇨Transform⇨Move. Then you can specify 1 inch in the dialog box's Horizontal field. Figure 12-2 shows the Move dialog box and where to enter that number 1.

Okay, so you may wonder how Illustrator knows to move the flower just an inch to the *right*, instead of to the left. Well, Illustrator knows because the number you entered in the text field is a *positive* number. If you enter a negative number, the object moves to the left. In fact, the *only* way to move something to the left in the Move dialog box is to enter a negative number in the Horizontal text field. If you do that, the Angle field automatically changes to 180 degrees, which is to the left (0 degrees is to the right).

You can use any unit of measurement to move objects. Whenever you enter a number, just follow it with the appropriate unit symbol: **"** or **in** for inches, **p** for picas, **pt** for points, or **cm** for centimeters.

Figure 12-1:
The original illustration (left) is modified (right) by using the Selection tool to move the bird. (Suddenly the parrot seems to defy gravity.)

Figure 12-2:
The Move
dialog box.

Move

Position
Horizontal: 0 pt
Vertical: 1 pt

Distance: 1 pt
Angle: 90 °

OK
Cancel
Copy

Options
☑ Objects ☐ Patterns ☐ Preview

Scale

To make something bigger or smaller in Illustrator, you *scale* it. Illustrator has a Scale tool, a Scale dialog box, and a scale function as part of the "bounding box" that surrounds an object after you select it with the Selection tool. Not only can you make an object bigger or smaller, but you can also "squish" an item to change its size. So, for instance, you can make an item twice as high but the same width as it was originally. Figure 12-3 shows an item and what happens when you scale it.

Figure 12-3:
The original
artwork
(left) scaled
smaller and
larger.

The easiest way to scale art is *not* to use the Scale tool, but to use the "bounding box" that appears around objects after you select them with the Selection tool. The bounding box enables you to both scale and rotate artwork. To scale artwork, click and drag the handles (big, black squares) around the outside of the artwork.

If you hold down the Shift key as you drag the bounding box handles, you constrain the sizing of the bounding box (and the artwork) so that the width and height are scaled proportionately. This is typically a good thing; it prevents your artwork from getting really, really fat or really, really skinny as you scale it.

TIP

Holding down the Shift key as you use any of a variety of tools, tends to keep the object more controlled. For instance, with the Rotate tool, holding down the Shift key constrains rotation to 45-degree increments (a nice angle sideways, another nice angle upside-down, another nice angle sideways the other way, and finally one more lovely angle straight up).

The bounding box is nice and all, but you don't find Illustrator Knights of the Galaxy using it, because they *like* doing things the hard way (you know, greater evidence of artistic prowess, more prestige). The Scale tool is definitely more difficult to use than the bounding box for resizing artwork, but the Scale tool also has all sorts of capabilities that the bounding box doesn't have (accessed by double-clicking the tool in the Toolbox) — such as scaling from a specific origin, using specific values, and copying as you scale.

As a certain short, green philosopher once said, "Try not. Do. Or do not. . . ." Well, okay, you can just *try* the technique, as shown in Figure 12-4, if you want to. The galaxy isn't at stake here.

To scale your artwork by using the Scale tool, just follow these steps:

1. **Select your artwork using the regular Selection tool.**

2. **Choose the Scale tool.**

   The Scale tool icon is supposed to look like a small box being resized into a bigger box. Really. (Call it artistic license.)

Figure 12-4:
Using the Scale tool: (left to right) the original artwork selected, the hairline preview that appears when you drag with the scale tool, the final enlarged artwork.

3. **Click at the corner of the artwork and drag.**

   By default, the Scale tool scales from the center of the selection. When you drag, a hairline preview of your artwork appears, indicating the size and shape that your graphic will be after you release the mouse.

   Drag away from the graphic to enlarge it, drag toward the center of the graphic to shrink it.

4. **Release the mouse button when the art is the size you want it to be.**

   The artwork scales to that size.

All you accuracy addicts out there (you know who you are) can double-click the Scale tool slot in the Toolbox to indulge your habit: A Scale dialog box appears and offers a nice blank space in which you can type an exact scale percentage. (Some folks just have a hankering to know what an object looks like at 183 percent or 0.5597 percent of its current size.)

But wait, there's more! You also have an option for choosing a Uniform or Non-Uniform scale change. Well, no, choosing Uniform won't dress up the object in khakis. Instead, the object acts as if you pressed some super Shift key and ends up looking like a bigger or smaller version of the original, identically proportioned (nary a squish anywhere).

Not content with scaling from the center? The two-click method of using the Scale tool may soothe your yearning for alternatives. The two-click method enables you to move the origin point around the screen before scaling. The *origin point* is a place tacked to the artboard around which the rest of the artwork scales. Normally, the origin point is in the middle of the selection, but you can put the origin point anywhere, even outside the selection! Just select the Scale tool from the Toolbox and click once before you do the click-and-drag routine to scale the object. Illustrator resets the origin point to the location where you single-clicked.

If you drag back across the origin point (or the middle if you didn't set one) while using the Scale tool, you may well "flip" the artwork over. That's a little disconcerting, but as long as you don't release the mouse button, you can always drag back and fix it. If you *do* release the mouse button, you can undo (choose Edit⇨Undo).

Rotate

Spinning your artwork around in circles is a good way to whittle away an afternoon. Sometimes, we just sit, click, and spin, watching the artwork rotate on the screen. It's mesmerizing. Then again, we don't really get out all that much.

You can use the funky "corner arrows" in the bounding box (which shows up when you have something selected with the regular Selection tool) or by using the Rotate tool. The Rotate tool (like the Scale tool) enables you to set the origin point, which is the location the artwork rotates around. Double-clicking the Rotate tool also enables you to set a specific angle of rotation. Figure 12-5 shows artwork before and after it's rotated with the Rotate tool.

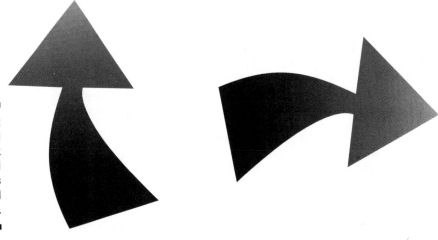

Figure 12-5:
The original artwork (left) and after it's rotated (right).

Reflect

Using the Reflect command, you can flip a selection over any axis, making a mirror image. Figure 12-6 shows original artwork before and after it's flipped over a 90-degree axis.

To use the Reflect tool to create a mirror image, just follow these steps:

1. **Select the artwork to be reflected.**

2. **Choose the Reflect tool from the Toolbox.**

Figure 12-6:
Reflecting artwork by using the Reflect tool.

3. **Press and hold down the Shift key (you release it after you release the mouse button in Step 5).**

   The Shift key constrains the reflection to a 45-degree angle, which makes a "horizontal" reflection easier to accomplish. (Who knew it took so much work to be a beam of light? Other than Einstein. . . .)

4. **Click the far-right edge of the selected artwork and drag to the left.**

5. **Release the mouse button (and then the Shift key) after the artwork "flips" over.**

But that's not all! If you act now and double-click the Reflect tool, you get the Reflect dialog box (shown in Figure 12-7) absolutely free! Here are its exciting capabilities:

✔ **Horizontal:** This radio button flips the image upside-down as you reflect it.

✔ **Vertical:** This radio button flips the image over as you reflect it.

✔ **Angle:** This setting rotates the image to a specified, um, *angle* as you reflect the image.

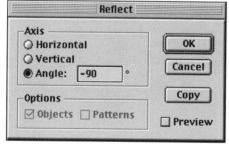

Figure 12-7:
The Reflect dialog box.

Shear

Most programs call this "skew," but Illustrator takes the high road and uses a lofty aviation term. It's commonly used for creating cast shadows (the kind that fall away from an object, like your own shadow does on a sidewalk on a sunny afternoon, also known as perspective shadows) or cast reflection (like trees reflecting a still autumn lake).

The Shear tool is one of the easier tools to use, but it can be tricky to use at first. When you click and drag with the shear tool, everything on the side of the origin point moves to where you drag it to, while everything on the other side of the origin point moves an equal distance in the opposite direction. The artwork in between distorts accordingly, and you get a "slanted" version of your artwork.

To make the Shear tool easier to use, always use the two-click method. Before you drag with the Shear tool, click at the edge of the selected artwork to set the origin point. When you do this, you only have to pay attention to your artwork shearing in one direction. The overall effects are the same, but you don't have to worry about the artwork shearing in both directions.

To use the Shear tool:

1. **Select the artwork to be sheared.**

2. **Choose the Shear tool from the Toolbox.**

   The Shear tool typically hides behind the Reflect tool in the Toolbox. Click and hold on the Reflect tool, and the Shear tool pops out from behind it.

3. **Click once at the edge of the artwork to be sheared.**

   This sets the origin point, making the Shear tool easier to control.

4. **Drag with the Shear tool.**

   The artwork "shears" or distorts to look slanted, as shown in Figure 12-8.

Figure 12-8:
Original art-
work (left)
and after
shearing
(right).
Yeah, that's
attractive.

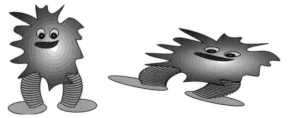

Additional Transformation Tidbits and Distortions

All of this transforming may seem like some pretty amazing stuff (with the exception of Shear). What's *really* amazing is the bevy of little extras that Illustrator has thoughtfully provided to make transforming easier and faster. The following sections in this chapter show you how to use these extras. Here's a list of what you can do:

- ✔ **Use the Transform palette.** This palette keeps all the transformations in one handy place, where you can apply them by typing in numerical values.

- ✔ **Copy as you transform.** Being able to rotate a *copy* of your artwork is pretty snazzy.

✔ **Transform each piece of artwork separately.** The Transform Each dialog box lets you apply transformations to individual objects, instead of to everything at once. This feature is useful, believe it or not.

✔ **Repeat the last transformation.** Do it again . . . and again . . . all with a simple menu command (or keystroke).

✔ **Transform a portion of a path.** That's right, you can select just a few points and move, scale, rotate, reflect, or shear them. (This capability is especially useful if you want to give that virtual caterpillar a Mohawk.)

The Transform palette

The Transform palette, shown in Figure 12-9, is a one-stop shopping location for all your transformation needs. Access the palette by choosing Window⇨ Show Transform. The palette's quite powerful, as long as you don't mind the math.

Figure 12-9: The Transform palette in all its glory.

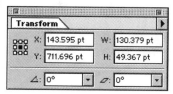

By entering values in the Transform palette's text fields, artwork can be moved, scaled, rotated, and sheared. The palette's pop-up menu has options for reflecting. The W and H (width and height) fields can take both *absolute measurements* (sizes specified in inches, centimeters, whatever) or *relative measurements* defined by percentages. Just type the little extra bit after the number that specifies what kind of measurement the number represents — **in** for inches, **cm** for centimeters, or % for a percentage.

If you have to crunch numbers or go nuts, rejoice! The Transform palette does the math for you! For instance, if you want an object to be one-third as wide as it is now, just type **/3** after the current value in the text box for width, and the artwork will shrink to 1/3 of its original width.

Copying while transforming

All five of Illustrator's transformation functions enable you to copy objects as well as transform them. To accomplish this dazzler, Illustrator applies the transformation to a *copy* of the original selection, just as if you used cut-and-paste to copy the object, pasted it directly on top of the original, and then applied the transformation. In Illustrator, you can do all that in one step.

When using the transformation tools, you can press the Option [Alt] key to make a copy of your selection while transforming. Just press the Option [Alt] key *after* you start dragging (not before) and hold it down until after you release the mouse button. Illustrator creates a duplicate of the selection.

Illustrator users do this sort of thing so often that they invented a couple of terms (*Option-drag* for Macs, *Alt-drag* for PCs) to mean *copy an object*. (Nine times out of ten, it means *move a copy*.)

Figure 12-10 shows the way a sample of type looks after you transform it with the Shear tool while holding down the Option [Alt] key. The result is a cast shadow that appears in front of the original type (which Illustrator treats as an object). For additional information on creating shadows, see Chapter 20.

Figure 12-10:
To get this utterly cool cast-shadow effect with the Shear tool, we duplicated the text object and set the Fill to a gradient.

If you're using a dialog box to accomplish a transformation, click the Copy button instead of the OK button to create a *transformed duplicate* of the object. The original artwork stays untransformed.

Transform Each

The Transform Each dialog box (Figure 12-11), accessed by choosing Object⇨Transform⇨Transform Each does two things: First, it brings most of the transformations together into one dialog box. Second, it applies transformations to *each* of the selected objects separately, instead of all at once.

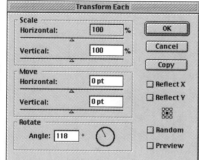

Figure 12-11:
The
Transform
Each
dialog box.

Oddly enough, this approach results in an effect that bears almost no resemblance to transforming everything at once. Figure 12-12 shows the results of regular rotation versus the results of rotation using the Transform Each dialog box. (Just don't say we didn't warn you.)

Figure 12-12:
The original
artwork
(left) after
it's rotated
with the
Rotate tool
(middle) and
using the
Transform
Each dialog
box (right).
(Oops!
There go
the letters.)

Transform Again

After you transform something, you can repeat the transformation quickly by choosing Object⇨Transform⇨Transform Again. This action simply repeats the previous transformation — whether by tool or dialog box or palette — and applies that transformation to the current selection. You can even deselect something, select something else, and apply the same transformation to the new selection.

Transform Again also works with copying selections, as shown in Figure 12-13.

Figure 12-13:
The tick marks on this clock were made with the Transform Again function by rotating a copy around the center in 6-degree increments.

Partial transformations

If you select just a section of a path, you can apply the five basic transformations to it, just as you do with an entire object. The result can be quite ordinary (as when you move a few points around) or rather unexpected (as when you scale, shear, or reflect just a few points), as shown in Figure 12-14.

The following steps select, move, and scale *just a few points* on a path (with some interesting results):

1. **Using the Direct Selection tool, click and drag over a portion of a path.**

   As you click and drag with the Direct Selection tool, a rectangular marquee appears. Only the points inside this marquee are selected.

2. **With the Direct Selection tool still selected, click a selected (solid) point and drag.**

   All the selected points move along with the one you clicked and dragged. Be sure to click directly on a point that is selected (indicated by a solid square) otherwise, you'll accidentally drop the selection and select something else.

3. Choose the Scale tool, and then click and drag.

Dragging toward the middle of the selected points brings them closer together. Dragging away moves them farther apart.

Don't click too near the middle of the points, or they get all cantankerous and hard to control.

Figure 12-14: Moving and scaling a portion of a path.

Punk and Bloat

Well, no, this isn't a how-to on slam-dancing while you're eating too much pizza. The Punk and Bloat filter, accessed by choosing Filter⇨Distort⇨Punk & Bloat, squeezes and bulges paths by moving points and handles in the opposite directions from each other. Figure 12-15 shows what happens to text outlines when they get punked and bloated.

Figure 12-15: Punk and Bloat. Can you guess which is which? No peeking, now. Oops. Too late.

The Punk and Bloat filter is related to the number of points on a path. The more points, the more punk spikes and bloat bubbles. You can add points via the Add Anchor Point tool (in the slot with the Pen tool) or by choosing Object⇨Path⇨ Add Anchor Points.

Roughen and Scribble and Tweak, oh my!

For making artwork look messy, the Roughen filter and the Scribble and Tweak filter are your best bets. (To access these filters, choose Filter⇨Distort and then choose either Roughen or Scribble and Tweak.) Roughen adds additional points to your paths and moves those points around, making the artwork look, well, rougher, as if it were drawn with a very shaky hand. Scribble and Tweak moves existing points and handles around. This option can make the artwork look a lot looser, as if it were hastily scribbled. What's unique about these filters is that the results are totally random, so the graphic they produce appears much less rigid and more natural. Applying these filters to existing artwork can result in unique effects, as shown in Figure 12-16.

Figure 12-16:
This artwork has been roughened to give the appearance of sketchily drawn artwork.

Zig Zag

Zig Zag adds points and then moves every other point in, and the remaining points out, to give an evenly bumpy appearance. Use Zig Zag to quickly create special effects such as the graphic shown in Figure 12-17. To access the Zig Zag filter, choose Filter⇨Distort⇨Zig Zag.

Blending: The Magic Transformation

This section covers what may well be the oddest feature in Illustrator. Illustrator can "blend" one path into another. So for instance, you can blend the shape of a fish into a lowercase letter *f*. The result is a series of paths that slowly transform from one path into another. In addition to the shape changing from one path to another, the color (and style, if one exists) changes as well.

Figure 12-17:
Points are
added and
then moved
in and out
via the Zig
Zag filter to
create
effects
like this.
(Nervous?
Who's
nervous?)

Sound familiar? No surprise. The results look a lot like the "morphing" effect you see in every werewolf-vampire-alien-shapeshifter movie made in the last ten years.

Only paths can be blended together. You can select any number of paths (no more than two or three, though, for the best results) and blend them together, as shown in Figure 12-18.

To create a blend that takes the artwork from one path to another, just follow these steps:

1. **Create two paths on opposite sides of the document.**

2. **Choose the Blend tool from the Toolbox.**

3. **Click one path, click the other path, and watch the blend appear.**

   The number of objects between the two original paths depends on how different the colors are.

4. **(Optional) To specify the number of steps between the paths, double-click the Blend tool. In the Blend Options dialog box, select Specified Steps from the Spacing pop-up menu and enter the number of steps you want between the two paths. Then click OK.**

   Illustrator creates the number of objects you specify between the two original paths.

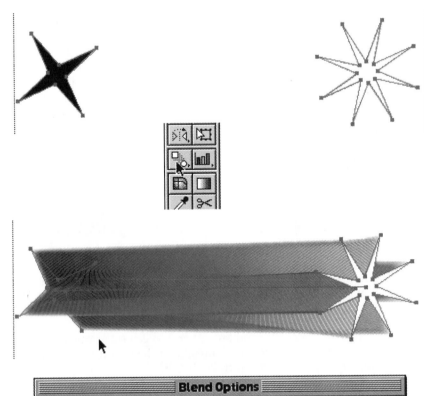

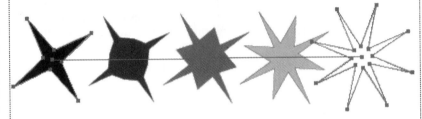

Blend Options

Spacing: Specified Steps ⊕ 3

OK

Cancel

Orientation:

☐ Preview

Figure 12-18:
Creating a
blend
between
two paths.

Chapter 13

Organizing Efficiently

- -

In This Chapter

▶ Understanding how objects can be above and below each other

▶ Moving objects in front of and behind other objects

▶ Using the Layers palette

▶ Changing the "stacking" order of objects with the Layers palette

▶ Naming objects, groups, and layers

▶ Organizing artwork with groups

▶ Taking advantage of Illustrator's grid

▶ Letting Smart Guides do the work for you

▶ Working with guides

▶ Aligning objects

- -

*I*llustrator is certainly not a 3-D program, but oddly enough, you may spend a good deal of your time placing your objects correctly in front of one another. A good way to think about how Illustrator relates to the 3-D world is to consider Illustrator objects as construction paper cutouts. You can arrange them any way you want, but in all likelihood, some will start to overlap. Each piece of paper can then be tucked behind another piece or pulled out in front of another piece. Doing so results in totally different effects.

This chapter focuses primarily on stacking objects — tucking them in behind each other or bringing them forward to upstage each other — and shows you how to deal with stacking as easily as possible. In addition, a later section scrutinizes precision placement and aligning of objects (in normal 2-D space).

Stacking Illustrator Artwork

Illustrator automatically accomplishes its front-to-back positioning for you, in a fairly straightforward, logical way. Each new object that you draw, place, or paste is positioned in front of the last object that you drew, placed, or pasted, resulting in a stack of artwork.

Unless you apply Transparency (a setting that allows underlying objects to show through an object, detailed in Chapter 10), objects positioned in front of other objects tend to "knock out" the portions of the objects that they overlap. Figure 13-1 shows Illustrator objects stacked in three different arrangements. Oddly enough, the objects are in the same locations, but their stacking order is different. The result is completely different artwork in each example.

Figure 13-1: These arrangements of artwork are a result of changing the stacking order of the objects.

Stacking order

Illustrator treats onscreen objects as if they were playing cards stacked neatly on a table. (You'd be standing next to the table and looking straight down on them.) The "cards" themselves are invisible. You only see the artwork. *Stacking order* is the order of objects in the stack. The order of the objects in the stack is typically determined by when they're created or placed in the document, although this order can be changed using the Object⇨Arrange commands (more on the Arrange commands later in this chapter). The first object created sits at the bottom of the stack. Illustrator refers to this as the Back. The next object created is in front of that object, and the most recent object created sits on top of all the others. Illustrator considers this topmost position to be the Front.

Figure 13-2 shows a basic illustration and an imaginary "edge-on" view of that artwork as it would appear from the side, if the stack were as tangible as a pack of playing cards (which it isn't, but you knew that). This concept is just a harmless metaphor. Right.

Even when two objects appear visually side-by-side and do not overlap in any way, Illustrator still considers one object to be "in front of" the other — as if each object that you create in Illustrator were painted on a separate piece of transparent plastic. Often, the only time you can know the stacking order is when you move one object in front of another. To be honest, that is the only time you *need* to know the stacking order, because stacking order only makes a difference when objects overlap. When objects overlap improperly (such as when the big yellow triangle hides the word "YIELD" when you really want the word to be in front of the triangle) you can use the Arrange commands to change stacking order.

Moving art up front or back down in the stacking order

Illustrator offers four commands that you can use to move objects up and down through the stacking order:

Object⇨Arrange⇨Bring to Front: This command brings selected artwork to the top of the layer you're working on (more about layers in the next section) by putting that artwork in front of the other objects.

Object⇨Arrange⇨Send to Back: This command moves selected artwork to the bottom of the layer you're working on by putting that artwork behind the other objects.

Object⇨Arrange⇨Bring Forward: This command brings selected artwork forward (that is, upward in the stack) one step at a time.

Object⇨Arrange⇨Send Backward: This command puts the selected artwork farther back (that is, downward in the stack) one step at a time.

Figure 13-2:
The original illustration (left), shown from a "sideways" view (right). The space between the stacked objects on the right is not only imaginary, it's exaggerated!

Illustrator uses stacking order to keep track of all the objects onscreen, even when they don't overlap. The Bring Forward and Send Backward commands affect the stacking order regardless. Whether you send an object backward or bring it forward, you may not see any apparent difference if nothing's overlapping. Don't panic! The object really did move in the pecking order.

Managing the Mess

Although the four commands for moving artwork may seem fairly flexible at first, that's only true if you keep the number of objects way down. Once you start creating artwork with dozens (or even hundreds) of objects in it, the fab four commands start showing their limitations and creating frustration. For instance, think of the hassle of putting an object in a precise order when you have a hundred different levels in the stack ("Move it from level 94 to level 63? No problem . . . I *hope* . . . "). Not to mention the challenge of selecting one object from among hundreds!

That situation is where the Layers palette comes in. Not only does it enable you to organize your artwork into layers, but it also gives you a much more flexible method of arranging your artwork within the stacking order. You can also do fiendish things to layers — hide them so you can't see them, lock them so you can see them but can't change them, or duplicate them (along with their artwork) in a different document. This flexibility brings a great deal of sanity to working with complex illustrations.

Imagine that you are creating an image of a flock of birds in a maple tree. Your client wants to see the tree change according to the four seasons. She also wants to see the tree with and without the birds. You have one tree, fifty birds, and hundreds of leaves — and the whole image is set in spring. Oh, and the client is coming over to see all the finished artwork in fifteen minutes! Do you panic? No, you use layers! You separate the tree, the birds, and the leaves into their own layers. Then you can hide and reveal the bird layer to show the tree with and without the birds. Hide the layer with the leaves on it, and you have your maple tree in winter! To simulate seasons, duplicate the "leaves" layer twice. Then, again using the Layers palette, you can select all the leaves in one layer and change the Fill colors to summer colors. Then go to the third leaf layer and change those colors to fall colors. By showing one layer while hiding the other two, you can create your fall, spring, and summer trees. There you have it! Eight pieces of artwork from one piece, in about as much time as it takes to tell about it!

Using the Layers palette

The Layers palette, shown in Figure 13-3, provides you with the means to do as much (or as little) organization as you want. You can split your artwork into layers, sublayers, and sublayers of those sublayers. Then you can view, hide, select, rearrange, or delete any number of the layers and sublayers.

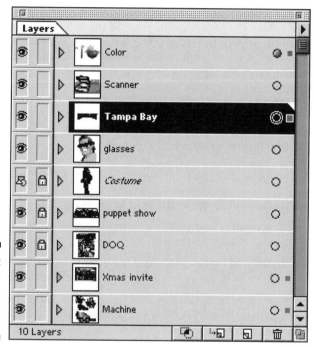

Figure 13-3:
The Layers palette with multiple layers.

Thumbnails

The thumbnails on the Layers palette show what objects are on each layer. You can quickly select everything on that layer by clicking the Target circle once. Double-clicking the Target circle enables you to apply Transparency settings and effects to that layer, as discussed in Chapter 10.

Is the thumbnail too small to get an accurate view of the artwork? Choose Palette Options from the Layers palette flyout. The thumbnail size is determined by the Row Size. Choose from small, medium (the default size), or large; or choose other and type in any pixel size for your thumbnails.

We call it Surprise Layer Cake . . .

If you haven't opened the Layers palette before, you may be surprised to find that you've been working with layers all along. Whenever you create a new document, Illustrator automatically creates a layer to contain your artwork.

When you start working with multiple layers, you may have to get accustomed to the Arrange commands, such as Bring Forward and Send to Back. These commands work *within* layers but don't move objects from one layer to another. After you select an object and choose Object⇨Arrange⇨Bring to Front, Illustrator brings the object to the front of the layer it currently occupies — but not all the way to the front of the document. So if another object is hanging around in a layer in front of the selected object and you use Bring to Front, the selected object may still be behind another object in the document. If this happens, use Steps 3 and 4 in the following exercise to move artwork into another layer.

A good way to get a feel for the Layers palette is to break a piece of existing artwork into several layers, as shown in Figure 13-4.

To separate your artwork into multiple layers, just follow these steps:

1. **Decide how you want to organize your artwork.**

    You may want to split it into similar elements — such as type, pixel images, graphics, and a background.

2. **Create the additional layers you need for your artwork by clicking the Create New Layer button — click once for each additional layer.**

    The Create New Layer button is the third button from the left at the bottom of the Layers palette; it looks like a sheet of paper with the bottom-left corner folded up to reveal a second sheet of paper underneath.

3. **With the Selection tool, select the graphic element in your artwork that you want to move to one of the other layers.**

    After you select the art, a little square appears to the right of the layer that currently contains the selected artwork.

4. **To move the art to another layer, click and drag the little square up or down in the Layers palette to the layer you want.**

    When you release the mouse button, the artwork has already changed layers. You may not see any apparent change in the artwork, but moving the artwork into a new layer changes the color of the selection highlights (the tiny, onscreen squares and lines that appear along the points and paths after you select something with any Selection tool. The color changes to the selection highlight color for the new layer. It's a dead giveaway.

5. **Repeat the previous two steps until all your artwork is in the correct layers.**

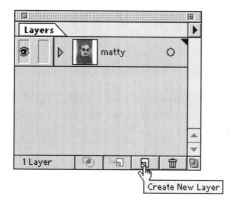

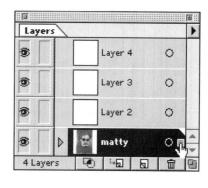

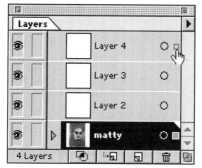

Figure 13-4:
Placing
existing
artwork
into multiple
layers.

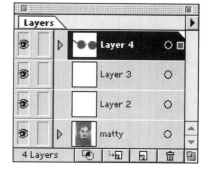

Changing the stacking order of layers

Layers, like individual objects, also have a stacking order. This order is reflected in the Layers palette. The contents of layers at the bottom of the palette appear in back of the contents of layers at the top of the palette. To change the stacking order of a layer, click the name of the layer or its thumbnail and drag upwards or downwards in the Layers palette. As you drag, a black bar appears between layers to indicate where the layer will be moved to after you release the mouse. When this black bar is at the position you want the layer to occupy, release the mouse. The layer and all its contents move to that position.

Lock and Unlock, View and Hide

Well, no, we aren't suddenly writing rhythm-and-blues lyrics. You can lock Layers by clicking the Lock/Unlock toggle button (the square just to the left of the Thumbnail). A *toggle* is an either/or type of button. Clicking it causes it to do the opposite of whatever it's currently doing. If a layer is unlocked, for example, clicking the Lock/Unlock button locks the layer. If a layer is already locked, clicking the Lock/Unlock button *unlocks* the layer. So far, so good. But potential frustrations lurk.

When a layer is locked, you can see it, but you can't select it or alter it in any way. If you try to select anything in a locked layer, you only select whatever object is behind it. After you get accustomed to this state of affairs, you find that layers are a great way to get things out of the way that you aren't working on, and to preserve any artwork that you don't want accidentally changed.

Just to the left of the Lock/Unlock button is the View/Hide button (which looks like an eye). Why hide all that work? One word: safety. This button not only hides the artwork in the layer, it also locks the artwork so you can't accidentally change it. The View/Hide button is also a great way to get things out of the way and to prevent accidents. It's also a great way to create multiple versions of artwork by showing and hiding different elements. (You know — trees with several sets of leaves for different seasons, football players with several uniforms, depending on their contracts . . .)

Hidden artwork is always locked artwork. If it weren't locked, you could change that poor, hapless object without meaning to — because you can't see hidden artwork. (Wow. Sometimes obvious stuff is so *comforting*.)

Copying layers (quickly and completely)

You can copy a layer — along with all the artwork it contains — by clicking the layer and dragging it on top of the Create New Layer button, which is just waiting around at the lower edge of the Layers palette, hoping somebody will give it something to do. This technique is also a great way to create multiple versions of artwork. You can duplicate one element many times, and then change the appearance for each layer. Show and hide the layers to compare and contrast the different versions.

Viewing objects and groups

After you click the little triangle to the left of a layer's name, you see an instant panorama of the groups and objects on that layer, as shown in Figure 13-5.

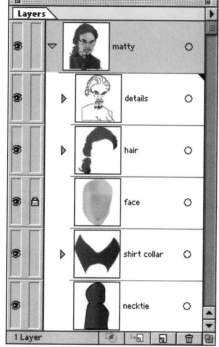

Using your options on layers, groups, and objects

You can give each layer, group, and object in Illustrator a name. If you don't name them, they wander around despondently, lugging their default names (such as <path> and Layer 1). Naming layers can be a great help for locating different objects. (Those teensy Thumbnails can be awfully hard to tell apart!) Naming the layers provides you with instant recognition.

To change a layer's name, double-click that layer in the Layers palette. To change the name of a group, double-click that group in the Layers palette. And finally, to change the name of an object, double-click that object in the Layers palette. (Is there an echo in here? Nope, just consistency — part of good software design.) The Layer Options dialog box appears, as shown in Figure 13-6.

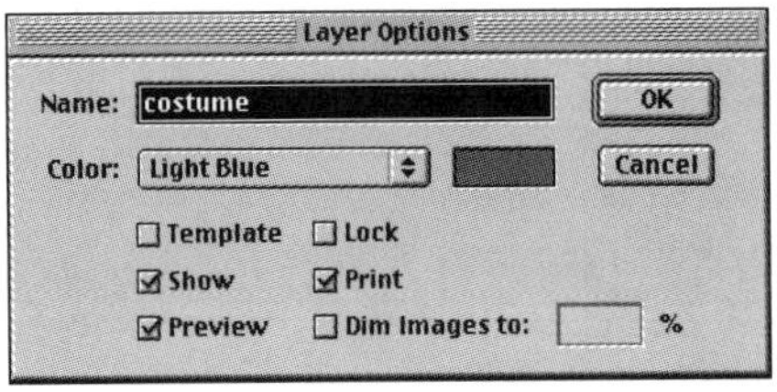

Figure 13-6:
The Layer
Options
dialog box.

The Layer Options dialog box offers several other options beyond just naming layers.

✔ **Name.** This option lets you type in a descriptive name for the layer.

✔ **Color.** This option lets you set the selection highlight color. Changing this option does not change any color in the artwork — just the color used to show that something is highlighted.

✔ **Template.** This option lets you give the layer a special designation and the following unique set of behaviors (which tells you that the layer is a template):

• The layer is automatically locked so nothing on it can be selected or changed.

• Pixel-based artwork shows as dimmed. This lets you focus on your own artwork better while still being able to see the template artwork. Think of the layer as virtual tracing paper.

• The names of the Template layers are italicized, so they're easy to spot in the Layers palette.

• Template layers do not print, and they aren't included with your artwork when you use the Save for Web command.

• You can create a different version of a particular piece of artwork and put the existing artwork in a Template layer where it's out of the way. It won't print but you can still see it.

✔ **Lock and Show.** These options can be checked and unchecked to let you perform the same function as selecting the Lock/Unlock and View/Hide buttons in the Layers palette.

✔ **Preview.** This option, when checked, lets you see your artwork in Preview mode. This option, when unchecked, displays the current layer's artwork in Outline view; all other artwork in the document remains in Preview view.

✔ **Print.** This option can be checked or unchecked to make the layer printable or not printable.

✔ **Dim Images to:** This option lets you dim pixel-based artwork to any set percentage. You may want to do so for tracing purposes — so you can focus on your Illustrator artwork while using the faded pixel artwork as a guide.

You can move objects, groups, and layers around inside the Layers palette, doing all sorts of strange things to your artwork. You can move objects from one layer to another, move groups inside other groups, and even "nest" layers by dragging them inside each other. Try doing this and watch out for surprises.

Imposing Slavish Conformity with Groups

Grouping objects is a great way to organize your artwork; it gives several objects a common "address" where Illustrator can find them. After you click any one of them with the Selection tool, you automatically select all the objects in the group.

To create a group of objects, select the objects that you want to include and then choose Object⇨Group. You won't see any physical change in the artwork, but from that point onward, all objects in the group are selected at once (provided you use the regular Selection tool to select them).

The main difference between layers and groups is that grouping organizes objects *by their relationships to other objects,* rather than by their position inside a layer. As any ex-high-school student can tell you, belonging to a group means you have to conform to its rules. Consider these rules, for example:

- ✔ **Grouped objects must exist in the same layer.** If you select two objects in different layers and group them, the bottommost object gets moved into the layer that the topmost object inhabits.

- ✔ **Groups can be grouped together** by selecting two or more groups and then choosing Object⇨Group. If you have two groups called Football Team and Cheerleaders, for example, you can group them in another group called Stadium.

- ✔ **Grouped objects can be ungrouped** by selecting the group and then choosing Object⇨Ungroup. (Or maybe you *could* get an object in the group to do something uncool . . .)

See Chapter 6 for more information on selecting groups.

Lining Up

Illustrator provides several ways for you to make things line up as neatly as possible. Instead of just eyeballing the things in the line (which sounds sort of icky), you can have Illustrator help you make sure everything lines up just right. In fact, so many ways to align things exist that you don't need to figure out all the different methods. Just pick the one that makes sense to you and use it.

Two of the more-arcane-but-useful functions in Illustrator are tricky to find and use, but worth the effort:

- ✔ **Snap to Point.** This function (choose View⇨Snap to Point) "snaps" your cursor to a nearby point (on a path) whenever you're near to it. This function is perfect for butting objects up against each other.

- ✔ **Constraining via Shift.** This function (hold down the Shift key *after* you make your selection) constrains movement of objects to 0, 45, or 90 degrees (and all sorts of combinations thereof).

If you want your objects to move in a constrained fashion, make sure that you hold down the Shift key *after* you make your selection and that you keep holding it down until after you release the mouse button. If you hold the Shift key down *before* you make your selection, you add that selection to anything else that is already selected. If you let go of the Shift key before you let go of your mouse button, you release the constraint, and the object is positioned someplace far from where you want it to be.

Electronic graph paper

Choose View⇨Show Grid. Suddenly your background turns into graph paper. If you also choose View⇨Snap to Grid, your objects snap to the grid corners whenever you move them or whenever you create new objects. When we say "snap" we don't mean that the objects automatically jump to the grid corners. What happens is a lot more subtle. As you drag an object using any selection tool, it just sort of sticks a little when an edge of the object is over a grid corner. If you don't want the object to reside at that point, you can keep dragging. The "stickiness" is just enough to help you align the object. Figure 13-7 shows a document with the Grid option turned on.

Guides that are truly smarter than most of us

What if Illustrator knew what you were thinking? Science fiction? Maybe. But Illustrator is smart enough to know what you want to align, if you turn on Smart Guides (by choosing View⇨Smart Guides). These little helpers come out and start drawing temporary guides for you all over the place. Suddenly you can align objects in all sorts of ways.

Figure 13-7:
A document
(in this case,
a cartoon)
with the grid
behind it.

Here's how this feature works. When the Smart Guides feature is on, it watches you work. As your cursor passes over different objects, Smart Guides draws lines from the points you drag over, showing you how they align. Figure 13-8 shows Smart Guides in action.

Figure 13-8:
The Smart
Guides
feature
gives
alignment
information.
The figure
on the left is
being
dragged.
The Smart
Guide
shows how
the point
where the
cursor is
aligns with
the top of
the hair of
the figure on
the right.

Although Smart Guides can come in handy, they cause enough busy blinking of objects and lines to compete with the Saturday morning cartoons. We advise that you keep them turned off unless you're doing some serious organizing or drawing and can use the visual cues.

Let the rulers guide you . . .

You can create a guide of your own if you drag out from one of the rulers (click the ruler and drag from it into the document). Think of these guides as individual grid lines. You can use them to align artwork horizontally or vertically wherever you want, without having your whole screen littered with grid work as you do whenever you choose View⇨Show Grid.

Unlike Smart Guides, Guides give you no additional information about your artwork. They are just lines that hang out behind your artwork for you to use as a point of reference. When View⇨Snap to Grid is turned on, objects snap to Guides as well (even if you aren't using a grid).

You can drag out as many of these guides as you want or need. To move a guide that you've dragged out, choose View⇨Guides⇨Unlock Guides and then click and drag the guide that you want to move. You can also press the Delete key after clicking a guide to remove it altogether. This action lets you customize your guides so that they are in the exact position you need to help you with the specific artwork you are creating.

Locking your guides after you move them, by choosing View⇨Guides⇨ Lock Guides, is a good idea.

I'm a path, I'm a guide

You can turn any path into a guide by selecting the path and choosing View⇨Guides⇨Make Guides.That means circles, squares, wavy lines, or an entire logo can be used as a guide. You can also turn any guide back into a path (even the ruler guides) by selecting them and choosing Guides⇨ Release Guides. Guides need to be unlocked and selected for this to work.

If you need to move or delete a single guide, you can press ⌘+Shift [Ctrl+Shift] and then double-click the guide to both unlock it and change it into a path. (Just press Delete afterward to make it disappear.)

You can always clear out all the guides in a document by choosing View⇨ Guides. (Or, you can tell them that the meanest grizzly in the park is loose again. . . .)

Alignment

Illustrator's Align palette, shown in Figure 13-9, enables you to align and distribute selected objects just by clicking a button. Open the Align palette by choosing Window⇨Show Align. The little pictures on each button in the palette show what the button does after you click it.

The top row of buttons aligns objects. You can align objects horizontally or vertically. If you align objects horizontally to the left, Illustrator aligns the left-most points in the objects. If you center objects horizontally, Illustrator aligns the centers of the objects.

The final location of the objects may seem a little random at times because the Align command aligns them to a point that is the average of the locations of the objects. For instance, if you are aligning two objects vertically by their centers, and one object is on the right hand side of the page and the other is on the left hand side, the objects will align somewhere near the center of the page. To get them *exactly* where you want them, you may need to click and drag the objects with the Selection tool after you align them. Still, the Align palette does save you a whole lot of time getting there.

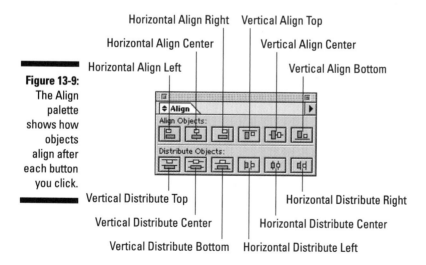

Figure 13-9:
The Align palette shows how objects align after each button you click.

Horizontal Align Right   Vertical Align Top
Horizontal Align Center   Vertical Align Center
Horizontal Align Left   Vertical Align Bottom

Vertical Distribute Top   Horizontal Distribute Right
Vertical Distribute Center   Horizontal Distribute Center
Vertical Distribute Bottom   Horizontal Distribute Left

The bottom row of buttons distributes objects. In other words, these buttons move selected objects so that they are the same distance apart. The Distribute Objects option takes the two objects that are the farthest apart and distributes the remaining objects between these two objects.

The Align palette is a good way to align things that you've already created in Illustrator and simply need to straighten up a bit. If everything you've created is all helter-skelter (or just helter work with), Align adjusts your artwork until it looks just right. Or left. Or centered. (It's pretty handy and politically neutral.)

Part IV
Weaving Beautiful Typestries

The 5th Wave

By Rich Tennant

"OK, TECHNICALLY, THIS SHOULD WORK. JUDY, TYPE THE WORD 'GOODYEAR' IN ALL CAPS, BOLDFACE, AT 700-POINT TYPE SIZE."

In this part . . .

1n this visually-oriented culture, the way words *look* can be as fraught with meaning as what they say. Small wonder that creating fancy, artistic type is one of the most popular uses of Illustrator. Maybe that's because it offers easy (and practically limitless) ways to create *wow-look-at-that* artwork with a few simple steps. This part covers all the basics (and some of the beyond-basics) of type, from aligning your characters and changing their size to making type flow around a circle or inside a shape. You also unlock the secrets of utter mastery over the appearance of your type, as you edit the minutest part of a letter by using the Create Outlines command.

Chapter 14

Introducing Letters and Such
(Type 101)

*T*ype is undoubtedly one of Illustrator's strongest areas. All the things that Illustrator does best — logos, advertisements, posters, Web-page graphics — depend on text and typography. Many Illustrator features interact with type in some way; and the program's type capabilities are pretty straightforward, once you know where they are and what they can do.

This chapter introduces you to the basics of Illustrator type. (If you're already familiar with controlling type in Microsoft Word or some other piece of word-processing software, you're already familiar with many of these terms.) To ease the journey, this chapter covers locating the Illustrator controls — and deciphering the "Illustrator way" of doing things. Chapter 15 takes off from there, getting into nifty tricks such as type-on-a-path that Illustrator is (typographically speaking) world famous for.

Using the Word Processor from Outer Space

If you think of Illustrator's type capabilities as an extended word-processing program, you're in the right ballpark; people frequently mention Illustrator's amazing typographical control. The basics of type (such as fonts, size, and alignment) work much the same in Illustrator as they do in most software programs out there. But Illustrator also packs some advanced typographical capabilities — such as saving files in three of the most universally recognized file formats (EPS, GIF, and JPEG). What sets this program apart from the rest is that you can do wonderful things with type and use it just about anywhere.

Controlling type in Illustrator

Illustrator has three basic places where you can work with type options: the Type menu, the Character palette, and the Paragraph palette, as shown in Figure 14-1. These three locations are essential knowledge for Illustrator users; so is a good grasp (so to speak) of the Type tool in the Toolbox.

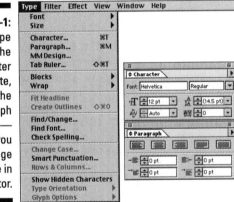

Figure 14-1:
The Type menu, the Character palette, and the Paragraph palette — where you massage your type in Illustrator.

The Type tool

You don't actually need anything but the Type tool to create type (as shown in Figure 14-2) — although the Type tool by itself won't let you change anything about your type.

Figure 14-2:
Creating
type in
Illustrator.

Point type

Starting with the Type tool, follow these steps to create type:

1. **Choose the Type tool (which looks like a letter *T*) from the Illustrator Toolbox.**

2. **Click (once) where you want the text to start.**

   A flashing insertion point appears. (If you accidentally click and drag at this point, you create a text box that contains your type. For more information on the text box, see the next series of steps.)

3. **Start typing.**

This process is the most basic way to create type. What you actually do in the preceding steps is to create *point type,* which is a single line of type that doesn't wrap (move to the next line) automatically. You have to press Return (that is, Enter) if you want to add a line beneath this line; otherwise, the line you're typing continues to infinity.

You can also create "rectangle type" (type that is confined within a rectangular area) with the Type tool, as shown in Figure 14-3. Just follow these steps:

1. **Choose the Type tool from the Illustrator Toolbox.**

2. **Click and drag with the Type tool.**

   As you drag, a rectangular marquee grows from the cursor. Text can only be typed inside the area of the marquee.

3. **Release the mouse button.**

   A flashing insertion point appears in the upper-right corner of the text box.

4. **Start typing.**

   As you reach the right edge of the text box, the text wraps to the next line.

Figure 14-3:
Creating
rectangle
type in
Illustrator.

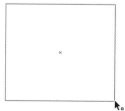

In both cases, you create a type object. You can treat this type object as any other Illustrator object (after you select it, the familiar path and point symbols show up to indicate the selection).

With both point type and rectangle type, you can always get to the next line by pressing Return (Enter) on the keyboard.

The Character palette

The Character palette, found by selecting Type⇨Character, is the place where you make changes to individual characters (letters, numbers, and punctuation, usually). Figure 14-4 shows the Character palette with all the pieces labeled.

Font Family   Font Style

Figure 14-4:
The
Character
palette in
Illustrator.

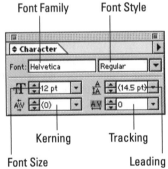

Kerning   Tracking

Font Size   Leading

To make text changes by using the Character palette, you first need to select the text you want to change. You can select text in three ways:

✔ **Click the text with a selection arrow.** This action selects all the text in the text object. Even though the text isn't highlighted (it has a simple underline for a highlight, as if the text object were a straight path), you can still change the size, font, and alignment.

✔ **Click and drag the Type tool across the type you want to select.** As you click and drag, a black box appears behind the selected text to indicate that the text is selected. This is what Illustrator means by *highlighting*. Only highlighted text is changed. But watch out ! If you click and drag too far away from your targeted text, you make a new text box instead of selecting the text.

Pay attention to the Text tool's cursor; it always tips you off about what the tool is going to do. When the cursor is in position to create a new text box, a dotted rectangle appears around it. If it's in the right place to *select* text, the dotted rectangle disappears. To select text, click and drag when you see *just* the I-beam text tool cursor with no box around it.

✔ **Double- or triple-click with the Text tool.** Double-clicking a word selects the entire word. Triple-clicking selects the entire paragraph in which the word appears.

The Paragraph palette

The Paragraph palette (shown in Figure 14-5) is the place to make type changes that affect whole paragraphs. If you haven't dealt with this feature in other software, you may be in for a bit of a tussle. At least the palette is easy to summon; simply choose Type➪Paragraph. Then things start to get a little strange.

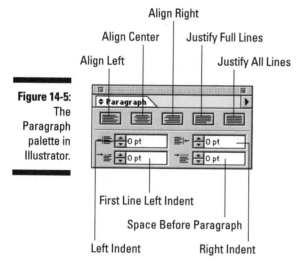

Align Right

Align Center   Justify Full Lines

Align Left   Justify All Lines

Figure 14-5:
The
Paragraph
palette in
Illustrator.

First Line Left Indent

Space Before Paragraph

Left Indent   Right Indent

As Illustrator sees it, a _paragraph_ consists of _the type contained between two returns._ Even if you type only one letter and then press Return (Enter), Illustrator considers that single letter a paragraph. Or you can type a thousand words without pressing the Return (Enter) key, and Illustrator considers all those words to be a single paragraph. (Nope, this definition of a paragraph isn't grammatically correct, but Illustrator duzn't kare a hute abowt gramer.)

A lot of people are under the impression that you have to select an entire paragraph for the Paragraph palette functions to make changes. Actually, the exact opposite is true. Paragraph palette changes affect the entire paragraph, _regardless_ of what you select. For instance, even if you highlight only a single letter, changing a Paragraph option affects the entire paragraph, not just that single character. Most of the options on the Paragraph palette work this way, so applying them to individual characters simply wouldn't make sense.

Introducing the Strange Land of Type

Although much of Illustrator may seem new and different, it describes type with a language steeped in centuries of tradition. For example, consider the term *leading* (rhymes with *bedding*), which means the space between lines of type. In centuries past, the term referred to the precisely sized pieces of lead placed between lines of movable metal type so the printed lines would be just that far apart on the page. Such was the work of typesetting when it actually meant setting metal letters in a wooden tray; the Character and Paragraph palettes name their features with traditional typesetter's terms. The lingo may seem nonsensical right now, but as words like "font" and "kern" and "baseline shift" start to crop up in your everyday conversation, you'll be joining an ancient and respected occupational culture. (The secret handshake comes later.)

Just so you know what you're getting into here: Once you become immersed in this world, you start picking out typefaces on signs, wincing when you see bad kerning, and generally holding the rest of the world in contempt for not using proper typographical procedures. (It's an ancient occupational hazard.)

Fonts, typefaces, and font families

You often hear these terms used interchangeably. Fonts, typefaces, and font families actually have somewhat distinct meanings; but for this book's purposes, you deal primarily with *fonts* (and if you happen to call them *typefaces*, we can nod knowingly, wink, and let it go). Fonts are sets of common letterforms that give consistent, distinct designs to the entire alphabet, all the numbers, and a boatload of symbols. Figure 14-6 shows a variety of fonts.

Figure 14-6:
Several different fonts, with each name printed in the font that bears the name of the font it's printed in . . . uh, is there an echo in here?

Helvetica

Arial Black

Courier

New Baskerville

Sand

Skia

You can change fonts in Illustrator quite easily, as shown in Figure 14-7, by following these steps:

1. **Using either the Type tool or a Selection arrow, select the type you want to modify.**

2. **Choose Type⇨Character.**

   The Character palette appears. The family name of the currently selected font appears at the upper left of the Character palette. Beside the Font Family name is the Font Style box, with a downward-pointing triangle just to the right.

3. **Click the downward-pointing triangle next to the Font Style box.**

   A pop-up menu presents you with a list of all the fonts on your computer.

4. **Pick a font from the list and click its name.**

   After you release the mouse button, the selected text changes to the font you chose.

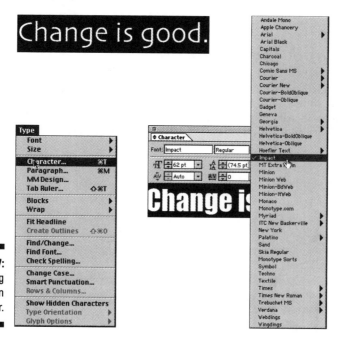

Figure 14-7:
Changing
fonts in
Illustrator.

As you peruse the list of fonts, notice that the font styles appear in submenus of the main list. This brand-new Illustrator 9 feature shows you related versions of a particular font. For instance, Figure 14-8 shows samples of three font styles in the same family. Top to bottom, they are Times Roman, Times Bold, and (first two words of the third line) Times Italic. All are in the same submenu of the Times menu item. Font styles in the same font family have a similar look and (as a general rule) work well together.

Figure 14-8:
These font styles are all part of the Times font family and look rather nice when placed together.

Change is good.
Bold is better.
I agree, he thought.

Serif and sans serif

Fonts are generally divided into two categories: serif and sans serif. *Serif* fonts have little doohickeys called serifs on the tips of letters and numbers; *sans serif* fonts don't have them (in this case, *sans* means "not gonna happen here"). Figure 14-9 shows examples of serif and sans serif fonts.

Figure 14-9:
Serif (top) and sans serif (bottom) fonts. Serifs are circled to show what they look like.

Goodbye.
Hello.

Why Illustrator refuses to fake a font

It's not a bug, it's a feature! Honest! Some folks who are new to Illustrator but have worked with type in word processing programs (and certain disreputable page-layout programs) are miffed to find that Illustrator doesn't have buttons for making fonts bold and italic. Believe it or not, this situation is a blessing! Programs that have such features are usually faking it. Not every font family has genuine bold and italic versions. If a program takes the non-italic version and tilts it, or takes the non-bold version and thickens it, the resulting false impression can waste money big-time. The _faux_ bold and italics may look okay onscreen — and even print out decently on an inkjet printer. But when an _imagesetter_ (a professional high-resolution printer) rejects them as fake, they show up on the page as the ordinary non-bold, non-italic fonts they are — _after_ you've had costly films made.

Besides, it's _tres gauche_ to fake a font; a good font is a work of art. Each and every letter has been lovingly handcrafted to look exactly the way its creator meant it to, and to work well with every other letter in the alphabet. Imagine the Louvre deciding that the Mona Lisa isn't tall enough or skinny enough. (_Let's just stretch the canvas so she looks better!_ Shudder.) By refusing to make a good font look like a distorted version of what it isn't, Illustrator has just spared you a _faux pas_ (or is that _fonts pas?_) _and_ a chunk of change.

Why serif and sans serif? Traditionally, serif fonts are used for large areas of text, because the serifs make the text easier to read than the sans serif fonts (part of the magic that those ancient typesetters discovered). Sans serif fonts are used for headlines because they stand out more boldly; normally nobody wants to read a _paragraph_ that stands out boldly. (It'd be like having the evening news yelled at you by a drill sergeant.) However, as wider ranges of fonts have become available to wider ranges of users, more people are breaking the rules and getting away with doing so. Traditional usage just isn't always the case anymore. Books and magazines still use serif fonts (more than sans serif fonts) for long passages of text, but you can find many exceptions to the rule. Sans serif type is often easier to read onscreen; those little serifs are frequently just too small to display properly on low-resolution computer screens.

When you are creating for print, a wise idea is to print your Illustrator text now and then throughout the creative process, to see what the end result _really_ looks like. The printed page can differ substantially from what you see onscreen. If you're creating text for Web graphics, consider yourself lucky; when you've got your graphics and the text looking good onscreen, mission accomplished!

To make Illustrator show as closely as possible what your text will look like on the Web, choose View➪Pixel Preview.

The biggest Don't Do It that we can think of

Back in 1987, when Illustrator and PageMaker had just hit the scene, many computer users without an artistic bone in their bodies began creating documents and graphics. They got carried away with the computer's magnificent ability to mix and match fonts. The printed results often looked *way* short of professional: Busy. Trashy. Hard to read. Lately, font madness has struck again — with Web pages — so your loyal authors make this impassioned plea:

> **Don't use too many fonts** on the same page the way **we just did.**

What's too many? Well, the awful no-no we just inflicted on the page has five. If you run out of fingers (on one hand) while counting fonts, you have too many. If you have to count at all, you probably have too many. The classic limit is three fonts (*including* any bold or italic versions of the main font you're using).

Exploring Size, Leading, and Other Mysterious Numbers

The world of type has a lot of measuring associated with it. You have to keep in mind point size, leading, x-height, kerning, baseline shift, tracking, horizontal scale, vertical scale, em-width, and other arcane matters that only the Secret Brotherhood of Typesetters really cares about. All these numbers affect the appearance of your type. Some of these measurements are important; fortunately some of them are less so. The following sections let you in on which is which — and on how to understand and use each type setting in Illustrator. Figure 14-10 shows where to find some of these measurements on the letters themselves.

Measuring can be just plain odd

The size of type is measured in *points*. An inch has 72 points. A quarter inch has 18 points. That's the easy part. The hard part is that type isn't measured from top to bottom. Rather, type is measured from its ascenders and descenders *for the entire font*. You know those cute little tails that hang down from the lowercase g, j, p, q, and y? Well, those tails are called *descenders;* the *ascenders* are the upper parts of letters like lowercase d and k and of UPPER-CASE letters.

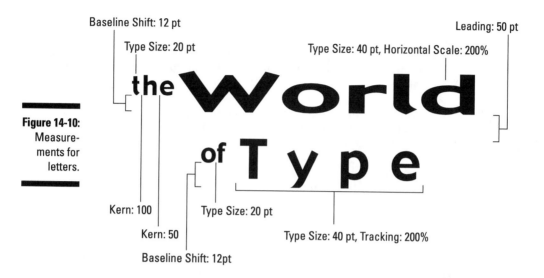

Figure 14-10:
Measure-
ments for
letters.

Words like "anon" (all lowercase, no ascenders or descenders) can _seem_ to
have a smaller type size than words like "Mr. Ripley," even though they are
the exact same type size. Type is measured from the uppermost point to the
lowermost point that is possible to create using that font. Even if you aren't
using any ascenders and descenders in the words you are typing, the font
size has to leave room for them (see Figure 14-11) in case words like
"Rumpelstiltskin" or "syzygy" show up in the sentence.

Figure 14-11:
Font size
has to allow
enough
space to
accommo-
date all the
possible
ascenders
and
descenders
in a font,
including
those in
lowercase
and upper-
case letters.

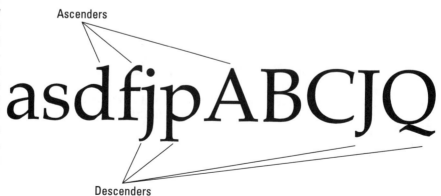

Things get really wacky when you start mixing different fonts. Each font can have completely different heights for its ascenders and descenders, creating the appearance of completely different font sizes, even though the actual space from the topmost point to the lowest point *for both entire alphabets* is identical.

For another example and a timely reminder, sneak a peek at the mishmash of fonts we stuck in "The biggest Don't Do It that we can think of" section (earlier in this chapter): They're all 12-point fonts.

You can set the point size of your type in the Character palette, right below the font. Either pick a value from the pop-up menu or type in a value in the field provided and then press Enter.

A good guideline is that capital letters are about two-thirds the point size and that lowercase letters without descenders or ascenders (like our esteemed friend the lowercase *a*) are about one-half the point size. So if you want a letter *A* that's one inch (72 points) high, you have to specify it as 144 pt (two inches) tall.

Measuring can be just plain annoying

The space between rows (lines) of letters has an even stranger story. First, the space is called *leading* (pronounced "ledding"), which makes sense if you're setting type by using pieces of metal. Second, the space is measured not between the descenders of the line you're on and the ascenders of the line below (which would make sense), but rather between the *baseline* of the line you're on and the baseline of the line *above* the line you're on. The baseline is the line on which most letters rest (those that don't have descenders). Figure 14-12 shows how leading appears in a typical paragraph.

You set the leading in the spot to the right of the font size in the Character palette. If a number appears in parentheses, that's the automatic value of the leading — 120 percent of the point size, rounded up to the next half point.

If the amount of leading matches the point size, the descenders of one line touch the ascenders of the line below. In the vast majority of cases, that's a *large* no-no.

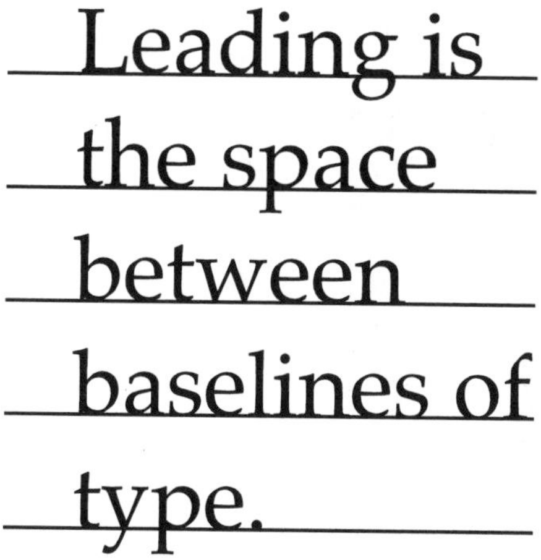

Leading is
the space
between
baselines of
type.

Figure 14-12:
Leading is
the space
between the
baselines
of type.

Spacing out while staring at type

Yet another thing to worry about (or ignore, if you choose to) is the space between individual letters that are next to each other. This space can be called two things (specifically to confuse the novice):

- **Tracking** is the space between letters in a series of letters.
- **Kerning** is the space between two specific characters.

Figure 14-13 shows the difference (sorta) between these two.

Tracking

Kerning

Figure 14-13:
Tracking
and kerning
in Illustrator.

Change the kerning by placing your cursor where you want to change the space between two characters. Change the tracking by highlighting a series of characters. Then change the appropriate field, as indicated in Figure 14-14.

Kerning   Tracking

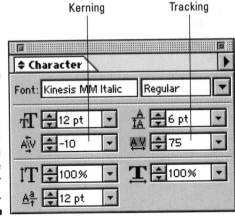

Figure 14-14:
Where to
change the
kerning and
tracking
values in the
Character
palette.

Typically, you can leave these values alone. However, when setting short sets of large type, for example, the type can look much better when it's kerned tighter. Many rules and guidelines exist for proper kerning and tracking, but the best designers set these by eye. If the type looks nice, it's probably kerned correctly.

Putting type on the rack

If you like, you can stretch your type to make it wider or taller; doing so is up to you. By changing the values in the Vertical Scale and Horizontal Scale boxes (shown in Figure 14-15), you *can* reshape type into all manner of oddness, but . . .

In general, this sort of modification is frowned upon, unless used sparingly and only to produce a small degree of change.

Moving on up and down

While leading sets how far apart the lines of text are, the baseline shift controls the vertical position of the text after it's been moved via the leading value. You use the field at the bottom of the Character palette to change the baseline shift. Positive numbers move selected text up; negative numbers move selected text down. Figure 14-16 shows a paragraph with a word of text that has a shifted baseline.

Figure 14-15:
Vertical
Scale and
Horizontal
Scale text
boxes in the
Character
palette,
along with
examples in
type.

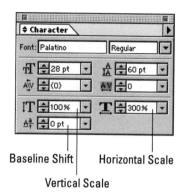

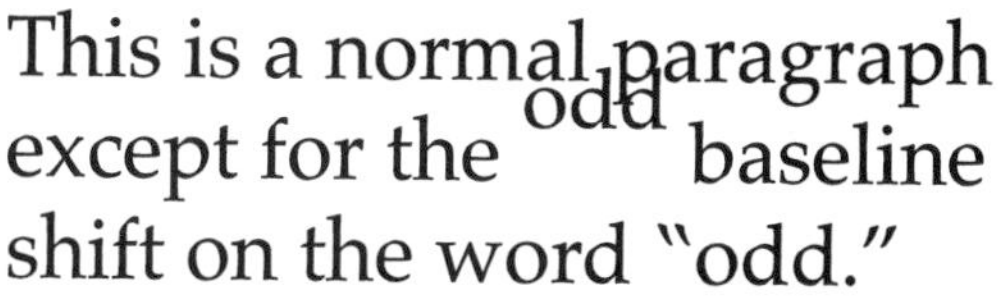

Baseline Shift | Horizontal Scale

Vertical Scale

Figure 14-16:
Using base-
line shift
within a
paragraph.

This is a normal paragraph except for the ᵒᵈᵈ baseline shift on the word "odd."

Adjusting Entire Paragraphs

The Paragraph palette provides controls for modifying *all* the text in a para-graph at once. These controls are quite different, of course, from those in the Character palette. (Don't want any silly old consistency to spoil the fun, now do we?)

Changing the alignment of a paragraph

At the top of the Paragraph palette are five buttons that set the alignment of paragraphs. Although the buttons are tiny, if you squint hard enough at them you can see that the tiny graphic image on each one mimics the alignment that they create. You don't have to guess at what each graphic is trying to represent (unless you're inventing a party game); simply position the cursor over the button without clicking — *et voilá!* — a tooltip appears and *tells* you what it is. To align a paragraph, click anywhere inside it with the Text tool; then click the alignment button in the Paragraph palette. By default, para-graphs are aligned to the left side of whatever you're typing in. This setting (called Align Left) results in text that looks smooth along the left edge of a series of rows; the right edge looks ragged and uneven. Another setting is called Align Right, and the opposite is true (right edge smooth, left edge ragged). Yet another setting is Align Center in which the left *and* right edges are ragged, but the lines of text are centered. The Justify Full Lines setting keeps both the left and right edges straight, except for the last line. Finally, the Justify All Lines setting keeps all lines (including the bottom one) even on both the left and the right. Figure 14-17 shows examples of these alignments (and which buttons to click to get them).

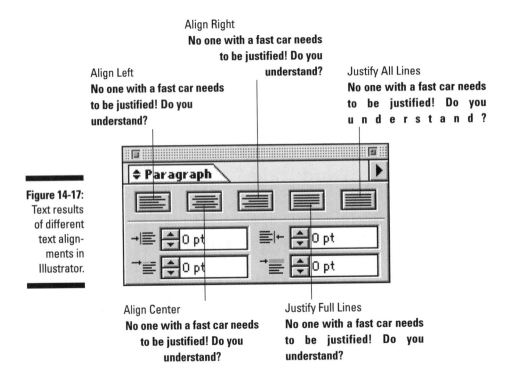

Figure 14-17:
Text results
of different
text align-
ments in
Illustrator.

Align Right
No one with a fast car needs
to be justified! Do you
understand?

Align Left
No one with a fast car needs
to be justified! Do you
understand?

Justify All Lines
No one with a fast car needs
to be justified! Do you
u n d e r s t a n d ?

Align Center
No one with a fast car needs
to be justified! Do you
understand?

Justify Full Lines
No one with a fast car needs
to be justified! Do you
understand?

Changing the space around the paragraph

The Paragraph palette in Illustrator offers three options for adjusting the space around a paragraph, plus an option to set how far from the left edge of the paragraph the first line starts. Figure 14-18 shows these options.

Left Indent

First Line Left Indent

Right Indent

Space Before Paragraph

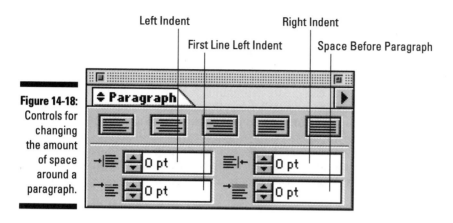

Figure 14-18:
Controls for
changing
the amount
of space
around a
paragraph.

The Left Indent setting is for modifying the position of the left edge of the paragraph. The larger the number, the farther to the right the left edge moves.

The First Line Left Indent setting moves the first line of the paragraph left or right relative to the left edge of the paragraph. Use a negative number to make the first line come "out" from paragraph's left edge, as shown in Figure 14-19. Use a positive number to push the first line in to the right of the paragraph's left edge.

Figure 14-19:
Bringing
"out" the
left edge of
a paragraph
with a
negative
number.

He appeared to a woman in the parking lot of a grocery store. She was putting her groceries into her car.

He asked: "Do you have the time?"

She looked up and there he was. Elvis. The King! Alive!

The Right Indent setting adjusts the paragraph's right edge. The larger the number, the farther to the left the edge moves.

The Space Before Paragraph setting adjusts the amount of space *before* the current paragraph. If you select a bunch of paragraphs, changing this setting puts space between each one of the paragraphs.

Using just the basic options available to you in Character palette and the Paragraph palette, you can create astounding feats of typestry. These two palettes provide the core for nearly everything you do with type in Illustrator. Using them, you can equal or surpass just about anything you can create on a single page in any word-processing or page-layout application. (For a crash course in how to do just that, fasten your seat belt and take a look at Chapter 15 — which grabs these basics and pushes them to their limits, creating the fanciest type tricks this side of the Typesetters' Inner Sanctum.)

Chapter 15

Studying Advanced Typography (Type 1,000,001)

Chapter 14 talks about the type in Illustrator. This chapter tells you how to get the most out of the type and how to turn Illustrator from some glorified word-processing software into an astounding type-modifying tool that can do just about anything to type — put it on irregularly shaped paths, wrap it around objects, give it an irregular shape, put objects in it — and that's just for openers.

Typing on a Path

To many people, Illustrator *is* paths. And putting type on a path has long been one of Illustrator's greatest capabilities. That said, you're up against a bizarre learning curve when using type in Illustrator. Initially, getting the type onto the path is pretty straightforward — but manipulating the type after it's there is a bit harder, and the effort required for doing things like putting type on both sides of a circle is downright silly.

Getting type to stick to a slippery slope

To place type on a path (what the heck, it may as well be the rollercoaster dip shown in Figure 15-1), just hang on tight and follow these steps:

1. **Using the Pen or Pencil tool, create the path on which you want to place your type.**

   For more information on creating paths, see Chapters 7 and 8.

   Don't be concerned with the fill and stroke of the path; they become invisible as soon as you type on the path.

2. **Select the Path Type tool from the Toolbox.**

   The Path Type tool is hidden in the Type toolslot.

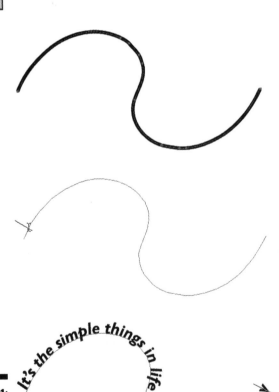

Figure 15-1:
Creating
type on a
path.

3. **Click the path at the place where you want the text to begin.**

   A blinking insertion point appears at that juncture.

4. **Start typing.**

   The text runs along the path as you type.

Once the type appears, you can edit it just like "regular" type, with the small exception that the type is stuck to a path. However, with the type attached to the path, you can move the type along the path in either direction, as shown in Figure 15-2. Just follow these steps:

Figure 15-2:
Moving type
along a
path.

1. **Using an arrow selection tool, click the path that contains the path type.**

   An I-beam cursor appears at the left edge of the type.

2. **Click the I-beam and drag it along the path.**

   The type moves as you drag.

3. **Release the mouse button when the type is where you want it.**

Be careful as you drag the I-beam cursor along the path. If you accidentally move the tip of your cursor below the path, the type "flips" upside down on the path. (As industry wags say of weird stuff that happens *consistently* onscreen, "That's a feature, not a bug!" In this case, it *is* a feature, believe it or not.) Don't panic; move the cursor back above the path and watch as the type rights itself.

Press the Option (Alt) key to duplicate text as you drag it along a path. Doing so duplicates both the type and the path. (Even though you don't actually see the duplicated path, it's most definitely there.)

In the next section, you find out how to use this technique to create type on both the top and bottom of a circle.

Solving the age-old type-on-a-circle mystery

To place type on a circle, you simply click a circle (path) with the Path Type tool and begin typing. That's easy enough. Okay, but what really bugs a lot of Illustrator users is that putting text on both the top *and* the bottom of a circle (without having half the text turn upside-down) doesn't seem very easy to do. That's because all the type on a path must have the same orientation, which can be either right side up or upside down, but not a mix of the two.

So without further ado, the following steps tell you how to place type on the top of a circle (shown in Figure 15-3), and the next set of steps tell you how to put type on the bottom of the same circle (shown in Figure 15-4).

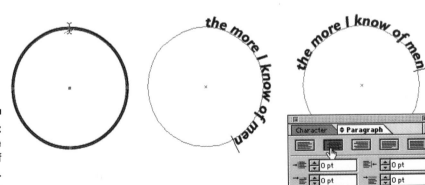

Figure 15-3: Putting type on the top of a circle.

Here's how to put type on the top of a circle:

1. **Select the Ellipse tool (which looks like an oval) from the Toolbox to draw a circle. Press the Shift key as you draw to make the oval into a perfect circle.**

   See Chapter 4 for more info on the Ellipse tool.

2. **Select the Path Type tool from the Toolbox and click the top of the circle.**

   A blinking insertion point appears on the top of the circle.

3. **Type your text.**

   Notice that the type starts to run down the right side of the circle. Don't worry; it's all part of the plan.

4. **In the Paragraph palette, click the Align Center button.**

   You can find the Paragraph palette by choosing Type➪Paragraph. The Align Center button is the second button from the left along the top row of buttons in the Paragraph palette. After you click the Align Center button, the text centers itself on the top of the circle.

Here's how to put type in the bottom of a circle:

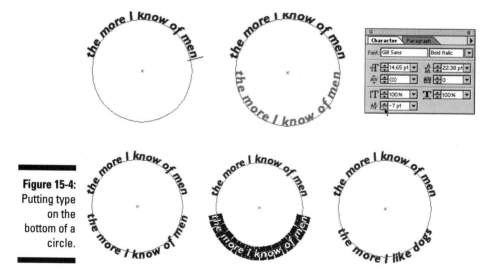

Figure 15-4:
Putting type on the bottom of a circle.

1. **Select the regular Selection tool from the Toolbox (select the type that's currently on a circle, if you haven't already done so) and click the circle text you created in the previous steps.**

   An I-beam cursor appears at the point where you clicked.

TIP

2. **Press the Option (Alt) key, hold down the mouse button, and drag the I-beam to the bottom of the circle.**

   Don't release the mouse button until you move the cursor up into the circle just a bit.

   Holding the Option [Alt] key duplicates the text as you drag it. Doing so also duplicates the circle the text is on, but since that circle is invisible, you won't see it. Moving the cursor into the circle "flips" the type so that it can be read right-side up on the bottom as well as the top of the circle.

3. **In the Character palette, click the down triangle of the Baseline Shift field until the type appears *outside* (below) the circle.**

   The Baseline Shift field is at the bottom left of the Character palette; if it isn't visible, choose Show Options from the Character palette's pop-up menu.

4. **Select the Type tool from the Toolbox and then select the type at the bottom of the circle.**

5. **Type the text you want to appear at the bottom of the circle.**

In this set of steps, you actually create two separate circles with type on them but since the circles overlap precisely, you get the illusion that the type is on just one circle. If you click and drag the circle with the Selection tool, you drag away the circle with the text in the bottom, thus destroying the illusion.

Typing Inside a Path

An interesting feature in Illustrator is the typographical capability to flow text within any shape; the shape acts as a container for the text, and the text fills the shape — matching it as closely as possible, left to right and top to bottom. For example, you may have a listing of the members of the California House of Representatives flow within a shape of the state of California.

To get text to flow within a specific shape, as shown in Figure 15-5, follow these steps:

Figure 15-5:
Flowing text
within a
path.

1. **Create a path using the Pen, Pencil, or any of the basic shapes tools. tools (see Chapters 4, 7, and 8 for more info).**

   The one shape you *shouldn't* flow text into is a rectangle, because this would be identical to creating a text box (see Chapter 14) and would kind of defeat the point.

2. **Select the Area Type tool from the Toolbox.**

3. **Click the path through which you want type to flow.**

4. **Start typing.**

   As you type, text flows within the object.

For best results with text, make sure you turned on Justify All Lines in the Paragraph palette (see Chapter 14 for details). This feature forces type to the left and right edges of the path. In addition, use fairly small type; large letters usually can't fill in the details of the path.

You can adjust the path of area type just as you do any other path, by clicking and dragging a point with the Direct Selection tool (Chapter 6) or by using the Pencil tool (Chapter 8) to edit the path.

Typing Around a Path

Typing around paths is sort of the opposite of typing within an area; type flows around the outside of a shape (or shapes) rather than within a shape. You don't have a special tool for flowing type around paths, but you do have a command to choose with both the type and the path selected. Figure 15-6 demonstrates text flowing around a shape.

Figure 15-6: Regular type with Type Wrap applied. (No, he doesn't know everything . . . they're hornets, not bees.)

"I think I know a little bit about bees," he added vigorously. "In fact, I fancy myself something of an expert." Of course, by the time we'd all stopped caring and were just ready to go home we nodded our heads and but nobody was really paying attention. He just blathered on about bees and all matters apiary.

"I think I know a little bit about bees," he added vigorously. "In fact, I fancy myself something of an expert." Of course, by this time we'd all stopped caring and were just ready to go home. We nodded our heads and smiled, but nobody was really paying attention. He just blathered on about bees and all matters apiary.

To flow text around the outside of a shape, follow these steps:

1. **Create a text box by clicking and dragging with the Text tool.**

2. **Type text into the box until it is full.**

3. **Create a path using any of the Illustrator tools and place the path *in front of* the text.**

   You get the best results by using a closed path rather than an open one. You can use as many paths and text boxes as you want, as with the multiple bees, er, *hornets* in Figure 15-6. All text wraps around all paths.

4. **Choose the Selection (black arrow) tool from the Toolbox.**

5. **Select the text and the path by holding the Shift key while clicking each of them.**

6. **Choose Type⇨Wrap⇨Make.**

   The text flows around the shape.

The most important thing to keep in mind when you wrap text around a path is that the path must be in front of the text. Typically, if you try to make text wrap around a path and the procedure doesn't work, the shape is probably behind the text. If this happens, click the path with the Selection tool and choose Object⇨Arrange⇨Bring to Front. This moves the object in front of the text. Select the path and the text again and again choose Type⇨Wrap⇨Make.

You can use several shapes for the text to wrap around, or you can add a shape later by selecting the new shape with the Selection tool, along with the existing text and/or shape objects, and again choosing Type⇨Wrap⇨Make.

Flowing Type from Path to Path

Any text that's within a shape (either area type or rectangle type) can be linked to other paths, so that the text flows from one path to another. For instance, a story about the pesky fruit fly can start in a path the shape of a banana and continue automatically into normal rectangular columns of text. Whenever changes occur in the banana's text, the text in the rectangle moves accordingly.

This process works by selecting the path that currently has text in it along with another path (or paths). You then choose Type⇨Blocks⇨Link. Figure 15-7 shows text that's linked, so it flows among several different shapes. The text flows from shape to shape in the chronological order that they were created. If you don't see any change when you choose Link, your first text box probably does not have enough text in it to overflow into the linked box. Just type some more in the first text box, and you will prevail.

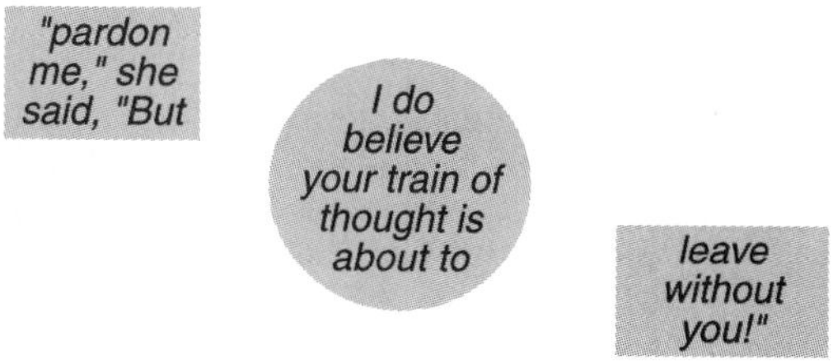
"pardon me," she said, "But
I do believe your train of thought is about to
leave without you!"

Figure 15-7: Type that's flowing among several paths.

Adjusting the Path (Not the Type)

After you create path type, area type, wrapped type, or linked blocks of type, you may discover situations in which you want to change *just* the path, and not the type. By default, if you select the path and the type together, you actually change only the type. So how can you change the path?

The secret to changing the path is to use the Direct Selection tool to select the path and then make your changes to the fill and stroke. Figure 15-8 shows how you can color circle type (refer to Figure 15-4) by using different fills and strokes on the circle to which the type is attached.

the more I know of men
the more I like dogs

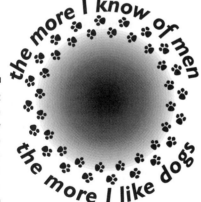

Figure 15-8: Circle type with a new fill (gradient) and stroke (pattern) on the circle.

Using Type as a Mask

Illustrator lets you do a remarkable number of things to your type, but some modifications seem *verboten*. For example, if you try to fill type with a gradient (see Chapter 5), the type just turns black. And what if you wanted to get really fancy and fill text with another piece of artwork you created in Illustrator? There's just no way you can do that!

Or is there?

Using the Clipping Mask feature (also seen in Chapter 10), you can create the appearance that text is being filled with a gradient, or artwork, or anything that you can put the text in front of. And what *can't* you put text in front of? Absolutely . . . nothing! (Say it again, ya'll. . . .)

A clipping mask is a special feature of Illustrator. It uses the frontmost object (called the clipping object) to hide the objects behind it in a unique way. Everything outside the clipping object is hidden, and the fill and the stroke of the clipping object become transparent, so that you can see whatever is behind the clipping object appears to be filling the clipping object. A type mask is what you get when you use type as your clipping object. This may sound strange, but it'll make a lot more sense after you create a type mask of your own.

Creating a type mask is oh so simple. Here's how:

1. **Create the stuff you want to fill your type with.**

   This can be absolutely anything. The only catch is that it must be bigger than the type you want to fill.

   For example, if you want to fill your text with a gradient, you create a rectangle (or any other object provided it is larger than your type) and fill it with a gradient. (See Chapter 5.) Or create the artwork that you want to fill the type with. There really are no limits here, provided that whatever you fill the text with is larger than the text. It may help to think of the text as a cookie cutter and the object you are going to fill the text with as cookie dough. You are going to cut away everything outside the text.

2. **Create type in front of whatever you want to fill the text with.**

   Create your type using the ordinary Type tool. Using the Character palette (see Chapter 14) choose a font size large enough so that the type is almost (but not quite) as large as the artwork behind it. If you already created your type, select it with any selection tool and choose Object⇨Arrange⇨Bring to Front and drag it in front of your object.

3. **Use any selection tool to select the text and the object or objects behind the text and then choose Object⇨Clipping Mask⇨Make.**

   To select multiple objects, just hold down the Shift key while clicking each of them with any selection tool.

   After you choose Object⇨Clipping Mask⇨Make, the fill and stroke of the text disappear and are replaced by the contents of whatever is behind the text. Anything outside the area of the text becomes invisible, or "masked out." Figure 15-9 shows the process in action.

Figure 15-9:
The type mask in action: (top) text in front of objects and (bottom) type masking the objects.

One very neat feature of type masks is that the text is still ordinary text. You can highlight the text, change the font, type in different words, and so on, while retaining the masking properties.

Any time you want to make the text stop masking out what's behind it, select the text and choose Object➪Clipping Mask➪Release.

Converting Type to Paths

The type possibilities in Illustrator are nigh infinite. To make them truly infinite, you need take only one step — convert the type to paths. You gain absolute control over every point of every letter of every word of type.

Edit carefully and spell-check your text before you convert it. After it's converted to paths, you can no longer edit it as type. (You can't highlight it with the Type tool and retype it, change the font, or anything like that. Your text becomes as frozen as the print on a sign in a snapshot.)

You may want to make this conversion for one or both of the following two reasons:

- ✔ **To manipulate type as you do any other object in Illustrator:** Type stops being type and becomes just another Illustrator path, at which point you can do absolutely anything to it that you can do to other paths.

- ✔ **To bypass the need for the font files associated with the type:** If you give someone a graphic file that contains type, a hassle is in store if the font you used to create the type isn't installed on the recipient's computer. The graphic won't display or print properly if opened in Illustrator or placed into a page-layout program. Converting the type to paths creates a file that displays and prints exactly as you created it, regardless of the fonts installed on the recipient's computer. This action is also a good way to "lock down" text, making sure it can't be retyped. You should always convert text to paths for any logo that you send to other people, since doing so helps guarantee that the logo will always look the way you created it.

To convert type to paths, as shown in Figure 15-10, follow these steps:

Figure 15-10: Converting type to paths. Left: The letter A as type. Right: The letter A converted to paths (note the anchor points).

1. **Use the Selection tool to select the type you want to convert to a path.**

   Okay, you are altering type, so you *should* be able to do this using the Type tool, but you can't and that's just one of those little frustrations that have been around for years in Illustrator, so you may as well get used to it.

2. Choose Type⇨Create Outlines.

All the points that make up the type suddenly appear, enabling you to edit the Type as you edit any other object in Illustrator as shown in Figure 15-11. Why Create Outlines? Only some long-gone Adobe programmer knows for sure. A better name might be Create Paths from Text (that's what this command really does).

Figure 15-11: Type gets down and funky. Here's the letter *A* from Figure 15-10 after the points are moved one-by-one and a gradient fill applied.

Part V
Getting Art to Print, to the Web, and to Other Applications

The 5th Wave   By Rich Tennant

In this part . . .

This part is the polar opposite of everything else in the book. Everything else is all about getting things *into* Illustrator. This part is about getting things *out of* Illustrator and into the rest of the world. You can do so in one of three ways — by printing the artwork, by putting it on the World Wide Web, or by bringing it into another program. You find out about all three options in this part. You find out how to print your Illustrator artwork in a variety of ways, how to prepare it in different styles for the World Wide Web, and how to save your files in multiple formats to be opened or placed into other applications.

Chapter 16

Printing Your Masterpiece

*I*f you design artwork to be printed at some point, the best thing you can do as you design is to think about how the artwork is going to look when it's printed. If you have a clear idea of what you're going to print your artwork on as you create it, you can save yourself all sorts of time. For instance, if you create a stunning logo that depicts the neon manhole covers your company manufactures, full of vibrant colors and subtle hues and reflections, you probably can't use that logo for black-and-white work. This chapter provides some great ideas to keep in mind as you create your artwork — and you can also refer to it when you actually arrive at the printing process.

If you just want to print, read the following section, "Printing Quickly." If you want to discover all the stuff *behind* what goes into printing, check out the "What You See Is *Roughly* What You Get" section. Or if you want all the nitty-gritty about setting up Illustrator for printing (plus even more details on printing), skip ahead to the "Setting Up Your Page to Print (You Hope)" section.

Printing Quickly

If you have a printer hooked up to your computer or network, you can print just about anything that you can create in Illustrator.

Before you start to print, make sure your artwork is inside the printable area. A dotted gray line indicates the printable area (which your selected printer will actually print out); anything outside the dotted line won't print.

To print your artwork, Choose File➪Print. When the Print dialog box appears, press the Return or Enter key on the keyboard, or click the Print/OK button. After a few minutes, assuming the computer gods smile on you, whatever you created in Illustrator prints on a piece of paper in your printer. Hitting Return or Enter without adjusting any settings in a dialog box is known in the trade as "running with the defaults." *Defaults* are settings that are made automatically when Illustrator is installed — and it is surprising how often they work just fine for printing artwork from Illustrator. When things don't print as you expect them to, you need to adjust the other settings discussed throughout this chapter.

What You See Is Roughly What You Get

Whatever you create onscreen, you can print (at least, theoretically). And what you print looks pretty much like what you see on your monitor. Note that we say *pretty much* and not *exactly*. Here's why:

- ✔ Your monitor resolution is much lower than your printer resolution. You may think this should make everything you print look better than it does onscreen, and in most cases, that's correct. In other cases, however, that extra resolution makes problems that you can't see onscreen stand out in print.

- ✔ By default, Illustrator displays art and text on your monitor as *anti-aliased* (anti-aliasing is the process of making the edges where colors meet blend slightly together, producing a more visually appealing image onscreen). Whenever you print, edges aren't blurred but print smoothly and cleanly.

- ✔ Your monitor displays color images by lighting up little red, green, and blue phosphorescent squares called *pixels,* whereas printing produces color images by applying dots of ink on paper. Creating colors by completely different physical processes causes a major difference between what you see onscreen and what you get in print.

With these points in mind, you should regularly print out your artwork as you create it, to make sure the printed result is as close as possible to what you're designing onscreen. That way, you can modify your artwork so you have no surprises when you print the final product. After some practice, you develop an eye for what a printout is going to look like, even when you're working entirely onscreen.

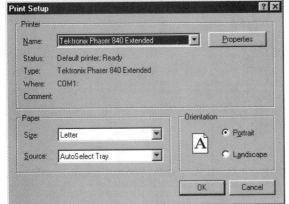

Figure 16-2:
The Print
Setup dialog
box in
Windows.

For Mac users, Page Setup contains the information that Illustrator needs about what type of printer you're printing to, how big the pages are, and other information such as whether the printer is color or black and white. Print Setup does the same song and dance for Windows. You actually have dozens of options, but don't panic — some are specific to the Macintosh and others to the PC using Windows.

The only options you need to care about

Imagine a chance to establish an oasis of simplicity in the sea of everyday confusion. You're almost there if you concern yourself with only these few options in the Page Setup or Print Setup dialog box:

✔ **Format For (Mac) Name (Windows):** The top of the Page Setup or Print Setup dialog box indicates the printer you plan to print to. Click this, and a pop-up menu appears listing all the printers you have access to (in an ideal world, where your software and networked hardware are set up properly). If you have access to only one printer, this setting remains the same all the time. The printer that you are currently printing to should always be selected here, because this actually sends important information to the rest of the Page Setup or Print Setup dialog box, such as the page sizes that are possible with the currently selected printer.

✔ **Page (Mac) Size (Windows):** This pop-up (or drop-down) menu lets you see the available page sizes for the printer that is selected in the Format For or Name pop-up menu. Make sure that you select the right page size for the paper you plan to print on.

✔ **Scale:** This value (located in Page Setup on the main panel and in Print Setup after clicking the Properties button and then the Graphics tab) controls the size of the illustration. The value is defined as a percentage of the artwork's size inside Illustrator. For example, if you have a logo that's 1-inch-by-1-inch in Illustrator, changing the scale to **250** percent results in the logo scaling up to 2.5-inches-by-2.5-inches when printed.

✔ **Orientation:** This setting determines whether your page prints the tall way (represented by button with an androgynous human figure standing upright on the Mac, and by the Portrait radio button on the Windows side) or the wide way (represented by the button with an androgynous human lying down on the Mac, or by the Landscape radio button in Windows).

Check the Page Setup or Print Setup dialog box settings *whenever* you choose a different page size, or print to a printer other than the one you were using before. Doing so will save trees, frustration, and nearby delicate ears.

Printing Mechanics

After you make sure that your Page Setup settings are correct (typically they're fine unless — ahem — *somebody* mucks them up), you're ready to send your masterpiece to paper.

Printing composite proofs

Printing a composite proof is really printing what you see onscreen to a single sheet of paper. This kind of printing is simply what you do all the time (given a fancy name). If you have a color printer, your result looks really close (hopefully) to what's onscreen. If you have a black-and-white printer, you get a black-and-white version of what's onscreen.

The other kind of printing is called *printing separations*. Printing separations means generating a separate sheet of paper (or, more likely, film) for each ink to be used when the artwork is printed. Separations are discussed in more detail in the "All About Way-Scary Separations" section later in this chapter.

You can print composite proofs by just following these steps:

1. **Choose File⇨Print from the menu.**

   The Print dialog box appears.

2. **Select the appropriate printing options (discussed in the following "Important printing options" section).**

3. **Click the Print or OK button.**

Important printing options

The Print dialog box (Figure 16-3 is a mug shot of the Mac and Windows versions) has all sorts of options, but only a few of them are worth noticing. Fortunately, the default settings are usually what you want anyway — for example, one copy of whatever you send to the printer of your choice. However, for situations in which the current setting is not what you want, the following handy options are lurking in the Print dialog box:

- **Printer:** The top of the Print dialog box indicates the printer you intend to print to. If you have only one printer, this setting is most likely right all the time. If you have more than one printer, you can see which one you're currently printing to. You can change the printer setting here as well.

- **Number of Copies:** This option shows the number of copies of your artwork that you want to print, each on a separate sheet.

- **Print Range:** Illustrator can't really have multiple pages (a page one, two, three, and so on). It can, however, print one page across several pages (in effect, a very large single page). Before you choose File➪Print, choose File➪Document Setup and then click the Tile Imageable Areas radio button in the Document Setup dialog box. Artwork that hangs outside the Artboard prints on separate pages. You can then print the artwork on multiple pages, tiling it so that you can cut and paste the artwork by hand into a *really* big poster, if you want. (Using these options, you can make your artwork larger than your page size by as much as 18 feet!)

Unfortunately, the implementation of this feature is abysmal (which is why we don't mention it anywhere in this book beyond this paragraph). For instance, you have no way of telling *which* pages your artwork is on, even though you are to specify the pages in the Print Range option in the Print dialog box. This inevitably leads to much wasted paper. Even when you do get the thing to print out properly, you still have to cut up your pages and tape them together. If you need poster-sized output, you're much better off printing it at your local service bureau on a large-format output device.

In addition, you want to consider three other options. These are found in the main Print dialog box in Windows, but on the Mac, you need to click the pop-up menu in the upper-left corner of the Print dialog box just beneath the Printer selection pop-up menu (this menu has no name but usually displays the word General) and choose Adobe Illustrator. Either way, you get three options:

- **Output:** This option controls whether you print composites or separations.

- **PostScript:** If you're printing to a PostScript printer, change this to the correct version of PostScript in your printer (you can find out what version is in your printer by printing a test page from the printer). Illustrator 9 is designed for PostScript 3 printing. Keep in mind that each version of PostScript adds features and enhancements. Illustrator can still print to lower levels (and even to non-PostScript printers). However, some features, such as Gradient Meshes and Object Blends, print out at a lower quality than with PostScript 3 printers — and everything prints a lot slower. So if you have the option, print to PostScript 3 printers or, when the time comes to buy a new printer, lobby for one that supports PostScript 3. The increased speed and quality quickly offset the extra cost.

✔ **Separation Setup:** If you want to print separations, you can access the Separation Setup dialog box by clicking the Separation Setup button. After you make your changes, you return to the Print dialog box.

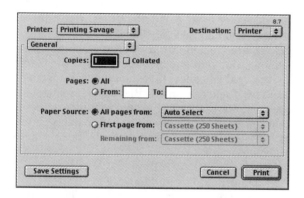

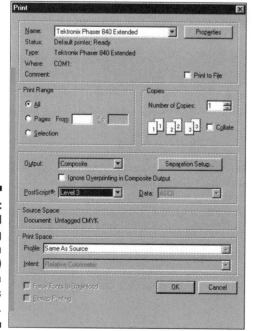

Figure 16-3:
A typical
Print dialog
box for a
Mac (upper)
and for a
Windows
PC (lower).

All About Way-Scary Separations

Separations print a separate page for each color of ink you use in a document. Printing separations is a good way to double check your work before you send it to a service bureau to be made into film or plates. If you never do that, skip this section.

If you do send your work to a service bureau to be made into film or plates, printing separations can save you great pain. For example, suppose you plan to print a job using black ink and the spot color Pantone 185. After printing separations, you get pages for cyan, magenta, yellow, and Pantone 185, rather than just pages for black and Pantone 185. You know immediately that some of the colors you used were created as CMYK process colors, not as spot colors. On closer examination of the pages, you see that the black type you used exists on all pages, and you know that the type was specified as Registration, not as Black. Registration and Black *look* identical onscreen, but Registration is a special color that's used exclusively by printers (for those little marks that help center the content on the page). Registration is totally unsuitable for artwork. (Ack! No! Don't print that ink drawing in Registration! You'll only get a page full of gunk.)

You can fill a book with information about looking at separations to find out information about potential problems in your artwork. The book would be a painfully long and boring book, however, and one we don't want to write. So we tell you how to print separations and leave it at that. Perhaps the best place to find out more about separations is your service bureau. They can help you "read" your separations. In fact, many service bureaus require that you provide them with separations when you give them a job to print!

The concept behind printing separations from Illustrator is actually quite straightforward. Because printing in color requires different inks, which are applied to paper sequentially on a printing press, each ink gets its own printing plate. Illustrator generates film, paper, or even the individual plates themselves — one for each color of ink.

Traditionally, "full-color" artwork is printed using four different inks (and therefore four plates): cyan, magenta, yellow, and black. If you have a CMYK document in Illustrator, you're actually working in the environment that's perfect for full-color printing. Figure 16-4 shows a composite image and the four separations used to create it (all are shown here in black and white, of course).

In addition to standard full-color printing (also known as process printing), you have the concept of spot-color printing. Spot colors are colors that print on their own plate. A good example is a can of Coke. Rather than full-color

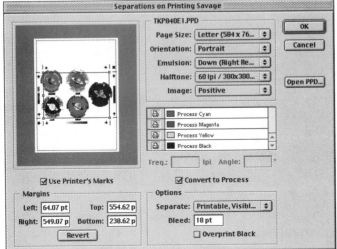

Figure 16-5:
The
Separations
Setup dialog
box.

1. **Choose File⇨Separation Setup.**

   The Separation Setup dialog box appears.

   If most of the fields are grayed out, that means you have never selected a PPD (Printer Prep Document). Every printer has a PPD (unless some vile knave deleted it or never installed it on your computer). The PPD contains information that applications need to print to it properly.

2. **Select the PPD for your printer by clicking the Open PPD button and choosing your printer's PPD.**

   If you can't find the PPD that matches your printer, you can find sample PPDs in the Adobe Illustrator folder. After you choose a PPD, you can change the other settings in the dialog box.

3. **Make sure the settings (Page Size, Orientation, Emulsion, Halftone, and Image) are correct.**

   If you aren't sure whether they're correct, leave the default settings and check with your commercial printer.

4. **In the text area beside the scroll bar (where the colors appear), click the printer icon to the left of any color you want to keep from printing.**

5. **Click OK after you finish making changes.**

To print separations (rather than a composite), be sure to choose Separations (not Composite) in the Print dialog box (on a Mac, you have to choose Adobe Illustrator Settings to change this).

By the way, if you need a quick refresher on the uses of CMYK and RGB (no, they aren't rock bands from the '60s), sneak a peek at Chapter 1. We won't tell a soul.

Chapter 17

Putting Your Art on the Web

· ·

In This Chapter

▶ Designing for the Web in Illustrator

▶ Differentiating between raster and vector formats on the Web

▶ Saving JPEG, GIF, and PNG for the Web

▶ Exporting Flash and SVG

· ·

*I*llustrator is the perfect tool for creating and designing graphical elements for Web pages. That statement may surprise you, since most Web graphics are pixel-based and Illustrator is a vector-based graphics tool. In Illustrator, however, the big advantage to creating Web graphics is in the resolution independence of vector graphics (discussed in Chapter 1). You can create a graphic once, then scale it to be any size you need it to be, even use it for print in addition to the Web, and it will always be a high-quality rendition of your creation.

In this chapter, you peer into the myriad ways of preparing Illustrator graphics for the Web and figure out how to determine the options that best meet the needs of individual graphics. You also find out about how some new file formats, such as Flash and SVG, help you put vector graphics *on the Web* — preserving the advantages of vector graphics (such as small file size and maximum quality, no matter at what size you view or print the graphics).

From Illustrator to the Web

When you create a graphic in a pixel-based program such as Photoshop, you have to decide how big you want the graphic to be from the very start. If you want to enlarge the graphic, you add pixels; if you want to make the graphic smaller, you throw away some pixels. Either way, you can get a blurry, lower-quality image. But with Illustrator, you don't have these problems. Even though you ultimately create pixel-based graphics, your graphics don't become pixel-based until you save them or export them. You can save the Illustrator file many times at different sizes, and each one will be at the best possible quality!

The differences between creating for the Web and creating for print happen when you save your graphic. Whenever you create artwork in Illustrator for the Web, you work just as always. The key difference is in how you save your work after you create it. The only other difference you may find is in the color choices whenever you're creating a graphic for the GIF file format. (More on that in a moment.) Otherwise, the creative processes for Web and print are identical.

Because Web graphics live onscreen, you have a much better idea of how they're going to look after you put them on a Web site than you would if you were going to print them. Colors onscreen (and on the Web, which is always displayed on a screen) consist of red, green, and blue pixel combinations. So if you create graphics just for the Web, RGB documents (see Chapter 1) are your best bet. In fact, if you create things for both screen *and* print, RGB gives you the greatest flexibility.

Using Web colors only

You're in a room full of Web designers, and you hear them talk about "Web-safe color space" and the "Web palette." You look around discreetly. A dapper man in a dark suit steps out from behind the potted plant and tells you, "You're traveling through another dimension. . ." and a weird guitar riff starts to play. . . .

Granted, Web design can seem pretty weird. At least the numbers are relatively small. *Web-safe color* refers to a set of 216 colors that look the same in all Web browsers and on all computer platforms. If you've been creating for print for any length of time, you may be used to using an almost unlimited range of colors. A mere 216 colors may seem strange at first, but there's method in the madness.

One key benefit of the GIF-file format command is that you can specify exact colors to use in your artwork *after* the artwork is created. The catch is that you can only choose from the 256 colors that the GIF format supports. (Other formats support up to 16.7 *million* colors. Yikes.) So how do you get 216 out of 256? Well, unfortunately, only 216 colors actually display the same on all Web browsers and computer platforms. That's what makes them Web-safe.

What happens if you use a color outside of those 216? Whenever a computer encounters a color it can't display, the computer *dithers*. No, it doesn't start nervously talking nonsense. The computer takes the colors it *can* display and tries to emulate the missing color by putting alternating squares of the colors the computer *can* display close together — so that if you look at the monitor from a distance and squint, you see a color that looks very similar to your original color.

Dithering is especially noticeable in large areas of solid color. The effects vary from computer to computer and browser to browser. Sometimes the effects aren't noticeable at all. Sometimes you get an obvious plaid or striped pattern. Still other times, you get plaids and stripes together (and that is *such a fashion faux pas*).

Bottom line: If it's critical that your colors display consistently (and without dithering) to as many viewers as possible (as in the case of a corporate logo on a home page), use Web-safe colors. You can use these Web-safe colors when you save your Illustrator graphic for the Web or when you first create your graphic in Illustrator. You can change the colors in your previously created Illustrator artwork by choosing File⇨Save for Web. Or you can use Web-safe colors to build your artwork in the first place (which may save some hassle down the line) by choosing Window⇨Swatch Libraries⇨Web. The Web color palette is shown in Figure 17-1.

Figure 17-1: The Illustrator Web color palette.

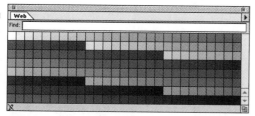

Just click any color in this palette and add it to your Swatches palette, so that you can use it just as you do any other color. If you only use colors from this palette, you ensure that your artwork uses only Web-safe colors. However, many Illustrator features (such as blends, color filters, and transparencies) can quickly turn even these colors into *unsafe* colors. Illustrator *likes* millions and millions of colors. . . .

Don't let all this talk of Web-safe colors make you gun-shy. In some situations, Web-safe colors are vital (for example, in logos and large onscreen areas of solid color) — in other situations, they just don't matter. Dithering is most obvious in large areas of solid color; if your graphic is made up of many small parts, the dithering won't really be noticeable.

The Save for Web command lets you decide at any time whether to use Web-safe color when you save your illustration.

Working in Pixel Preview mode

The majority of graphics created for the Web are pixel-based. The two most widely supported graphics file formats on the Web are JPEG and GIF, and these formats only save pixel data, not vector data (see Chapter 2). When your graphics are in either of these formats, the majority of people in the world who have Internet access will be able to view your graphics. Fortunately, Illustrator can save graphics as both JPEGs and GIFs. Since pixel-based and vector-based images can look quite different, Illustrator has a special preview mode designed for when you are creating graphics for the Web. It's called Pixel Preview mode. Pixel Preview lets you see what your vector artwork will look like when it is turned into pixels for display on the Web. That way, you get a better idea of what the final artwork will look like on the Web (rather than waiting to be surprised when you see it on the browser for the first time).

To turn on Pixel Preview mode, choose View⇨Pixel Preview. You may not notice anything different onscreen until you zoom in closer than 100%. Try 200% to really see the pixel detail. Figure 17-2 shows Pixel Preview turned off and turned on at 200%.

Figure 17-2:
Pixel
Preview
turned off
(left) versus
Pixel
Preview
turned on
(right).

This approach is much more convenient than using the File⇨Save for Web command to convert your graphic into pixels to see how it will look, and then having to re-save it if it looks awful. With Pixel Preview mode, you can edit the graphics "live" while you're viewing the pixels.

Choosing a file format

Deciding what file format to use is almost as perplexing as picking between paper or plastic in the checkout line. (Plastic is easier to carry than paper, paper is easier to recycle; plastic takes up less space in a landfill, the kids can cover their schoolbooks with the paper bags. . . . Meanwhile, the guy behind you is fuming). It's a classic case of a modern syndrome known as Too Many

(Expletive Deleted) Choices. Annoyingly, no single "right" answer exists when you have to decide which file format to use for the Web. What works best for your purpose normally turns out to be a compromise between what you want and what you can have.

Well, okay, what can you have? You can use any of five file formats to put your graphics on the Web: GIF, JPEG, PNG, Flash, and SVG. The basic difference is in how each format presents your artwork. Consider this thumbnail comparison:

- ✔ GIF, JPEG, and PNG require that path-based files be converted to pixel-based artwork. The results look sketchier but load faster.

- ✔ Flash and SVG preserve the paths you create in Illustrator — sometimes complete with humongous file sizes.

Each format has unique benefits and drawbacks. And here they come now.

GIF

GIF is a great format for "traditional" Illustrator graphics — which means almost no gradients, blends, or fine details. GIF (which stands for Graphics Interchange Format) uses a maximum of 256 colors, but typically you want to use even fewer. The fewer colors you use, the smaller your files.

GIF works best with simple graphics that have large areas of solid color. GIF compression encodes an area of solid color as though it were one big pixel. The more solid colors you have (almost regardless of how much onscreen area they cover), the smaller the file size. But if you use gradients, soft drop shadows, or really complex graphics, you introduce more instructions into the file; and the file gets a lot bigger.

In the process of compressing all the different colors in your image (sometimes thousands or millions) down to 256 or fewer, you can get banding and dithering. *Banding* happens when a range of different colors gets compressed into one solid color and looks like a big stripe in your image where you didn't intend to put one. *Dithering* is Illustrator's way of simulating missing colors by putting tiny squares of the remaining colors close together. Of course, the result isn't always too realistic (corduroy suntans, anyone?). This type of dithering is separate from any additional dithering that happens when you don't use Web-safe colors.

GIF files differ from JPEG files in two important ways: They can have transparent areas, and you can specify the exact colors you want (such as Web-safe colors) when you save the file.

GIF is one of the most widely recognized graphics formats for the Web. If you use a GIF file, you virtually guarantee that all your site's visitors can open it in their browsers.

JPEG

JPEG is among the most widely recognized graphics formats for the Web. Anything you save in JPEG can be viewed by almost everyone. The JPEG format (created by the Joint Photographic Experts Group) provides the best compression possible for digitized photographs. It does so by throwing information away. Don't fret too much about this situation. JPEG does so intelligently — examining the image and removing data where the human eye is least likely to notice the absence. What this amazing feat of mathematics means to you as an artist, however, is that your graphics files should start out with a lot of information — so that if you have to throw out a lot of the information, you still have a lot left. Unlike GIFs, JPEGs can't have transparent areas and offer no way to specify exact colors.

Complex images with lots of gradients, blends, and soft shadows make good JPEGs. Alas, this format is really lousy for graphics that have big areas of solid color. No way exists to hide the loss of information. Basically, if the image looks good as a GIF, it may well look bad as a JPEG — and vice versa. Fortunately, you can decide which format works best by using the Save for Web command.

PNG

PNG (Portable Network Graphics format) has a split personality — PNG-8 and PNG-24. The graphics quality you can get with simple GIFs is also available with PNG-8 graphics. PNG-24, on the other hand, is as adept at handling complex images as JPEG. PNG-8 and PNG-24 files can have transparent areas — and PNG-24 compression is *lossless,* which means no reduction in image quality.

Okay, so why don't we just use PNG for everything? Well, first, PNG offers no way to control how much compression is applied to the image; you can't make the image smaller if you want to (as you can with a JPEG). More importantly, PNG is not as universal as JPEG and GIF; you don't see PNG format nearly as often on the Web. So if you use this format, not all your visitors can view the graphic on their browsers. Some may need to install a special piece of software called a *plug-in,* so their browsers can read PNG graphics. This situation creates enough hassle that some visitors just click away from Web pages that use PNG graphics. They don't want to invest the time to download and install the PNG plug-in.

If your primary concern is image quality, use PNG-24. If you want the maximum number of people to view your work on the Web, and the maximum control over file size, use GIF or JPEG.

Flash (SWF)

Flash (also referred to as *SWF* for Shockwave File, *not* Single White Female), a file format created by Macromedia, is one of the cooler things to happen on the Web in recent years. Flash is the current standard for vector graphics on the Web. Not only does it support vector-based graphics, but also animation, sound, and interactivity. Of course (as per Murphy's Law of Innovation), something so cool would *have* to have the occasional "unfortunately" tacked to it. The first is that nearly every browser in existence requires a plug-in to view a Flash file, which limits your audience from the start. The second is that Flash doesn't support cool Illustrator features such as transparency, object blends, and gradient meshes. Lastly, Flash files don't play well with others (just ask Ming the Merciless). If you try to tie them into other non-Flash aspects of your Web site, you may run into difficulty.

SVG

SVG (or Scalable Vector Graphics) format is the upcoming standard for vector graphics. It's the coolest thing to happen to the Web in the near future — which means that you still have a while to wait. As they do with Flash graphics, the current versions of most browsers need a plug-in to read SVG files.

Ah, but the upside is tantalizing. SVG supports anything you can create in Illustrator, as well as animation and interactivity. SVG files can interact with HTML pages and work in conjunction with XML-driven Web sites. A long list of companies, including Adobe and Corel, are fully behind SVG. It may well become the dominant vector-graphics format in a few years (say, by the time the International Space Station is complete). Unfortunately, the following couple of pitfalls exist:

- ✔ Although the industry has great expectations for SVG by 2005, it may not seize the vector-graphics crown on schedule.

- ✔ Although SVG is, hands down, one of the coolest formats out there, it is so new that only a few people have the plug-in, and hardly any support exists for SVG *right now*.

Still, you optimists can take heart: Illustrator 9 is one of the very first applications that can create SVG files. Whenever the touted SVG revolution comes, you (as an Illustrator user) can say you knew it all along.

So which file format is best, already?

Sorry. The answer depends on what you need the file format to do and what tradeoffs you're willing to live with. That's the most practical answer for now. However, a summary may help ward off the Too-Many-Choices headache, so here goes:

- ✔ Use GIFs and JPEGs if you want maximum compatibility with as many people as possible.

- ✔ Use GIFs for simple graphics with large, solid colors or for transparency.

- ✔ Use JPEGs for more complex graphics with gradients and so forth.

- ✔ Use PNG for maximum-quality complex graphics when compatibility is not an issue.

✔ Use Flash when you need to publish vector-graphics on the Web and want as much compatibility as possible (but don't require as much compatibility as with GIFs and JPEGs).

✔ Use SVG when you want as many bells and whistles as possible and are willing to throw compatibility to the wind.

If we're all lucky, everyone will eventually adopt SVG as the standard, and we won't have to worry about such issues as which file format to use. (Of course, you gotta ask yourself: Do I feel lucky?) Until then, choosing the right file format is a juggling act that balances features, quality, and compatibility.

Creating Web-Specific Pixel Graphics

Most of the graphics found on the Web are not vector but pixel-based, for reasons of compatibility. Regardless of which pixel format you plan to use, Illustrator gives you the same dialog box from which to export your artwork. Choosing File⇨Save for Web displays the Save for Web dialog box, as shown in Figure 17-3.

The Save for Web dialog box may appear a bit intimidating at first, but it's actually quite easy to use. Although you do have to wade through a lot of settings, the dialog box provides you with a preview of the image, so that you can see how the settings affect the image's quality. The dialog box also gives you the file size and an estimate of how long the graphic will take to download — important considerations in creating graphics for the Web.

Figure 17-3:
The Save for Web dialog box.

The dialog box is slightly different, depending on the file format you're working with, but the following few features remain consistent in any format you use:

- **Original, Optimized, 2-Up, 4-Up.** These tabs let you view the image at different settings. Click the Original tab to view the image before any settings are applied. Click the Optimized tab to see how the image will look after you save it with the current settings. Click the 2-Up and 4-Up tabs to see the image at multiple settings at once. These last views are the most useful. Your goal when saving your image, no matter what format you use, is always to resemble the original as closely as possible while maintaining the smallest file size (and lowest download time). The ability to compare the image at different settings with the original is vital to achieving this goal. To use the 2-Up and 4-Up settings, click either of the tabs. Then click one of the images to select it. Any settings you make apply to that selected image only. Click a different image to apply different settings. Illustrator saves whatever image is selected (at whatever settings) after you click OK.

- **File Size and Download Time.** These features tell you how large your file is and how long that file will take to download over a 28.8 modem. This information is very important. Think of every second required for a graphic to download as another second the viewer has to get bored and click away from your page. Weigh this download time against the quality of the graphic and ask yourself whether having those extra colors, a little less banding, or a better-looking graphic is worth the download time.

- **File Format.** This pop-up menu is where you choose the format — GIF, JPEG, PNG-8, or PNG-24.

- **The Rest of the Settings.** The rest of the fields around the File Format pop-up are the file settings and the unique settings of that format. After you choose a format, the rest of the settings change to match the features of that format. These are covered in-depth under each file format in the next few sections of this chapter.

- **Color Table.** This tab shows you the exact colors that will be used when you save the file in GIF or PNG-8 format. Here you can delete colors (or shift non-Web-safe colors to Web-safe colors).

- **Image Size.** This tab lets you set the size (in pixels) of the image as you save it. This setting is the actual physical size of the image as it displays in the browser, not the file size.

GIF

To save your graphic as a GIF, follow these steps:

1. Choose File⇨Save for Web.

The Save for Web dialog box appears.

2. **Select GIF from the File Format pop-up menu (refer to Figure 17-3).**

3. **Click the 2-Up or 4-Up tab at the top of the graphic.**

   After you choose either 2-Up or 4-Up, the first graphic is your original image, and the second is selected as the Optimized image. As you change your file settings, this graphic updates to preview those changes. Clicking the third or fourth graphic (in 4-Up view) lets you make different settings and simultaneously compare and contrast them to find the best settings. Adjust your settings to find the best balance of small file size and best image quality. Every setting you change affects both of those things. Watch the image carefully to see how the changes affect it.

4. **Adjust the settings for the graphic:**

   • **Color Reduction Algorithm.** This delightfully descriptive setting simply means you take the many colors in your image and reduce them to 256 or fewer colors. How do you want to do that? Your choices are Perceptual, Selective, Adaptive, Web, or Custom. The first three are pretty much the same. *Perceptual* makes the colors as close as possible to whatever colors the human eye perceives in the original image (so they say). *Selective* does the same thing but uses as many Web-safe colors as possible. *Adaptive* makes the remaining colors as mathematically close to the original as possible. *Web* uses the closest Web-safe colors to the colors that are in the image. *Custom* is for power users who want to create their own color-reduction algorithms.

     Your choices, then, are really between Perceptual and Web. Perceptual gives you an image as close as possible to your original creation. Web gives you an image that looks the same no matter what computer or Web browser it's on. Unfortunately, Perceptual usually looks great, while Web dithers things substantially. But look at the Web choice this way: this is as bad as the image is going to look. With any other setting, the graphic is going to look better or worse unpredictably. With the Web setting, you know exactly how much dithering is going on, and nothing more will happen to the image. Compare the second image in Figure 17-4 to the third. The only difference between the two is the Color Reduction algorithm. Although noticeable dithering appears in the Web-safe image, it doesn't look unacceptably bad, and the file size is almost a third smaller.

   • **Dither method.** This is the actual shape of the dithering pattern. *No Dither* won't dither the image at all. *Diffusion* randomizes the dithering pattern to make it less noticeable. *Pattern* dithers in a fixed grid. *Noise* is even more random than Diffusion, making any dither even less noticeable. Sadly, the settings that produce the least noticeable dithering also create the highest file sizes. Noise produces the largest files, and Diffusion the second largest. Pattern produces small files, with noticeable stripes. No Dither produces obvious bands of color in the image. Notice the sphere and the

gradient around the word "Teenage" in Figure 17-4. A No Dither setting causes the stripes. Here again, your goal is to strike a balance
between the smallest size and the best quality.

- **Transparency.** How do you want to treat the parts of your image
  that have no graphics? Do you want them to be transparent or
  filled with the Matte color (explained later in this list)? Check this
  box to make them transparent.

- **Interlaced.** This setting makes the file larger so it seems to be
  downloading faster, which seems like a contradiction. When a
  graphic is interlaced, it loads a very low-resolution version to the
  Web browser, then the full-resolution version. It seems to load
  faster (actually it's just soothing the user by showing something
  useful happening). Without Interlacing, the whole thing has to
  download before you can look at it (it actually loads faster this
  way; it only *seems* to take forever). Impatient people may want to
  check this box (unless, of course, they already skipped this list).

- **Lossy.** This setting reduces file size by as much as 40% by eliminat-
  ing pixels, at the expense of image quality. Use as much Lossy as
  you can get away with, but don't ruin your image!

Lossy won't work with Interlacing turned on.

- **Colors.** This setting is the total number of colors used in the image.
  Sometimes, reducing the number results in a smaller image, but
  doing so doesn't usually have as much effect as the Dither and
  Lossy settings.

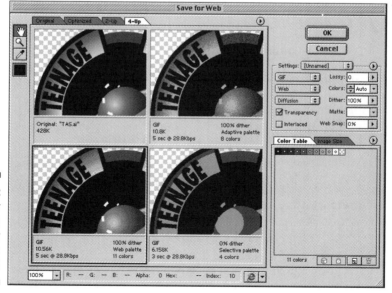

Figure 17-4:
The Save for
Web dialog
box set for
saving a
GIF.

- **Dither.** If you select Pattern, Noise, or Diffusion for a dither method, you can use this setting to turn down the amount of dithering. Lower amounts result in smaller graphics with more noticeable dithering patterns.

- **Matte.** If you don't choose Transparency, the Matte color fills areas of your image where there are no graphics. If you're using transparency and know what color you plan to use for the background of the Web page, you can set the Matte to that color and the edge pixels of your graphic will blend with the background, creating a more visually appealing image. If you don't know what the background color will be, set the Matte color to None. Otherwise, the edge pixels may blend to a different color from your background, producing an obvious fringe around the graphic, as if it were snipped hastily out of a different background.

- **Web Snap.** If you aren't using Web for your color reduction algorithm, you can use Web Snap to convert *some* of the colors (starting with the ones used most in the image) to Web-safe colors. This setting is a great way to achieve a balance between quality and compatibility. By changing just the largest areas of color to Web-safe, you can avoid the dithering problem in places where it will be most noticeable. The higher the setting, the more colors Illustrator converts to Web-safe.

After you make your settings on several images and decide which image works best for you, click that image and then click OK. The graphic saves as a GIF, ready for you to use on your Web page.

JPEG

JPEGs are easier to make in Illustrator than GIFs. You only need to worry about one setting: Quality. Of course, quality *can* be specified in two ways. (Simplicity? Well, almost.)

To save your artwork as a JPEG:

1. **Choose File⇨Save for Web.**

   The Save for Web dialog box appears.

2. **Choose JPEG from the File Format pop-up menu.**

3. **Click the 2-Up or 4-Up tab at the top of the graphic.**

   After you choose either 2-Up or 4-Up, the first graphic is your original image, and the second is selected as the Optimized image. As you change your file settings, this graphic updates to preview those changes. Clicking the third or fourth graphic (in 4-Up view) lets you make different settings and simultaneously compare and contrast them to find the best settings. Adjust your settings to find the best balance of small file size and best image quality. Every setting you change affects both of those things. Watch the image carefully to see how the changes affect it.

4. Choose a Quality setting.

There are two ways to choose the Quality setting, but the effects are identical: by choosing it from the Quality pop-up menu or by entering a number into the Quality field.

- **The Quality pop-up menu** offers you a choice of four preset values: Maximum, High, Medium, and Low. These options refer to the quality level of the image, not the amount of compression applied. A Maximum quality level produces (as you may expect) the largest file sizes and the highest-quality images.

- **The Quality field**, just to the right of the pop-up menu, lets you type in any value from 100 (maximum quality) to 0. Use the lowest Quality setting you can that doesn't destroy your image. You may notice that the loss of quality in your image shows up as weird patterns that weren't there before. These patterns are especially noticeable where two large areas of different colors meet. Notice the weirdness (called *artifacting*) in the area around the lettering in the fourth image in Figure 17-5. A little of this is tolerable in the name of smaller files, but too much becomes distracting. Note that entering settings in this field is identical to choosing values from the pop-up menu. In the pop-up menu, the values of Maximum, High, Medium, and Low correspond (respectively) to settings of 80, 60, 30, and 10 in the Quality field.

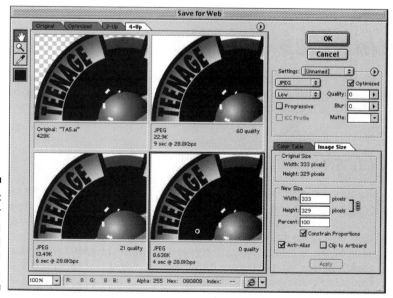

Figure 17-5:
The Save for Web dialog box being used to save a JPEG.

5. Adjust the other settings:

- **Progressive.** Like Interlacing for GIFs, Progressive creates the illusion that the image loads faster on Web browsers by loading a low-resolution version of the graphic first and then turning it into a higher-resolution image. In actuality, the image takes longer to load because Progressive files are larger, but viewers feel as though the download is going faster because they see things happening while they wait, rather than waiting for the whole download before they see anything.

- **Blur.** Blur is a fairly useless setting. The goal is to reduce the artifacting in the image by blurring it. Unfortunately, the setting blurs the whole image, not just the artifacts, creating problems where none existed before. Leave this set to zero and ignore it. (Unless, of course, you're feeling a little misty.)

- **Matte.** JPEGs can have no transparent areas, so wherever no graphic exists, Illustrator fills in with this color. A setting of None fills in with white.

PNG-8 and PNG-24

The settings for PNG-8 are identical to those for GIF. Read that section again and put PNG-8 wherever you see GIF. No settings exist for PNG-24; what you get is what you get. Choose that file format, and the compression scheme does its thing. Either you like the result (and click OK), or you don't (and choose GIF or JPEG instead).

Creating Web-Specific Vector Graphics

Vectors have several advantages over pixels. One of the chief advantages is their small size, especially for basic graphics like logos and buttons. Another advantage is their ability to be scaled without any loss of quality.

Flash •

Flash is a very versatile format developed by Macromedia Corporation. Not only can you use Flash to show vector graphics on the Web, you can also animate and add sound and interactivity to them. In Illustrator, you can create the graphic and do limited animation (see Chapter 20) with it. Beyond that, you have to use another application (such as Adobe LiveMotion or Macromedia Flash), to take full advantage of the format. For this reason, the Export to Flash command is really intended to prepare artwork for export to one of these other applications, rather than to create artwork to go directly to the Web. Not that you can't put a Flash file created in Illustrator directly on the Web. You certainly can, but then you're tapping into just a fraction of what Flash can do.

Still, if you want your Illustrator artwork on the Web as vector data, Flash is currently the way to go. The one drawback to the format is the previously mentioned need for a browser plug-in in order for people to see your graphic in their browsers. This situation can make your graphic inaccessible to some people. However, Flash is such a popular format that many people have the plug-in installed in their browsers. Chances are quite good that many people will be able to see your work without problems.

So if your primary concern is that your graphic appear on the Web with no-holds-barred top quality (and print with the best possible quality to boot), use the Flash format.

To save a graphic in Flash format, just follow these steps:

1. **Choose File⇨Export.**

   The Export dialog box appears.

2. **Specify a name, location, and file format for your document.**

   In this case, choose Flash (SWF) from the file format pop-up menu.

3. **Click Export or Save.**

   The Flash (SWF) Format Options dialog box appears, as shown in Figure 17-6.

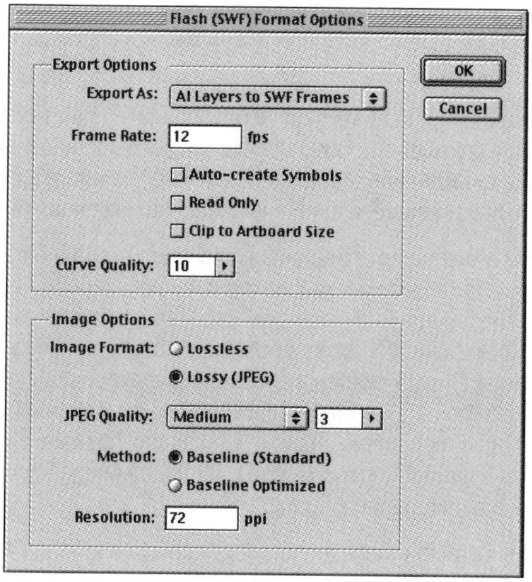

Figure 17-6:
The Flash
(SWF)
Format
Options
dialog box.

The Flash (SWF) Format Options dialog box gives you the following options:

- ✔ **Export As.** This is a pop-up menu with three options: AI File to SWF File, AI Layers to SWF Frames, and AI Layers to SWF Files. "AI" is short for Adobe Illustrator and refers to the file you are currently saving. SWF is another term for a Flash file. This option determines how Illustrator layers (see Chapter 13) are handled when they are saved. *AI File to SW File* flattens all the layers into a single image, just as if you were printing the illustration. *AI Layers to SWF Frames* builds a special file that, when loaded to a browser, displays each layer in sequence starting with the first layer and stopping with the last. You can use this option to create a slide show, by putting a different graphic on each layer, or to do simple animations. (For more information on animations, see Chapter 20 — it will move you.) The final option, *AI Layers to SWF Files,* exports each layer as a separate Flash file.

- ✔ **Frame Rate.** This setting determines how fast the Flash file flips through the different Illustrator layers after you choose *AI Layers to SWF Frames* in the Export As option. Each layer is considered a frame, and the number you enter here is the number of frames you want to appear every second.

- ✔ **Auto-Create Symbols.** This setting only matters when you intend to open up your illustration in Macromedia Flash (the program, not the format) for further editing. Checking this option lets the illustration work with some features available in the Macromedia Flash program. But if you aren't bringing the file into Flash (the program), you're just adding extra file size.

- ✔ **Read Only.** This setting creates a file that people can look at but not change in any way.

- ✔ **Clip to Artboard.** This option crops out any artwork that is off the Artboard.

- ✔ **Curve Quality.** The higher this setting (from 1 to 10), the closer the graphic is to your Illustrator file, and the larger your file size. Lower settings provide lower quality with smaller file sizes. Yet again, you're plagued by the agonizing compromise between file size and image quality!

- ✔ **Image Options** are a subset of the options in the Flash (SWF) Format Options dialog box. They may never come into play in the graphic you're exporting; they only matter if you created your artwork using features such as Illustrator's Transparency settings, *complex gradients* (gradients with more than 8 colors), gradient meshes, or Effects. (See Chapter 10 for more info.) The Flash format doesn't support these features, so it turns them into pixels in the final Flash file (your other Illustrator graphics remain vector-based). The following Image Options determine how to handle these pixel graphics:

  - • **Lossless.** This option saves the pixel graphics in PNG-24 format. Don't worry, the Flash plug-in takes care of any compatibility issues with the PNG format. Use this option if you're exporting your graphic for further editing in Macromedia Flash or Adobe LiveMotion, because you can apply further compression settings in those programs. Lossless lets you start with the highest possible quality.

- **Lossy.** This option saves the graphics as JPEGs. See the "JPEG" section under the "Choosing a file format" section. For more information see the "JPEG" section under the "Creating Web-Specific Pixel Graphics" section of this chapter.

- **Resolution.** This setting determines how much information the graphics contain; 72 ppi (pixels per inch) is perfect for onscreen display but may not be enough if you want people to be able to print your graphics as well. If the latter, you may want to go up to 150 ppi, or even 300. Watch out, though, because this high a setting makes your graphics have huge file sizes.

After you complete all your settings, click OK to save your file in Flash format.

SVG

Scalable Vector Graphics are great, but. . . well. . . futuristic. Look at it this way. You go to your local car dealer on a whim. There you find the car of your dreams, with every feature that you ever wanted and some you didn't know you wanted. The gas mileage is great, the color you want is in stock, and you can drive the car off the lot today! And the price? It's about half the price you're willing to pay! But just as you are about to sign on the dotted line, the dealer informs you that there's one little catch. The car runs on a special kind of gas. All the major gas stations have committed to start carrying the special gas in the future, but right now there's just no telling where you're going to be able get the special gas or how long before everyone carries it. What do you do? Take the risk and invest the money or purchase a car you know you can get gas for everywhere?

SVG is technically great. It offers everything that Flash does, with promises for a whole lot more, such as total support for everything you can create in Illustrator, for example. For another, the format is much more "open" than the Flash format. To create Flash files, you must use an application that specifically supports Flash format, such as Illustrator or LiveMotion. However, if you knew how, you could write SVG files in any word processing program. In the future, SVG files may integrate seamlessly with Web pages without requiring plug-ins or anything else. So you would get maximum quality and maximum compatibility, and issues such as file formats, dithering, and Web-safe colors would become concerns of the past.

Unfortunately, for now, you still have a hard time finding that special gas. All the major software companies have pledged support for SVG, but that support isn't there *yet.* The industry moves so fast that no one can say how long SVG may take to catch on. By the time you read this, that transformation may have occurred. On the other hand, it may be years from now (PNG format has been around for years and is only just starting to be adopted).

So, if you want to live a life of action and adventure on the bleeding edge of technology, start saving your files as SVG right now and create graphics so insanely great that people are forced to risk computer crashes and other frustrations to download and use the unstable plug-ins they need to view your SVG files. Go on. I dare you. I double-dare you. I double-*dog* dare you. If you can pull it off, you're the coolest kid in town and will be far ahead of everybody else. If you can't, you still have GIFs and JPEGs and Flash files to fall back on.

To create an SVG file, just follow these steps:

1. **Choose File➪Export.**

   The Export dialog box appears.

2. **Specify a name, location, and file format for your document.**

   In this case, choose SVG or SVG Compressed from the file format pop-up menu.

3. **Click Export.**

   The SVG Options dialog box appears, as shown in Figure 17-7.

SVG Options	
Font Subsetting:	Only Glyphs Used
Embedded Font Location:	Embed Subsetted Fonts
Raster Image Location:	Embed Raster Images
Decimal Places:	3
Encoding:	ISO 8859-1 (ASCII)
CSS Property Location:	Style Attributes

Figure 17-7: The SVG Options dialog box.

The SVG Options dialog box offers the following options:

✔ **Font Subsetting.** The SVG format lets you embed the fonts you used in the document in the SVG file. Fonts have traditionally been one of the major stumbling blocks for designers on the Web. Simply put, whoever has different fonts from yours installed on his or her computer may see your text, but not as you created it. Font subsetting eliminates this problem by making the fonts you used part of the SWF file. You have three choices for subsetted fonts: None, Glyphs Used, and All Glyphs.

   Glyph is just a weird name for letter; you've seen it before in the word *hieroglyphics.*

Choose None if you don't want to embed any fonts, if you didn't use text in your graphic, or if you converted your text to outlines. (For more information on converting text to outlines, see Chapter 15.) Choose Only Glyphs Used to embed just the font info for the specific letters you used. This option creates a smaller file, but the graphic is less editable than when you include All Glyphs, because you can only use letters that are already used in the file. All Glyphs includes all the characters of all the fonts you used. So even if you used just one letter out of Futura Condensed, all the letters A through Z, upper and lower case, and all special characters are included. If you just want people to see the graphic the way you created it, choose Only Glyphs Used. If you want people to be able to make changes to your text, choose All Glyphs. (Like All Glyphs, the other values — Common English, Glyphs Used+Common English, Common Roman, and Glyphs Used+Common Roman — are useful when the textual content of the SVG file may change.)

- ✔ **Embedded Font Location.** You can choose to have your fonts built directly into the file or collected in another location. The first choice results in a larger file, but you only have one piece to take care of. The second option results in multiple files.

- ✔ **Raster Image Location.** As with fonts, you can choose to have any placed pixel images in your document built into the SVG file or stored externally. The first option creates a larger file that is completely self-contained. The second option creates a separate folder for pixel graphics.

- ✔ **Decimal Places.** Higher values (from 1 to 7) for this setting result in better image quality with (what a BIG surprise!) larger file sizes.

- ✔ **Encoding.** The SVG format provides several Encoding methods to support alphabets in different languages, such as Kanji.

- ✔ **CSS Property Location.** This option lets you determine where your Cascading Style Sheet properties are located. Cascading Style Sheets are a standard method of imposing consistent display characteristics on HTML documents. Many Web sites use CSS as a dynamic and flexible way to format Web pages. Talk with your Webmaster about the best settings to use. (To find out more about Cascading Style Sheets, consult the stalwart *HTML 4 For Dummies,* Third Edition, from IDG Books Worldwide.)

This chapter focuses on a very specific part of Web graphics production: getting your graphic into a file format that can be displayed on the Web. This is just the start, however. Actually putting that graphic where people can see it is another saga entirely, one that involves Web-authoring tools (or hand-coding HTML), service providers, and a whole alphabet soup of FTPs, URLs, and other confusing TLAs (*three-letter acronyms,* not *true love always*). As you may have guessed, actually getting the graphic onto the Web in a real live Web page involves a process that goes beyond the scope of this one book. (For more information on *that* end of things, please see *Creating Web Pages For Dummies,* Fifth Edition, from IDG Books Worldwide.) The critical step in creating a Web graphic is to save the file. After you save a graphic for the Web, you have many, many options, all of which affect your graphic in different and significant ways. If you are not producing the Web site yourself, have a discussion with the site's Webmaster *before* you save the graphic to find out what formats and options work best for the site.

Chapter 18

Moving Files into and out of Illustrator

●●●

●●●

*A*lthough you can certainly take a file from concept to final printing using nothing but Illustrator, you probably shouldn't. It's a specialized program, created to be one small (but vitally important) part in a production cycle.

In a typical production cycle, text is created in a word processing program such as Microsoft Word, scanned images are edited in an image editing program such as Photoshop, and vector graphics are created in Illustrator or Macromedia Freehand. Finally, all these elements are combined in a page layout program such as InDesign or QuarkXPress or a Web-design application such as Adobe GoLive or Macromedia Dreamweaver.

Attempting to make Illustrator perform all aspects of the production cycle is like trying to build a house with a hammer as your only tool. You may be able to do it, but the task takes you a lot more time to complete, the result looks really awful, and you're a lot more tired and frustrated than if you'd used the right tools for the job in the first place.

Illustrator's mystical interconnection to all things is reflected in the fact that you can save Illustrator files in nearly *three dozen* different file formats! If you create something in Illustrator and save it properly, you can open your creation in just about any application that ever supported graphics on any platform — even bizarre and forgotten computer platforms such as Amiga!

The bottom line is that Illustrator is designed to receive graphics files created in other programs and to create files for use in other programs. Harnessing the full power of Illustrator means making the program work well (and play nice) with other programs — or in other words, getting files into and out of Illustrator.

In this chapter, you find out how to make Illustrator play well with others — by bringing files that weren't created in Illustrator into your Illustrator document and by moving Illustrator files into other applications.

Bringing Files into Illustrator

You can bring graphics or text into Illustrator in several different ways, but the most straightforward, Joe Friday way is to use the Place command in the File menu. Every type of graphic or text that can be placed in Illustrator can be placed with this command, making it the one-stop location for all file importing. The "Getting Files Out of Illustrator" section of this chapter contains a list of the most common file formats that Illustrator can both export and import.

When you place artwork into Illustrator, you usually have the option of either *embedding* or *linking* the artwork. Each of these processes has different implications for file size and storage:

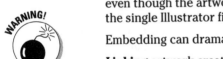

Embedding artwork makes the placed artwork part of the Illustrator file, even though the artwork was created elsewhere. That way, you only need the single Illustrator file for your artwork to print properly.

Embedding can dramatically increase the file size.

Linking artwork creates a link in the Illustrator document to the placed artwork. The file size of the Illustrator document is smaller as a result, and any change to the linked file is automatically reflected in the Illustrator document. Linking also enables the file to be updated outside of Illustrator (while maintaining the link). In order for linked files to print properly, both the Illustrator file and all linked files must be present.

To place a graphic in Illustrator, follow these steps:

1. Choose File➪Place.

The Place dialog box appears, as shown in Figure 18-1, so you can choose the file that you want to place.

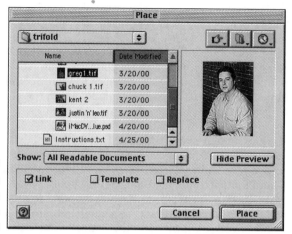

Figure 18-1:
The Place
dialog box.

2. **Select the file that you want to place.**

   If you don't have any files lying around, look in Illustrator's Samples folder and pick one of those files.

3. **Choose either to link or embed the file you want to place.**

   To create a link between the file you want to place and the Illustrator file (the default setting), make sure the Link box is selected. To embed the file you want to place in the Illustrator file, deselect the Link box.

4. **Choose either to use the graphic as an artistic element or as a template.**

   If you check the Template option, Illustrator creates a special layer for the Photoshop image (see Chapter 13). This layer is locked (you can't change anything on the layer), and the graphic is dimmed, making the graphic 50 percent lighter. Template layers also don't print and aren't included in the artwork when you use the Save for Web command. Template layers are especially useful when you plan to use the Photoshop image as a guide for tracing in Illustrator (see Chapter 20).

5. **Choose either to replace or to add the graphic to the rest of the placed graphics (if necessary).**

   This option is only available after you've already placed a graphic in the file and that graphic is selected. You have the option of replacing that graphic with the graphic you are about to place or bringing the new graphic in as a separate graphic. Just put a check in the Replace box to replace the selected graphic, or leave the box unchecked to leave the selected graphic alone.

6. **Click the Place button.**

But which is better, linking or embedding?

If you're just playing around to see how the program works, then whether you link or embed doesn't really matter. But if you're working on a production with tight deadlines and making rapid changes to your document, and money is on the line, *link whenever possible.* Linking makes the chore of changing placed images *much* easier for you.

When you embed something, it exists totally within a single Illustrator file. Your artwork is locked down. You can't do anything to it other than move it, scale it (and other such transformations), or run a Photoshop filter on it. That's all, folks — and that isn't much. You can't edit your artwork in another application; it's embedded in Illustrator and won't respond to other applications. The term *embedding* is quite literal — it's stuck in there. You can't get your artwork out unless you pry it out with the Export command (more on that in the "Getting Files out of Illustrator" section of this chapter).

Here's an example. You recently sent a completed job to your service bureau. They want to print your document, but they can't because your five Photoshop images are embedded, two in RGB mode and the rest in CMYK. They need all the images to be in CMYK for the job to print properly. Illustrator can't convert pixel data from RGB to CMYK (Illustrator can only convert vector data). You need to use Photoshop to convert the pixel images. If the images are linked, however, your service bureau can change them by opening the image in Photoshop, making the change, and then updating the link — a quick process that takes about a minute on a fast computer.

Because the images are embedded, though, you have two options. You can deliver the original Photoshop graphics over to the service bureau (assuming that your company has one, that you didn't send the job over at the last minute, and that the service bureau is still open). Or you can let the staff at the service bureau separate each of the images into its own layer in Illustrator, export the entire document as a Photoshop file, open the document in Photoshop, delete all the other layers, crop the image to the right size, change the color mode, save the image, go back to Illustrator, and replace the graphic (assuming the service bureau staff actually *knows* how to do this, which not many people do).

If you know beyond a doubt that your images are perfect, pristine, and final, and never need changing in any way, by all means embed them. If you have a shadow of a doubt, link your images.

The only hassle that comes with linking is that you have to provide all the linked images with your Illustrator file whenever it leaves your computer, because your file won't print properly without them. This procedure is a minor hassle, considering the amount of hassle it saves!

Managing links

Whenever you place an image into Illustrator and link it, the image isn't actually *in* your document — for the same reason that Dan Rather isn't actually *in* your house when you watch the news on TV. What you see in Illustrator is a preview of the file — an image of the image, so to speak. Think of the actual file as "broadcasting" an image of itself to Illustrator while the file itself sits somewhere else on your hard drive. You look at the preview on-screen; when the document prints, the actual file supplies the image for the document. If the actual file gets moved, modified, or deleted, then you have a problem — especially if you are printing — because Illustrator uses the preview image instead of the real file. The preview image that you see in Illustrator contains just enough info to be displayed on screen, but not nearly enough info to print with any quality. Fortunately, Illustrator provides you with a powerful tool to help you manage links: the Links palette. You can find the Links palette by choosing Window↪Show Links. What you get looks remarkably like Figure 18-2, even if you don't have thumbnails of all those people.

Figure 18-2:
The Links palette puts total management of links at your fingertips (in particular, the one on the mouse button).

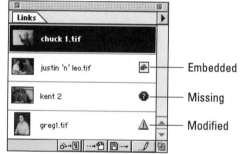

Embedded

Missing

Modified

The Links palette shows you all the placed images in your document; alerts you if anything is amiss; and lets you update, edit, or replace the images — all with the click of a mouse!

The Links palette includes embedded images as well, even though they aren't technically links.

To use the Links palette, you must first understand what the palette is telling you. The Links palette informs you about the status of the graphic through alerts. Alerts are tiny icons that appear beside the names of the graphics in the Links palette. They look a little like buttons, but they are strictly informative. Alerts warn you when there is a potential problem with the link. You can fix most problems by clicking the graphic within the Links palette, and then clicking the Replace Link or Update Link buttons at the bottom of the palette (more on these options in just a second).

The alerts provide the following information:

- ✔ **No icon means everything is okay.** This isn't really an alert. (Yeah, that would be pretty silly — *Warning! Everything is normal!*) But it's worth noting that when nothing is wrong with a linked image, the palette shows just the filename of the image, its thumbnail, and nothing else.

- ✔ **Embedded.** The Embedded icon shows a rectangle overlapping a triangle. This icon indicates that the image data is completely contained within the Illustrator document and not linked to an external file. This situation isn't necessarily a problem, but it can be. See the "But which is better, linking or embedding?" section earlier in this chapter. No "un-embed" button exists. The only way to turn this embedded image into a linked file is to click the Relink button at the bottom of the palette, locate the original file on the hard drive, and replace the file with the Link option checked.

- ✔ **Missing.** A question mark inside a red octagon (or stop sign) shows that the actual image file is missing. This is good to know, because the image still shows up in Illustrator even if the info the file needed to print properly is missing. You can fix this image by clicking the Replace button (more about this in a moment).

- ✔ **Modified.** A triangle with an exclamation point (sort of like an emphatic yield sign) indicates that the actual image has been changed outside of Illustrator. This information is also vital, because Illustrator still displays the original image.

After you identify the problems with the linked graphics, you can manage them using the buttons along the bottom of the Links palette. To do this, click the problem graphic in the Links palette; then click one of the following four buttons:

- ✔ **Replace Link.** This is the first button from the left at the bottom of the Links palette. Click this button when your image is missing or when you want to swap the selected graphic with another graphic on your hard drive. After you click this button, the Place dialog box opens. Choose a different file or locate the missing file on your hard drive, and then click OK. The new image replaces the old one.

- ✔ **Go to Link.** Second from the left, this button is handy for locating and selecting linked graphics. Click the linked graphic in the Links palette and click the Go to Link button. This action selects the graphic in the document as though you'd clicked it using the Selection tool. Clicking this button also centers the view on the graphic, making the graphic easy to spot whenever you have a lot of other graphics in the document.

- ✔ **Update Link.** Click this third button whenever you see the Modified warning beside a link. This action updates the selected link with the latest information from the original file.

✔ **Edit Original.** This fourth button is only available for linked images —
not for embedded images. After you click this option, the selected image
opens in the original application that created it.

The Edit Original option is a great way to modify images. After you place a
Photoshop image, click this button to launch Photoshop and open the image.
In Photoshop, you can make the necessary changes and then save your
image. When you go back to Illustrator, it asks whether you want to update
your modified image. Click OK to update the information.

Your goal, as you work with placed images, is to avoid all question marks and
exclamation points in your Links palette. Fix these problems by using the buttons at the bottom of the palette.

The Links palette offers a few more tidbits through its submenu to help you
manage links. Click the triangle in the upper-right corner of the palette to
access the Links palette submenu. Here you find Replace, Go to Link, Update
Link and Edit Original commands that duplicate the functions of the buttons
along the bottom. You also find various Sort commands, such as Sort by
Name, which alphabetizes the linked images within the palette. Or you can
reorganize the palette using Show commands such as Show Embedded,
which hides all linked graphics. The Show and Sort commands are only
useful when you have a lot of linked images. This situation is fairly rare in an
Illustrator document. The two most useful things in the Links palette submenu are Embed Image and Information. Here's what they do and why:

✔ **Embed Image.** Click a linked image in the Links palette and choose
Embed Image to embed the image into the Illustrator file.

✔ **Information.** Click an image in the Links palette and choose Information
to open the Link Information dialog box. This dialog box is strictly informative. You can't make any changes here, but you find out lots of information about the selected graphic, such as the location of the image on
the hard drive, the file size of the image, the image's file type, when the
image was created, and a whole lot more.

Getting Files out of Illustrator

Files that are native to Illustrator can't be read by every application.
However, these files are PDF-based, so any application that can read PDFs
generated by Acrobat 5 or a later version (including Acrobat Reader 5.0) can
also read Illustrator files. For the applications that can't read Illustrator-
native files, Illustrator can export a number of different file formats.

To decide which format to use, consider the eventual use of the file. For instance, if you're posting your artwork on a Web page, you probably want to use either JPEG or GIF formats (find out more about these formats in Chapter 7). If you want to place your file in a Microsoft Word document, you can use EPS, EMF, or BMP formats.

Typically, the manual that accompanies your software describes what file formats it accepts. Illustrator supports the export of eighteen different formats, so just choose a format that works in the "target" application from the list of available formats.

To export your artwork in a certain format, choose File➪Export from the File menu, choose the format you want from the Format list, and save the file. If you're saving the file as PNG, JPEG, or GIF, use the Save for Web command to save in these formats. Some Export formats open an additional dialog box for that specific file format after you click save.

Not all file formats support vector data! (See Chapter 2 for details.) If you use EPS, PDF, Flash, or SVG, then you preserve your paths; but most other formats convert your Illustrator files to pixels.

The following list is a brief summary of the most useful file formats available in Illustrator 9:

- ✔ **EPS.** Encapsulated PostScript files are accepted by most software packages. Raster and vector-based data are preserved in EPS files.

    For more about raster, vector, path, and pixel — they refer to types of graphics, not senior partners in a law firm — see Chapters 2 and 17.

- ✔ **GIF.** Graphics Interchange Format files are commonly used on the Web for files with few colors (good for solid-color logos and text).

- ✔ **JPEG.** Joint Photographic Experts Group files are highly compressible files that are used on the Web. They're especially good for photographs.

- ✔ **PNG.** Portable Network Graphic files are the most flexible of the Web formats, providing support for compression and detail in a single file format.

- ✔ **TIFF.** Tagged Image File Format files are the industry standard for pixel-based images for print work.

- ✔ **PDF.** Portable Document Format files are designed to keep the look and feel of the original artwork and can be read by anyone with a copy of the free Adobe Acrobat Reader.

- ✔ **PICT.** PICT files are the Macintosh's built-in pixel format. Export as PICT any graphics to be viewed on Macintosh screens.

- ✔ **BMP.** BMP files are the Windows built-in pixel format. Export as BMP any graphics to be viewed on Windows screens.

- ✔ **EMF.** Enhanced MetaFile formatted files are perfect for embedding graphics in Microsoft Office applications such as Word, Excel, and PowerPoint.

- ✔ **PSD.** Photoshop Document files are native Photoshop files, which can contain Photoshop layer information.

- ✔ **Flash.** Flash files are a vector graphic format for the Web.

- ✔ **SVG.** Scaleable Vector Graphics files are the up-and-coming Web standard of vector graphic formats.

Whenever you export files, use the same name as the original document file, but with a different extension (the three letters after a filename, traditionally required by Windows and DOS computers). These letters tell you the format of the file just by looking at its name.

Working with Illustrator and Photoshop

Illustrator and Photoshop, both from Adobe, provide truly unique and useful integration capabilities. You can take files from either application and put them directly into the other application in five ways: dragging and dropping, copying and pasting (almost identical to cutting and pasting), placing, exporting and importing, or opening. Each method produces slightly different results to meet your every need, whim, or desire. (Well, okay, just those desires that center on moving files between graphics applications. You have those *all* the time, right?)

If you ever bring something from Illustrator into Photoshop, or vice versa, and something weird happens (parts of the image are missing, odd lines streak through the image, nothing happens, or your computer crashes) try saving the file as an earlier version, such as Illustrator 8 or Illustrator 6. Close the file and open it again before you try to copy and paste. Adobe takes great pains to make the two applications as compatible with each other as possible, but whenever a new version of one application comes out, there is usually a lag time before the other application is updated to be compatible with the new features. Saving a file in an earlier version enables the application to "understand" the file.

Making life easy: Copy and paste, drag and drop

These methods of getting a file from one program to the other are so easy they should be criminal! Open a file in Photoshop. Open a file in Illustrator. Make a selection in either program, choose Copy from the Edit menu, and then go to the other application and choose Paste. Or simply click a selection in either program and drag the selection from that one application into an open window in the other application. In Illustrator, you can use any Selection tool to do the dragging. In Photoshop, you need to use the Move tool.

After you move graphics this way, they appear at the height and width they were when created in the other program. After you drag a graphic from Illustrator to Photoshop, the graphic rasterizes automatically. *Rasterize* is a two-dollar word for the process that converts vector data into pixel data.

Whenever you copy and paste a graphic from Illustrator into Photoshop, the Paste dialog box appears, as shown in Figure 18-3. You can paste the graphic as pixels or as paths. Your first impulse may be to paste the graphic as paths. After all, Illustrator uses paths, not pixels, so you expect this method to pre-serve your original Illustrator files as they are. Unfortunately, although Photoshop uses paths similar to Illustrator's paths, they work very differently in Photoshop than they do in Illustrator. For example, paths in Photoshop can't have strokes or fills, although paths can be used to fill or stroke an image in Photoshop and to do other important Photoshop-specific things. You just can't use the path to print or display information on the Web. So if you want your Illustrator image to show up in Photoshop, always choose the Paste as Pixels option.

Figure 18-3:
The Paste dialog box opens whenever you paste Illustrator data into Photoshop.

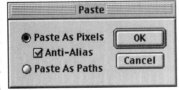

If you want to paste as pixels, you have the choice to anti-alias or not. (The opposite of anti-aliasing is *non*-anti-aliasing, not *aliasing*, believe it or not!) *Anti-aliasing* blurs the pixels where different colors meet to create a more natural transition between colors (as opposed to a jagged, "computery" edge). Images almost always look better after you anti-alias them. So you usually want to select the Anti-Alias check box.

Copying and pasting or dragging and dropping from Photoshop to Illustrator is easier than going from Illustrator to Photoshop (and that's pretty darn easy). You don't have to worry about the paths-to-pixels issue. Just make your selection and drag it over using the Move tool; or copy the image, go to an open Illustrator document, and paste the image. That's it!

If you assume (quite logically) that because moving Illustrator files into Photoshop rasterizes the files, then moving Photoshop files into Illustrator must "vectorize" them, you may be surprised to find that this is *not* the case. The pixels in a Photoshop file stay pixels, subject to all the laws and limitations of pixels anywhere else. For example, Illustrator vector data prints out at the highest quality no matter how much you scale, skew, rotate, or distort the data. But pixel data within Illustrator starts to *degrade* (the data gets blurry or worse) if you enlarge it or shrink it. Rotating, skewing, or distorting the pixel data has similar deleterious effects. Although you don't have to worry about resolution for vector data, you do have to make sure that your pixel data has a high enough resolution (72ppi for the Web and anywhere from 150ppi to 300ppi or higher for print).

Photoshop graphics that are dragged and dropped or copied and pasted into Illustrator files are *always* embedded.

Placing

Placing files into Photoshop or Illustrator is one of the more versatile ways of bringing data into the application. Each application provides a variety of options that aren't available using any other method.

Placing Illustrator files in Photoshop

To place an Illustrator file into Photoshop, open a Photoshop file and then choose File➪ Place. Select a saved Illustrator file (it doesn't need to be open) from the Place dialog box and click OK. The file opens in Photoshop inside a preview box (see Figure 18-4). The handiness of this preview box can't be overstated. While inside the preview box, the graphic isn't really "in" Photoshop yet. You can position the graphic, rotate it, and then scale the preview. Then double-click inside the preview box (or press Return/Enter) and Photoshop rasterizes the graphic at the best quality possible. If you rotate and scale the image *after* it's been rasterized, you can blur and otherwise degrade the image. Placing the image into Photoshop requires a couple more steps than copying and pasting or dragging and dropping, but doing so ensures that the image is the highest possible quality.

Placing Photoshop files in Illustrator

Placing Photoshop files into Illustrator is identical to placing any other graphic into Illustrator. See the "Bringing Files into Illustrator" section at the start of this chapter.

Figure 18-4:
The Place preview box in Photoshop provides the highest quality and greatest flexibility for Illustrator files brought into Photoshop.

Now opening in an application near you

Native files (files saved in the Illustrator format within Illustrator or the Photoshop format within Photoshop) can be read by the "opposite" application. In other words, Photoshop can read Illustrator files, and Illustrator can read Photoshop files. One advantage of this capability is that you don't need to have any document already open.

To open a Photoshop file in Illustrator, choose Open from the Illustrator File menu and select the Photoshop file. The Photoshop file opens in a new document within Illustrator, in the color mode of the Photoshop file.

To open an Illustrator file in Photoshop, choose Open from the Photoshop File menu and select the Illustrator file. The Photoshop Rasterize dialog box appears, as shown Figure 18-5. This dialog box may say "Rasterize Generic EPS Format" (if you saved the file as an EPS or if you saved it in Illustrator 8 or earlier format) or "Rasterize Generic PDF" (if you saved the file in Illustrator 9 format). Otherwise, the dialog box is identical, no matter which name you see.

Figure 18-5:
The
Rasterize
dialog box
that pops up
when you
open an
Illustrator
file in
Photoshop.

Rasterize Generic EPS Format	
Image Size: 93K	

Width: 2.083   inches

Height: 2.92   inches

Resolution: 72   pixels/inch

Mode: RGB Color

OK

Cancel

☑ Anti-aliased ☑ Constrain Proportions

In the Rasterize dialog box, you set the width, height, resolution, and color mode of your graphic. Your exact settings should reflect, as closely as possible, the final purpose of the graphic. The more you alter these settings after you rasterize the graphic, the more you degrade it.

Exporting

Exporting is almost the opposite of Placing. Instead of bringing a graphic into an application, you're getting it out of an application. Exporting has two big advantages. First, you don't need a copy of the other application to create the graphic in that format. Second, Illustrator layers export as separate Photoshop layers, instead of as one flattened graphic. (See Chapter 13 for more info on Illustrator layers.) Sadly, Photoshop layers don't export to layers in Illustrator.

You can export any path you create in Photoshop as an Illustrator file. To export paths from Photoshop, choose File⇨Export⇨Paths to Illustrator. A dialog box opens that lets you specify which paths to export. Select a path, click OK, and an Illustrator file is created that contains your path.

Exporting from Illustrator is much more powerful than exporting from Photoshop. Whenever you export a file in the Photoshop format from Illustrator, you can choose to export all your Illustrator layers as separate Photoshop layers. This option provides great versatility should you want to further edit your graphics in Photoshop.

To export your Illustrator graphic as a Photoshop file, choose File⇨Export. Name the file and choose Photoshop 5 as your format. After you click OK, the Photoshop Options dialog box appears, as shown in Figure 18-6.

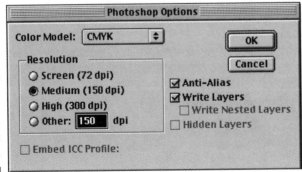

In the Photoshop Options dialog box, you set the color mode, resolution, anti-aliasing, and whether to export the graphic as a single, flattened layer or as multiple layers. Choose the Write Layers option to export the Illustrator layers as Photoshop layers. With this option unchecked, you export the file as a single, flattened layer. With this option checked, your layers will write as separate Photoshop layers.

When in doubt, select the Write Layers option. You can easily delete or flatten the layers in Photoshop (using the Photoshop Layers palette) if you decide you don't want them.

Using Adobe Illustrator with Nearly Everything Else

Illustrator works great with Photoshop. But what happens when you want to use Illustrator with products made by Adobe's competitors? To make your Illustrator files compatible with as wide a range of applications as possible, you need to go with the standards. Standard file formats are the formats that the majority of applications can use. Whenever you save something using a standard file format, you're almost guaranteed that anyone can open it, regardless of platform or application, just as long as he or she is using an industry standard application — such as QuarkXPress or Macromedia Dreamweaver — and not some weird, obscure application.

For Web graphics, the standard formats are GIF and JPEG. As of this writing, PNG, Flash, and SVG don't have the universal acceptance needed to declare them standards. Keep an eye on them, however; times change fast. For more information on saving files in these formats, see Chapter 17.

For printing hard copy, the standard format for vector graphics is EPS; the Illustrator options for this format appear in the dialog box shown in Figure 18-7. Virtually all page layout, word processing, and graphics applications accept EPS files. If the application that you're using doesn't accept EPS files, you may seriously want to consider abandoning it for one that does.

EPS Format Options

Compatibility: Version 8.0

Preview
Format: TIFF (8-bit Color)
● Transparent   ○ Opaque

Options
☑ Include Linked Files
☑ Include Document Thumbnails
☐ Include Document Fonts
☐ Use Japanese File Format
☑ CMYK PostScript
PostScript®: Level 2

Transparency
○ Preserve Paths (discard transparency)
● Preserve Appearance (flatten transparency)

OK
Cancel

Figure 18-7:
The EPS
Format
Options
dialog box.

Fortunately, saving EPS files is vastly simpler than saving for the Web. Choose File⇨Save As. The Save As dialog box opens. Give the file a name and choose Illustrator EPS for the format. Click OK, and the EPS Format Options dialog box opens (refer to Figure 18-7). Typically, *running with the defaults* (just clicking OK without changing any settings) works fine. But just in case you want to do something different, here's a little info about the other settings in the EPS Format Options dialog box:

✔ **Compatibility.** You can open and edit Illustrator EPS files just as you do any other Illustrator files. Suppose a friend is helping out with a graphics project and doesn't have the latest version of Illustrator. If you want to give an EPS file to this person for editing, you can set the Compatibility option to match whatever earlier version your friend is using. Otherwise, leave the file set to Version 9.

Saving your file to be compatible with an earlier version can alter your graphic. For example, Illustrator 3 doesn't support gradients. If you used gradients, they get broken up into separate objects for every different color in the gradient. The graphic looks the same, but editing can be a problem. The fact that you can save files in the Illustrator 3 format is a testament to Illustrator's compatibility with other applications. Illustrator 3 was outdated almost ten years ago! That's the computer equivalent of being fluent in ancient Greek!

✔ **Preview/Format.** This option determines how the Preview image, which displays when the graphic is linked to a document in another application, is created. Preview doesn't affect how the image is printed, only how it displays onscreen. Choose TIFF (8-bit color) for Windows (which most Mac applications can read) or Macintosh (8-bit color) for Macs (which most Windows applications can read).

✔ **Preview/Transparent or Opaque.** This option exists only when you choose TIFF (8-bit color) for your Preview. This option determines how transparent areas in your graphic are handled. Typically, you want to set this option to Transparent, but if you are using the graphic in any Microsoft Office application, you need to choose Opaque for full compatibility.

✔ **Include Linked Files.** If you have any linked files in your image, this option embeds them.

✔ **Include Document Thumbnails.** Have you ever noticed that in the Open dialog box of some applications, you get a thumbnail picture of the file, which lets you see the picture before you open the file? Check this option to create one of those thumbnails.

✔ **Include Document Fonts.** This option builds any fonts you used in your document into the EPS file. Although this option increases file size, it also ensures that your document displays and prints properly if the fonts don't exist on the computer used to open the file.

✔ **CMYK PostScript.** If you used any RGB colors in your document, this option enables them to print on a four-color, CMYK PostScript printer. This option is a good one to check, just in case.

✔ **PostScript.** This option sets the PostScript level at which the file prints. *PostScript* is the language that printers use. You want to use the highest level that the printer is capable of. The latest printers support Level 3, but these files don't print properly on older printers. If the file doesn't print, try using a lower level. Be aware, though, that lower levels can print more slowly and with less quality than Level 3. (But hey, that's better than not printing at all!) If you save your file with Illustrator 9 compatibility, you can't save it with Level 1 PostScript. Change the compatibility to Illustrator 8 (or an earlier version) to change to Level 1.

Quite frankly, if you have to print at Level 1, you may want to hunt down a better printer. Level 1 printers probably cost you money every time you print to them because they're slow and don't print well.

✔ **Transparency.** This setting appears whenever you set the Compatibility option to any version prior to Illustrator 9. Transparency is a new feature in Illustrator 9. (See Chapter 10 for more info.) This feature enables you to make an object semi-transparent, so that an object beneath it shows through as a blend of the two objects. Areas where a semi-transparent red circle overlap a blue circle appear purple, for example.

Because this feature is new to Illustrator 9, earlier versions don't support it. So when you save an Illustrator 9 file as Illustrator 8 or earlier, you use the Transparency option to determine how to translate transparent objects into something earlier versions can understand. You have two options: Preserve Paths and Preserve Appearance. Preserve Paths discards transparency altogether, keeping the same shapes that you originally created, but making the graphic look very different. For example, the two overlapping circles previously mentioned would look just like that, with no purple area where the two overlap. Preserve Appearance creates new shapes to maintain the look of the transparency. For instance, new paths would be created for the purple area where the two circles overlapped. Preserve Appearance is almost always the way to go; it keeps your artwork looking exactly the way you created it.

If you use the Transparency option when you save an Illustrator document in an older format, you may get some strange and unexpected results. Save in the latest format if you possibly can.

After you complete your settings, click OK. Your Illustrator file is saved as an EPS file, ready to use just about anywhere!

After you master saving your Illustrator artwork as an EPS, you can create graphics that are compatible with every major print publishing application there is. Saving graphics as GIFs or JPEGs (covered in Chapter 17) lets you make artwork that can be displayed in nearly every Web browser in existence. Add the ability to move files back and forth between Illustrator and Photoshop, as well as the many Export options, and you can create graphics that work anywhere.

Part VI
The Part of Tens

The 5th Wave — By Rich Tennant

ARTISTS Signature PCs

ANDY WARHOL   CHRISTO   ©RICHTENNANT

PICASSO   SALVADOR DALI

In this part . . .

This section is a mishmash of things that don't quite fit anywhere in the rest of the book. Some are so important that they need special attention. Some are so silly that we had to relegate them to the back pages. From hidden goodies to obscure trivia to quality-enhancing production techniques, this part has something for everyone!

Chapter 19

Ten Production-Enhancing Tips

*I*f you can picture something, you can probably create it in Illustrator. The only trick is knowing how to create it. People who've used Illustrator for years rely on thousands of little tricks to make their lives easier, make production faster, avoid unnecessary hassle and expense, and generally make their world a better place in which to live. Well, those thousands of tricks may not all fit in one book, but here are ten simple ways to jazz up your use of Illustrator. These tricks may not be obvious, but they get results.

Punching Holes

Take a close look at the two illustrations in Figure 19-1. In the image on the left, the hole in the center is actually a white circle that makes the life preserver *appear* to have a hole in its center. In Illustrator, white is a color that is really "there" — and it blocks out anything behind it. In the second illustration, the hole in the center *really* is a hole, revealing whatever is behind it (in this case, an alarmed passenger noticing just how few life preservers there are on the ship).

Figure 19-1:
A life preserver without a hole (left) and with a hole (right). They may look the same, but they aren't (just ask the guy on the right).

How is this remarkable feat accomplished? If you set the Fill color for the white circle to "none," then just that circle becomes transparent, revealing the gray circle behind it — so that won't work. The trick is to use Compound Paths. The Compound Paths command joins two or more paths in such a way that wherever the paths overlap, you get a hole revealing whatever is behind the paths. Incidentally, this is how the holes in letters like "O" and "P" are created, so that when you run type over an object you see the object through the holes.

All you need to create a compound path is two objects — one to serve as a cutting tool and one to serve as a place to put the hole. Then follow these handy do-it-yourself steps (no safety goggles required):

1. **Place the object that you'll be using to make a hole in front of the object in which you want to cut the hole.**

2. **Select both objects with any Selection tool.**

3. **Choose Object⇨Compound Path⇨Make.**

   Wherever the paths overlap, *shazam!* You get a see-through area — you know, a hole.

To make the paths behave normally again, select the objects and choose Object⇨Compound Path⇨Release.

Whoa! Don't Use That Photoshop Filter!

In the beginning, Adobe gave us Photoshop filters. These were features in Adobe Photoshop that let you manipulate pixel information in ways you never could before. You could take a scanned photograph and with a few simple commands make it look like a fresco painting, or like a reflection on rippling water. You could easily create things *nobody* had ever seen before, all using filters. And everybody thought Photoshop filters were *just so cool* when they came out. Especially the folks at Adobe, who decided to make it possible to use Photoshop filters in just about every application they made (including Illustrator) in an effort to make everything else seem as cool as Photoshop. This was a bad idea for a multitude of reasons:

- ✔ Photoshop filters are designed to work in Photoshop, so they run at a fraction of their normal speed when you use them outside Photoshop.

- ✔ Photoshop filters only work on pixels, not vectors (see Chapter 2) so most of the time the filters aren't usable in Illustrator.

- ✔ Whenever you apply a Photoshop filter to an image, Illustrator automatically embeds the image, even if you don't *want* to embed it.

- ✔ Most importantly, you have very little control over a Photoshop filter in Illustrator. In Photoshop, you can target the filter so it only affects a small part of the image. You can run the filter on different parts of the image with different intensities. In Illustrator, however, you can't target a small area and tell the filter to "change *that*, and only that." The tame, controllable Photoshop filter runs amuck — slathering the same intensity over the entire image. You can't fade the filter back after you apply it (as you can in Photoshop). Nope. Subtlety is not an option.

Unless you're doing a radical experiment in artistic frustration, leave those Photoshop filters in Photoshop. Of course, if you've made a wonderful mountain out of a molehill in Illustrator, you *can* bring that image into Photoshop and tweak it there. In the long run, you spend far less time if you open your Illustrator image in Photoshop, run your filter there, save the image, and then plunk it back into Illustrator.

This rather quirky workaround (quirkaround?) should not dissuade you from applying filters to your paths using the Effect menu. That's a different story entirely. These filters have all the coolness of the Photoshop filters, but they apply to vectors instead of pixels (and offer you a whole lot more control and flexibility than the Photoshop filters). The filters in the top half of the Filter menu are also fine to use because they apply to paths, not to pixels. Just don't use the ones in the bottom of the Filter menu (everything below Artistic, as shown in Figure 19-2) on pixel-based images (unless a mess is what you *want* to portray). For more information on using Photoshop with Illustrator, see Chapter 18.

Filter

Apply Neon Glow	⌘E	
Neon Glow...	⌥⌘E	
Colors	▶	
Create	▶	
Distort	▶	
Pen and Ink	▶	
Stylize	▶	
Artistic	▶	
Blur	▶	
Brush Strokes	▶	
Distort	▶	
Pixelate	▶	
Sharpen	▶	
Sketch	▶	
Stylize	▶	
Texture	▶	
Video	▶	

Figure 19-2: The Photoshop filters, selected from the Filter menu, that you normally shouldn't use on placed pixels.

When White Isn't Nothing

Double negatives aside, here's a little tip that can save you *beaucoups* bucks whenever you use gradients and spot colors in artwork you're creating for print.

If you work with print publishing for even a short time, you come to think of the color white as being *nothing*. In most of the familiar printing techniques, specifying the color white means *don't put down any ink* (or toner, or dye, or any of the methods for putting color on paper) for anything colored white. White ink doesn't exist (except in rare situations) — and no, correction fluid doesn't count. The white that you see in print publications is just the white of the paper.

This approach depends on an actual, tangible piece of paper to provide the white for the image. To save yourself untold woe, don't use the technique described here if your artwork is destined to live on the Web. It's strictly a hard-copy fillip.

Here's a scenario to keep in mind. Suppose you're creating a two-color publication using black ink and a nice blue Pantone 273 ink. The publication may be pretty dull in only two colors, but that's all you have a budget for, so you decide to spice things up using gradients. You create lovely gradients by blending Pantone 273 into white (logically assuming that white means "no ink"). Unfortunately, in terms of gradients, Illustrator thinks of a blend as a whole new CMYK color (see Chapter 1)— so the blend between white and a spot color such as Pantone 273 involves much more complicated instructions to the computer than you may have intended.

Sure, your graphics *look* perfect, but unbeknownst to you, your job has mutated from a two-color job to a *five*-color job. Usually, you only discover this after your job is already at the printer, and then you have to pay hundreds of extra dollars for a mistake you didn't even know you made.

The trick is to use the same Pantone color for all steps of the gradient (see Figure 19-3). Just follow these steps:

1. **Choose Window⇨Show Gradient.**

   The Gradient palette appears.

2. **Choose Window⇨Swatch Libraries⇨Pantone Coated (or another swatch library of your choice).**

   The Pantone swatch library opens.

3. **Click the color of your choice in the Pantone library and drag the color from the library onto a swatch in the Gradient palette.**

   Repeat this until all swatches in the Gradient palette are the same color (see Chapter 10 for more information on the Gradient palette).

   At this point, the gradient is one solid color. Not a gradient at all, really. But wait!

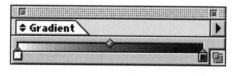

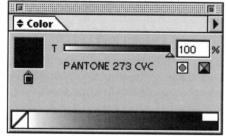

Figure 19-3:
The elusive spot-color gradient. The same color is used at two different tint percentages, specified in the Color palette.

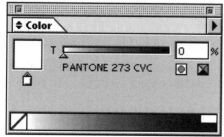

4. **Double-click a swatch in the Gradient palette.**

   The Color palette opens, showing the Pantone color set to 100%.

5. **Set the tint of the Pantone color to 0 percent.**

   This action gives you true, one-ink spot-color gradients that use the paper as "white" in that good old traditional way. See Chapter 10 for more info on gradients and spot colors.

Little things like this can drive Print designers to the Web!

Expanding for Simplicity

Sometimes you try to create fancy artwork and it just doesn't work out the way you planned (say, it doesn't print, or after you choose File⇨Save for Web, parts of your graphics are missing or displaying improperly). This kind of failure can lead to feelings of low self-esteem and low aesthetic self-worth. But don't blame yourself. Blame your computer. It rarely provides you with any warning or indication that what you're doing may not work. Worse yet, your computer almost never tells you what to do if your efforts don't succeed.

Fortunately, when your efforts don't work in Illustrator (including problems with printing, problems with copying between applications, or a selected object that contains an element you can't work with), the difficulties are almost always caused by the same culprits. Many of the more interesting features of Illustrator — such as gradients, patterns, custom brushes and object blends — are also very mathematically intensive. This situation can make the computer or printer choke at inopportune moments. Fortunately, the Expand command gives the Heimlich maneuver to the most complex graphics.

Expanding turns complex objects into simpler objects, making the objects easier for the computer or printer to understand. Expanding does this by making every color into a separate, basic object. Expanding also makes the objects less editable, so make a copy of any graphic that you expand!

To expand an object, follow these steps and examine Figure 19-4:

1. **Select the object with any selection tool.**

2. **Choose Object⇨Expand.**

   The Expand dialog box opens.

3. **In the Expand dialog box, choose to expand the fill, the stroke, and the object (if you selected an object blend) by checking those options.**

Figure 19-4:
Expanding
makes a
graphic
simpler
(believe it or
not). The
original
object with
a gradient
fill (top left)
is expanded
(bottom left)
to 20 objects
(with paths
showing)
and the final
object
(bottom
right).

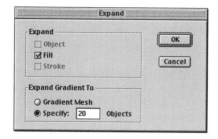

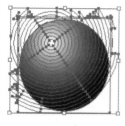

Check Fill to expand the fill and simplify gradients. Stroke for custom brushes, and check Fill or Stroke for patterns — or just leave everything checked to cover all the bases. After you expand a gradient, you need to specify the number of objects that the gradient is broken into. Choose the smallest number that doesn't produce visible banding. The default value of 255 objects is way too large for all but absolutely huge gradients! Click OK and your graphic is reduced to its basic components. Visually, the graphic looks almost identical, except that it now has many more paths. The graphic may *seem more* complex because it has more paths but it just looks more complicated because you can actually see those paths. In reality, when the object isn't expanded, all those paths have to be created anyway whenever you print the graphic or save the graphic for the Web. Expanding is a way of doing this work up front. While visually more complex (because of all the extra paths), the graphic becomes much simpler *mathematically*, and you should be able to work with it.

Quick! Hide!

Simply hiding things can greatly improve your productivity in Illustrator. Otherwise, you may have a hard time seeing your current creation for all the floating palettes and interface elements in the way!

You can hide all open palettes and the Toolbox by pressing the Tab key (unless you have the Type tool selected and are in a particular tool slot — then you just insert a tab into your text). Press the Tab key again to bring everything back.

If you're creating exclusively for the Web, hide the Artboard and Page Tiling. These features exist to show you the size of the page you're printing to and the printable area on that page. This information is useless if you aren't ever going to print! Choose View⇨Hide Artboard and View⇨Hide Page Tiling to make them go away.

Have you ever made an object that contains so many points that after you select it you can't tell what the object *is* anymore for all the highlighted points and lines? You can hide these, too, while keeping the object selected. Choose View⇨Hide Edges to make the highlights disappear.

You can hide everything you have open on your computer (including your Desktop) except for the current Illustrator document by clicking the Full Screen Mode with Menu Bar button in the Toolbox, as shown in Figure 19-5. To hide everything *including* the Menu bar, click the Full Screen Mode button. (You can toggle through these modes by clicking the "F" key.) To get a completely unobscured view of your artwork, switch to Full Screen Mode and hit the Tab key to hide your palettes. *Real* power users work this way, using keyboard shortcuts to access all their tools and menu items!

Figure 19-5:
The View
Mode
buttons.

Take a Tip from Illustrator

Illustrator has a feature called Tool Tips. If you hover over a tool with the cursor for a moment, a little yellow box of text pops up, telling you what the tool is. If the tool has a keyboard shortcut, that shortcut appears in parentheses after the name.

Tool Tips, despite the name, don't work with tools alone (and they don't give you tips, either — just the names of things. Go figure)! They work just about anywhere in Illustrator that you can position a cursor. Tool Tips give you information about whatever the cursor is over. Hover over a color swatch, and the Tool Tip tells you the name of that color. Hover over a brush, and it tells you the name of the brush. Not sure what some cryptic icon in the Pathfinder palette means? Just let the Tool Tip tell you.

Tool Tips can be invaluable whenever you're using the program, because there are just too many things to remember. With Tool Tips, you don't have to!

Change Your Units Whenever You Want

Do you feel as though no matter what you do, your units of measure seem to be wrong? Are they always set to points, for example, when you really want inches? Sometimes centimeters are so much easier to work with. Fortunately, Illustrator lets you change your mind on the fly. (Or is that "change the flies on your mind?")

To see your measurement options, choose View⇨Show Rulers and then click (right-click in Windows) any location on the rulers at the top and side of your screen. You get a pop-up menu that shows all the units of measurement that Illustrator understands. Choose the unit you desire, and from that moment on, Illustrator uses that unit of measurement.

You can reposition rulers by clicking [right-clicking] where the rulers meet at the upper-left corner. To reset them, double-click that corner.

However, you don't even have to change your unit of measurement in order to use a different one! In any field where you specify an amount (such as the Height and Width options in the Rectangle dialog box), just type in the amount you want, followed by the abbreviation of the unit of measurement that you want to use. If you don't know the abbreviation, just use the whole name. Illustrator makes the conversions for you. It's so smart, it's scary!

Reuse Your Brushes, Swatches, and Libraries

You went through all that work to create custom brushes, beautiful colors, and outstanding appearances, which you saved in the Styles palette. Unfortunately, these are all specific to the document that you created them in. But you don't have to settle for that! You can open the swatches, brushes, and styles you created in one document in any other document!

To get the brushes, for example, from another document, choose Window⇨Brush Libraries⇨Other Library. An Open dialog box appears. Choose the document with the brushes that you want to add to the current document, as if you were going to open it. Click OK. Instead of opening that document, Illustrator opens the custom brushes in their own palette, ready for you to use. Follow the same steps, choosing Window⇨Swatch Libraries⇨ Other Library or Window⇨Style Libraries⇨Other Library to add your swatches or styles.

Avoid Russian Dolls

Have you ever seen those cute Russian dolls? You know, the hollow doll that you open to find another smaller doll inside? And then you open that one to find an even smaller doll inside? And then you open *that* doll. . . oh it's just too cute! And so funny! Hours of fun for children of all ages! Who would suspected that inside such a joyous novelty lurks a heart of pure evil!

You see, Illustrator lets you create the digital equivalent of those Russian dolls. You place a Photoshop image into Illustrator, rotate the image, add text over the image, and then save the whole thing as an Illustrator file. Later on, you want to add more, so you create a new document in Illustrator, place the previously created Illustrator graphic (which also contains within it a Photoshop file) into the new document using the File⇨Place command. You save this Photoshop file within an Illustrator file within another Illustrator file as an EPS and place it within a page layout document. You have a Photoshop fill embedded four layers deep within the page layout document. While nothing prevents you from *creating* the digital equivalent of the Russian doll, the computer prevents you from ever *using* such files. Each time you place one file into another, you add a level of complexity to the file. Every time you rotate or scale that placed file, you add still another level of complexity, until you create a file that can never print or go out to the Web successfully.

Remember the KISS method (Keep It Simple, Sillygoose!). Avoid ever going more than three "places" from the original file (say a Photoshop file placed inside an Illustrator file, placed inside an InDesign document, with scaling only happening in *one* of those places). Two "places" are even better if you can limit yourself! If you need to bring Illustrator data from one Illustrator document to another, open both documents and then copy and paste the info rather than placing it.

Selecting Type When You Want

If you work with type and objects, you may discover how annoying it is to select an object that is lurking behind type. Even when you click where there is obviously no type, you still select the type instead of the object behind it. This situation is because one of Illustrator's most annoying features is turned on. Type Area Select automatically selects type when you click anywhere in its "area" — not just when you click directly on the type or its path.

Turn off this (ahem) "feature" by going to Edit⇨Preferences⇨Type & Auto Tracing. In the Type & Auto Tracing Preferences dialog box, remove the check mark from the Type Area Select checkbox. Click OK. Breathe easier. Henceforth, Type shall be selected whenever you click directly on a letter or on its path, and at no other time, by royal proclamation of the user.

Chapter 20

Ten Tantalizing Techniques

This book focuses on individual tools and features of Illustrator — which is fine, as far as it goes. After you have a handle on using the tools and features by themselves, the next level of mastery is to combine them. You can do so in almost infinite ways — to produce almost anything you can visualize. To harness the true power of Illustrator, you must use all its different capabilities in a synergistic whole that surrounds us and binds the galaxy together. . . oops. Got a bit carried away there. This chapter actually shows you how to use multiple features and functions to create specific results — ten of them — and you may think that's spectacular enough.

Making Text Three-Dimensional

Gradients are great for giving dimension to things. Unfortunately, gradients only work when you fill areas with them, and your only options are radial or linear gradients. Gradients don't flow along strokes, and you can't make them match complex shapes. Or can you? Using the Object Blend tool, you can create gradients in any shape your heart desires! In the following example, we use text, but this works with paths of all sorts.

1. **Create your text.**

   Any text will do, but large, fat, sans-serif text works best. We use 100-point Antique Olive Black, as shown in Figure 20-1.

Figure 20-1:
Basic text
can be the
starting
point for
many
fascinating
techniques.

2. **Select the text with the Selection tool and then choose Type➪Create Outlines.**

   As a first step in modifying your text to extremes, you have to turn it into paths.

3. **Set the Fill to None and the Stroke to Black using the Color palette (Window➪Show Color). Use the Stroke palette (Window➪Show Stroke) to set the stroke to 1 point.**

   This handy trick makes the paths of the text easier to see and work with. See Chapter 5 for more information on Fills and Strokes.

4. **Simplify the type.**

   Strategically delete path segments of the letters by clicking them with the Direct Selection tool and pressing the Delete key, one segment at a time. The goal here is to create letters that are single, continuous lines, as in Figure 20-2.

Figure 20-2:
The text,
after you
convert it to
outlines and
delete path
segments.

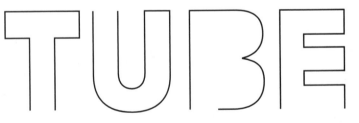

5. **Round off the corners and ends of the path.**

   Choose Window➪Show Stroke, click the Stroke palette's flyout menu, and then choose Show Options to access the palette's hidden options. Choose Round Cap and Round Join. Finally, set the Stroke to 10 points. By default, the corners and ends of Illustrator paths are sharp. This step gives you a nice rounded look for your tubes, as shown in Figure 20-3.

Figure 20-3: The full Stroke palette with settings for a 10-point stroke, Round Cap, and Round Join. Notice the effect these settings have on the text.

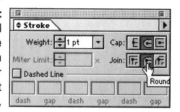

6. **Duplicate the text.**

   Select the entire text by clicking and dragging over it with the Selection tool; then duplicate the text and copy and paste it.

7. **Make the duplicated text lighter and narrower.**

   In this example the Stroke of the duplicated text was changed to white using the Color palette, and the stroke was set to 1 point using the Stroke palette. The Fill was left set to None.

8. **Move the white text in front of the black text, slightly offset, as shown in Figure 20-4.**

   The two sets of text are ready for an Object Blend!

Figure 20-4: The two sets of text, ready for an Object Blend.

9. **Select both sets of text with the Selection tool.**

   Click and drag with the selection tool over all of the text.

10. **Select the Object Blend tool from the Toolbox and blend the two sets of text.**

   To blend the two sets of text, click an end point of any letter in the white text. Then click the same end point of the same letter in the black text. It may help to zoom way in on the two points by clicking and dragging over them with the Zoom tool. (See Chapter 10 for more on the Blend tool.)

   The two paths blend together in a series of subtle steps, creating the appearance of a gradient flowing along a path! Totally tubular! (Eighties nostalgia, anyone?)

When you are in the proper position to make the first click with the Object Blend tool, a little multiply (x) sign appears to the lower right of the tool, as shown in Figure 20-5. When you are in the proper position for the second click, a little plus (+) sign appears to the lower right of the Object Blend tool.

Figure 20-5:
The Object Blend tool in action and the wonderful results.

Tracing Hastily

Tracing pixel-based images is one of the most common uses of Illustrator. By using a digital image as a guide and taking full advantage of the Layers palette and its arcane powers, you can create decent artwork with almost criminal ease! Just follow these steps:

1. **Open a new Illustrator document.**

2. **Choose File⇨Place. Select a pixel-based image.**

   Almost any image will do. Its visual resolution can be low (you don't need anything higher than 72 pixels per inch), out of focus, dirty, scratchy, or otherwise funky. Remember, the image is just a guide. You won't be printing it. As long as you can tell what the image is, it's good enough!

3. **In the Place dialog box, click the Template option.**

   Don't worry about linking the original image; it's destined for deletion after you trace it (insert villainous laugh here).

4. **Click OK.**

   The image appears in a Template layer, locked out and faded by 50 percent, as shown in Figure 20-6.

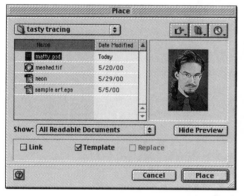

Figure 20-6:
Placing the image as a Template, and the results.

5. **If your Layers palette isn't already open, choose Window⇨Show Layers. Double-click the layer above the Template layer.**

   The Layer Options dialog box appears, enabling you to give the layer a name. For this example, name it **Pencil Sketch** and click OK.

6. **Double-click the Pencil tool to open the Pencil Tool Preferences dialog box and then un-check the Edit Selected Paths option.**

   Whenever you trace, you probably want to draw a lot of pencil lines close together. By turning off the Edit Selected Paths option, you make this task a lot easier, since you won't be replacing your last line with the next line you draw.

7. Change the Fill and Stroke color and the Stroke width to make seeing the lines you draw easier.

With the Pencil tool still selected, set the Fill color to None and the Stroke color to Black using the Color palette. Set the stroke width to 1 point in the Stroke palette. By changing the Fill and Stroke before you start drawing, you ensure each line has those Fill and Stroke values.

8. Using the image in the Template layer as a guide, trace the image in as much detail as you want.

Figure 20-7 shows the results of our efforts in this specific example.

Figure 20-7:
The image traced with the Pencil tool.

You can add color to your graphic by using the paths that you just created. The catch is that when you trace with the Pencil tool, the tendency is to make a whole lot of short, unconnected open path segments. They look great as lines, but when you try to fill them with color, doing so is virtually impossible, because you need long, closed paths. Fortunately, you can easily join the separate open path segments into closed paths. To make the graphic as editable as possible, create color in one layer and keep your original pencil sketch safely hidden in a different layer. The next step shows how.

9. Duplicate the Pencil Sketch layer.

In the Layers palette, drag the pencil sketch layer onto the Create New Layer button. This action creates a new layer with the same contents as the Pencil Sketch layer.

10. **Name the duplicate layer to avoid confusion.**

    Double-click this new layer. After the Layer Options dialog box opens, name this layer Color, and click OK.

11. **Click the View button in the Layers palette (the eye icon to the left of the layer name) for the Pencil Sketch layer to hide it.**

    Hiding the Pencil Sketch layer lets you focus on coloring the image. After you hide the Pencil Sketch layer, you join your various lines to create closed paths around all the major shapes in the artwork. You then fill those paths with color later on.

12. **Unite separate path segments into closed paths using the Join command.**

    To use the Join command, select two points in separate paths using the Direct Selection tool and then choose Object⇨Path⇨Join. This command unites the end points of two separate paths into a single point, as shown in Figure 20-8. In this example (or for any image of a face), you can join the hair into one closed path, the face into another, the lips into another, and so on. You may need to add extra lines using the Pencil tool in order to make your creation work, but you can close the majority of your paths with the Join command. Unfortunately, this command only works on two points at a time, so you need to repeat the Join command several times to create each closed path.

    At any time, you can choose a Fill color to test your path, to make sure it holds its color properly.

13. **After you create your closed paths, fill them with color using the Swatches palette or the Color palette, as shown in Figure 20-9.**

    See Chapter 5 for info on using these palettes to fill an object with color.

14. **Delete the Template layer.**

    In the Layers palette, click the Template layer. Drag it onto the Trash Can icon in the lower-right corner of the Layers palette. This removes the image you were tracing from the Illustrator document, reducing file size and giving you an unobscured vision of your artwork.

15. **View and position the Pencil Sketch layer.**

    In the Layers palette, click the View button for the Pencil Sketch layer. Click and drag the Pencil Sketch layer above the Color layer. When a dark bar appears above the Color layer, release the mouse button. The pencil sketch is positioned over the colors.

The illustration is now 98 percent done. You may need to make a few minor tweaks, but because your pencil sketch and the colors are in separate layers, you can quickly and easily target the areas to change by hiding or locking layers. The final illustration, shown in Figure 20-10, may not be absolutely perfect, but it took about 15 minutes to create! With a little practice, patience, and perseverance, you can create illustrations that put this one to shame!

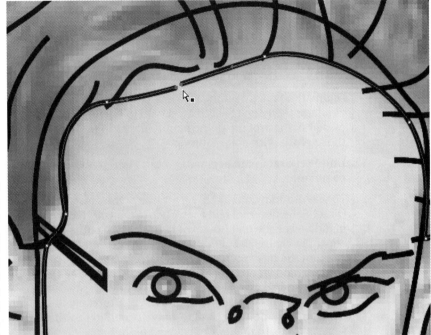

Figure 20-8:
Two endpoints, selected and ready to be joined with the Join command.

Figure 20-9:
The areas filled with color.

Figure 20-10:
The final illustration. The shading in the image was accomplished using nothing but basic gradient fills. (No funny business with object blends or gradient meshes here!)

Neon Glow

You can create a neon glow (the illusion that the graphic is made from neon lights) in many ways. This technique uses the Appearance palette to add multiple strokes of different colors to a single path. The technique is especially cool because it's a "live" effect and can be applied to the stroke of any path — even to text! You can change the path or enter in new text, and the glow matches the changes! Best of all, even though it may be labor-intensive to create, you can save the effect as a Style, to apply to other objects at any point in the future just by clicking in the Style palette.

For this technique, you need the Appearance palette, the Swatches palette, the Stroke palette, and the Styles palette. Find them all under the Window menu, open them, and you're ready to rock. Just follow these steps:

1. **Open a new document in Illustrator.**

2. **Create a piece of simple artwork.**

   In this example, we created a star using the Star tool (see Chapter 4 for info on basic shapes), but this technique works equally well with text, path segments, or any other object.

3. **Add additional strokes using the Appearance palette.**

   Choose Window⇨Show Appearance. From the Appearance palette's flyout menu, choose Add New Stroke. After you do this, you don't see any difference in the graphic itself, because the second stroke is identical to the first, but you see two strokes listed in the palette. Every object in illustrator always starts with one stroke listed in the palette. You don't need to worry about the color of the strokes at this point. You are just adding the strokes so that you can modify them later. Repeat the Add New Stroke command until you have five strokes total listed in the Appearance palette (see Figure 20-11). With all these strokes, you are ready to add color and change the width to "neonize" the text.

4. **Turn the bottom stroke into a thick red stroke.**

   The stroke that is listed at the bottom of the Appearance palette appears behind all the other strokes in the image. Click that stroke in the Appearance palette. Set the stroke's color to red (by clicking a red swatch in the Swatches palette) and its width to 20 points (in the Stroke palette).

Figure 20-11:
Add multiple strokes using the Appearance palette's flyout menu.

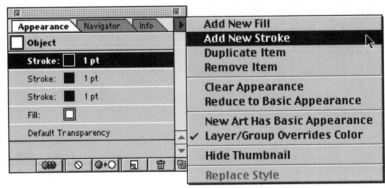

5. **Make the second stroke from the bottom dark orange.**

   In the Appearance palette, click the second stroke from the bottom; set its stroke color to dark orange (by clicking any dark orange swatch in the Swatches palette), and then set the stroke width to 20 points in the Stroke palette.

   This width is the same as that of the bottom stroke, so this stroke totally hides the red stroke. (Don't worry, we correct the problem shortly.)

6. **Make the third stroke from the bottom light orange, and narrower than the underlying strokes.**

   Click the third stroke from the bottom in the Appearance palette. Set the stroke color to light orange by clicking any light orange swatch in the Swatches palette. Set the stroke width to 12 points in the Stroke palette.

7. **Make the second stroke from the top yellow and narrower than the underlying strokes.**

   Click the second stroke from the top in the Appearance palette. Set the stroke color to yellow by clicking a yellow swatch in the Swatches palette, and set the stroke width to 8 points in the Stroke palette.

8. Make the top stroke white and narrower than all the other strokes.

Click the top stroke in the Appearance palette. Set the stroke color to white by clicking the white swatch in the Swatches palette, and set the stroke width to 2 points in the Stroke palette.

Your Appearance palette should look something like Figure 20-12. At this point, your object should look halfway decent as a neon glow effect. You could use steps 1 through 9 with very different colors to create striped text. This time, however, you complete the neon glow effect by softening the edges of the strokes using the Gaussian Blur effect.

Figure 20-12: The Appearance palette after setting stroke widths and colors, and the image that it produces.

9. Soften the edges to the white stroke using the Gaussian Blur effect.

With the top stroke selected, choose Effect⇨Blur⇨Gaussian Blur. The Gaussian Blur dialog box opens. Set the Radius to 1.5, and click OK. The white stroke is blurred.

10. Soften the remaining strokes one-at-a-time *except* for the bottom stroke.

Select the next stroke down by clicking it in the Appearance palette and apply the same Gaussian Blur effect that you applied to the white stroke. (see Figure 20-13).

Selecting the top menu item in the Effect menu (this is the name of the last Effect you applied) repeats the last Effect you used with the same settings.

Do not apply the effect to the bottom stroke. Remember, neon tubes glow, but they are still hard glass tubes!

The result is a neon stroke! You can save this stroke and apply it anywhere you want. To save this stroke, just click the New Style button in the Styles palette. Create any text or path you want and click the style in the palette to apply the neon stroke, as shown in Figure 20-14.

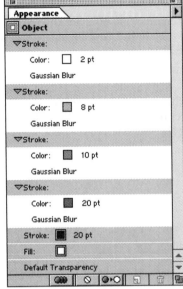

Figure 20-13:
The Appearance palette after applying Gaussian Blurs, and the new stroke that it creates.

Figure 20-14:
Saving the neon stroke by using the Styles palette, and the new style applied to different paths.

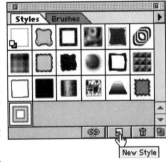

Ancient Type

One secret of top digital designers is to use the worst features of a program and make them work. This idea may seem illogical, but part of good design is to think of things that others don't. Most people never waste time deliberately using the *worst* part of a program! Well, you heard it here first: This technique for creating ancient looking type combines the Auto Trace tool (arguably, one of Illustrator's worst tools) with the Rasterize command (a command that you normally want to avoid) to create a happy accident! Just follow these steps:

1. Create some large text.

Any text will do, but fonts with big serifs, such as Adobe Garamond, work best, as shown in Figure 20-15. You also get better results if you use large text (say, 60 points or more).

Well, it's a start — but the Auto Trace tool only works with pixel data. Before we can use the text, we need to convert it to pixels using the Rasterize command. That's next.

Figure 20-15:
74 point
Adobe
Garamond
Bold is the
font at the
heart of this
technique.

Goth Talk

2. Convert your text to pixels using the Rasterize command.

Select the text with the Selection tool and choose Object⇨Rasterize. The Rasterize dialog box appears. As shown in Figure 20-16, choose 72 ppi, set the Background to White, select the Anti-Alias option, and then click OK.

Your text converts automatically to pixels. (Pretty neat, eh?)

Figure 20-16:
After the
Rasterize
command
converts
vector data
to pixel data,
select the
AutoTrace
tool.

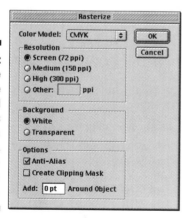

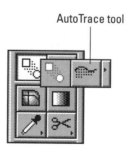

AutoTrace tool

3. Choose the colors for the Auto Trace tool to use.

The Auto Trace tool only detects the shapes of what it is tracing, not the color, so you have to determine in advance what colors to use. Click the

Auto Trace tool, set its Stroke to Black and its Fill to None. Because you do this before you start using the tool, the objects that the Auto Trace tool creates are set to these colors.

4. **Click the Auto Trace tool and trace the letters.**

The Auto Trace tool creates paths around highly contrasting areas (such as between the black text and its white background). You have the best luck with this tool if you remember the following:

- To Auto Trace a solid letter, click anywhere in the dark area of the letter.

- To Auto Trace a letter with a hole in it (like A, O, P, and such) first click the inside edge of the hole, where the dark meets the white. If you click the outside of the letter first, the whole thing fills in with black, hiding the inner hole!

By and large, the poor old Auto Trace tool isn't very consistent. Whenever you click a dark solid, Auto Trace traces the whole thing properly; but to trace a white area, you have to click its edge. Don't worry that the white holes fill with black when you Auto Trace them. You can take care of this later using the Compound Path command.

5. **After you trace all the letters, click the rasterized type with the Selection tool and delete it.**

Not to worry; the project doesn't use the rasterized type anyway (except as something to trace). It just gets in your way, so get rid of it!

You are now ready to add the finishing touches by using the Compound Path command to poke holes in your text.

6. **Put "holes" in letters like "P" "O" and "B" using the Compound Path command.**

Using the Direct Selection tool, click and drag over a letter that should have empty holes in it. Make sure the hole and the main part of the letter are selected. Choose Object⇨Compound Path⇨Make. This makes the holes completely see-through, as any hole should be. Repeat this step for each letter, one letter at a time.

Sit back and admire the results, as shown in Figure 20-17.

Figure 20-17:
The resulting text, looking positively ancient.

Goth Talk

Making Artwork on a (Shoe)String

The Scatter Brush is usually used to scatter objects randomly along a path, but you can rein in all the settings to make this brush place objects in an orderly manner along a path, as though they were strung like beads on a necklace. Just follow these steps:

1. **Create any object that you want to place along a path.**

   In this instance, we create a pearl to use in forming a pearl necklace. To create the pearl, we blend two circles — a small white circle and a larger white circle — using the Blend tool (see Chapter 12 for details on the Blend tool). This technique gives you a little more control than the Gradient Fill and also creates a simpler object.

   After you create the pearl using the Blend tool, it needs to be expanded using the Object⇨Expand command. Unfortunately, some artwork you create in Illustrator is just too complex to be made into a brush. Artwork created using the Blend tool just happens to be one of these objects. Fortunately, you can use the Expand command to simplify an object without changing its appearance. A blended object that has been expanded *can* be made into a brush. See Chapter 11 for more information on the Expand command.

2. **Choose Window⇨Show Brushes and click the New Brush button.**

   Before you can create a new Scatter brush, the artwork you want to use in the new brush must be selected. If the artwork isn't selected, the Scatter Brush option is grayed out in the New Brush dialog box.

   The New Brush dialog box appears.

3. **Choose New Scatter Brush and click OK.**

   The Scatter Brush Options dialog box appears.

4. **Specify the settings for the new brush.**

   For this example we set the Size and Spacing to 100 percent, and set the Scatter and Rotation to 0 percent so that the artwork doesn't change size or rotate when it is applied to a path.

   We set Size, Spacing, Scatter, and Rotation to Fixed to make sure the previous settings don't change.

   We set the Rotation Relative To option to Page. This setting makes the artwork keep the same rotation, no matter which way the path turns.

   Finally, we set Colorization to Tints, so the color of the pearls matches the Stroke color, as shown in Figure 20-18.

   Click OK and voilá — you have a new brush *based on* a blended object. (Is that sneaky or what?)

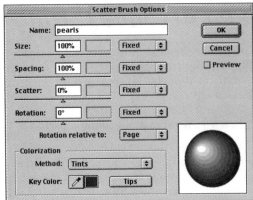

5. Test the new brush.

Choose the Paintbrush tool from the Toolbox and paint a loose loop, like a necklace. The result is a string of pearls, as Figure 20-19 lavishly depicts.

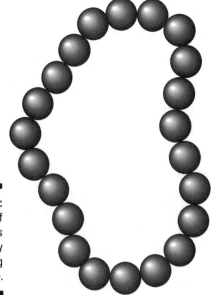

Figure 20-19:
A string of
pearls
(somebody
cue the big
band).

Cleaning Up After Illustrator

Although the other techniques in this chapter are creative techniques, this one is not. This technique prevents the creation of unnecessarily large files and extra work. You can build a whole bunch of information into a file, but that bulk of information makes the file slower to copy and print and less stable. A few commands are all you need to make a streamlined file that has just the necessary information and none of the fat. This is especially important whenever you give your file to other people. Here are the steps:

1. **With the finished document open, choose Object⇨Path⇨Cleanup.**

   The Cleanup dialog box appears, as shown in Figure 20-20, giving you the option of deleting stray points, unpainted objects, and empty text paths. Check all three options (if they aren't already checked) and click OK.

   After you click OK, everything taking up file space that doesn't appear in your document is deleted.

   The invisible, unnecessary elements can contain fill, stroke, and text information, even though you don't see them and they don't print. Illustrator doesn't know that; it leaves all that stuff in the document. Results: Great big files, long print times, and unprintable grumbling.

Figure 20-20:
The Cleanup command gets rid of unnecessary garbage in your illustration.

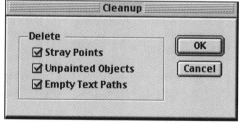

2. **Choose Window⇨Show Brushes. From the Brushes palette flyout menu (accessed by clicking the tiny triangle in the upper-right corner of the palette), choose Select All Unused. Then click the Trash button in the lower-right corner of the Brushes palette.**

   All brushes in the palette, whether you use them or not, are embedded in the saved file. Deleting the unused brushes saves some space.

3. **Choose Window⇨Show Swatches. From the Swatches palette flyout menu (accessed by clicking the tiny triangle in the upper-right corner of the palette), choose Select All Unused. Then click the Trash button in the lower-right corner of the Swatches palette.**

   All swatches in the palette, whether you use them or not, get embedded in the saved file. Deleting the unused swatches saves some space.

4. **Choose Window⇨Show Styles. From the Styles palette flyout menu (accessed by clicking the tiny triangle in the upper-right corner of the palette), choose Select All Unused. Then click the Trash button in the lower-right corner of the Styles palette.**

   All styles in the palette, whether you use them or not, get embedded in the saved file. Deleting the unused styles saves space. And hassle. And your faithful authors from having to say it again.

Yes, boys and girls, these few simple steps can save you time, improve your outlook on life, and prevent those awful headaches caused by stuffed-up files!

Getting Animated

Writing about animation is a little bit like dancing about architecture. Animation makes a lot more sense if you can see it happening. Fortunately, animating from Illustrator is so straightforward and clear that you don't have to see anything actually move until you *put* it in motion.

The basic principle in creating Illustrator animations is almost embarrassingly simple. Ever have one of those books of drawings that you can riffle to make the pictures move? Same thing. Whenever you export an Illustrator file in the Flash format, you can export each layer as a separate frame in a movie. What you wind up with is a stack of layered images. When the frames play, the effect is as though you were clicking through the layers (showing the next one and hiding the previous one) really fast. Play begins at the bottom layer and goes upward in order to the top layer.

For a simple (but entertaining) example of this effect, the following steps demonstrate how to animate text to make it look as though it's typing itself:

1. **Create a new document in Illustrator.**

2. **Type some spontaneous foolishness.**

   For this example, we use **Say what?** so it will seem to be *saying* itself.

3. **Highlight each letter with the Text tool and give each one a different Fill color.**

   Figure 20-21 gives you a look at the result. All our letters are gray here because we are very boring people (in fact, this whole book is printed in full color, but we just couldn't bring ourselves to use any color that wasn't a shade of gray). But feel free to make every letter a different, vivid color.

Figure 20-21:
In this animation, the text appears to magically type itself.

Say what?

4. **In the Layers palette, duplicate the layer by dragging it on top of the Create New Layer button**

   The Create New Layer button is the second button from the right at the bottom of the Layers palette. We duplicated the layer eight times, once for each letter, plus one extra. The idea is to have one more layer than the number of letters you have, as shown in Figure 20-22.

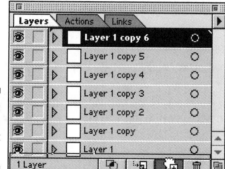

Figure 20-22:
Duplicating the Text layer.

5. **Hide all layers except for the second layer from the top by clicking the View button.**

   The View button is the eyeball to the left of the layer name in the Layers palette.

6. **Highlight the last letter in the text and press the Delete key.**

   In our case, we deleted the question mark.

7. **Hide all layers except for the third layer from the top and delete the last two letters.**

   We got rid of the question mark and the letter *t*. Figure 20-23 adroitly demonstrates this sleight-of-hand.

Figure 20-23:
The trick is
to delete all
the letters
you deleted
in the
previous
layer, plus
one more.

Say w

8. **Hide all layers except for the fourth layer from the top and delete the last three letters.**

   We exterminated the question mark, the letter *t*, and the last letter *a*.

9. **Keep going down through the layers in this way, deleting one more letter each time, until only one letter remains in the second layer from the bottom, and the bottom layer is blank.**

10. **Show all the layers.**

    Hidden layers won't export to the Flash file.

11. **Choose File⇨Export, and after the Export dialog box appears, select the Flash (SWF) format.**

    When you name your file, make sure its name ends with the **.SWF** extension. Flash files have a hard time playing when they don't have that extension (even on a Mac).

12. **Click OK.**

    The Flash (SWF) Format Options dialog box appears as shown in Figure 20-24.

13. **Choose AI Layers to SWF Frames under the Export As option at the top of dialog box.**

    Because this animation has few frames, use a slow frame rate, such as 3 fps (frames per second). For a more dynamic animation, create more layers and use a faster frame rate. If you are going to be editing this animation in Macromedia Flash, click the Auto-Create Symbols option. Otherwise, leave the remaining settings as they are.

14. **Click OK.**

15. **Test your animation by opening it in your Web browser.**

    If the animation doesn't play, you may not have the necessary Flash plug-in installed. Go to www.macromedia.com to find instructions on downloading and installing the plug-in for your browser.

Tune in next week when our hero Flash Format conquers the planet Mondo Cool.

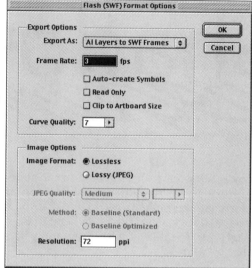

Figure 20-24:
The Flash
(SWF)
Format
Options
dialog box
contains
settings for
animating
layers.

Perspective Shadows

Perspective shadows are among the most popular artistic techniques ever. They almost magically add depth to any illustration. Although this example uses text, the technique works with any object. Illustrator has a built-in drop shadow filter, but it is rather limited compared to what you can do on your own with little trouble. To create drop shadows, follow these steps:

1. **Create text or an object to which you want to apply a shadow. Duplicate the text or object by copying it and choosing Edit➪Paste in Front.**

   This command places the copy directly in front of the previous object.

2. **Keep the copy selected and click the Free Transform tool in the Toolbox.**

   A control box appears around the text.

3. **Click the top control handle, drag it beneath the bottom of the text, and don't release the mouse button.**

4. **Still holding down the mouse button, press and hold the ⌘ [Ctrl] key and drag to the left.**

   By holding the ⌘ [Ctrl] key as you drag the center handles of the Free Transform box, you can skew the selection. That's the secret of creating a *perspective* drop shadow, as shown in Figure 20-25.

Figure 20-25:
The text
with a
perspective
shadow. Not
bad, but we
can do
better!

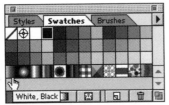

Granted, the shadow as shown is rather sharp. You can soften it by using a gradient — provided you're putting the shadow on anything *other* than text. Unfortunately, gradients can't fill text. If you use text for this technique, we have to stick an extra step in here: Convert your text to paths by choosing Type⇨Create Outlines. *Then*, apply the gradient, as shown in Figure 20-26.

Figure 20-26:
The White,
Black
gradient
applied to
the shadow.

5. **Set the Fill color to the default gradient (White, Black) by clicking this option in the Swatches palette.**

   Wait a minute — that doesn't look quite right. You need to set the direction of the gradient.

6. **To set the gradient's direction, choose the Gradient tool, click at the bottom of the shadow, and then drag to where the shadow meets the text.**

   Finally, the shadow is all set! Figure 20-27 tells the tale.

Figure 20-27:
With the
gradient
direction
set, the
shadow
fades
as a real
shadow
does.

Haunted by a Ghost (ing)

Many magazines use the *ghosting* technique to solve the age-old problem of keeping text legible when it overlaps a graphic. If the graphic image is complex or highly detailed, it can distract attention from the text and make the text hard to read. A ghost is a subtle fade that wafts over part of the image, keeping the text readable without losing the visual interest of the graphic.

Ready to ghost part of a graphic? That's the spirit! Here goes:

1. **Open the graphic in Illustrator.**

2. **Using the Rectangle tool, drag a rectangle over the part of the image that you want to fade and then fill the rectangle with White.**

3. **Choose Window⇨Show Transparency. Using the Opacity slider in the upper-right corner of the Transparency palette, set the Opacity to 70 percent, as shown in Figure 20-28.**

You may need to set a higher or lower opacity, depending on what you're ghosting.

Figure 20-28:
The original image, the rectangle, and the rectangle ghosted to 70% to create an area for text while maintaining the visual interest of the artwork.

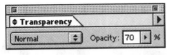

Cubing the Square

Although Illustrator may never go out and mow your lawn or do your taxes, you *can* get it to do some of your work for you. For example, you can begin creating a graphic image by using the basic shapes created with the Circle tool, the Rectangle tool, the Star tool, and so on. These simple shapes may not be the final form of what you want, but a little manipulation (using only the Transform tools) can turn them into an astonishing variety of shapes. In the following steps, for example, you use rectangles and the Transform tools to create a cube:

1. **Use the Rectangle tool to draw a square.**

   If you want a perfect square, hold down the Shift key as you draw.

2. **Select the square with the Selection tool. Click the square again and drag it. As you start dragging, hold down the Option [Alt] key.**

   Holding down the Option [Alt] key as you drag makes a copy of whatever is currently selected. This maneuver is one of the primary ways that Illustrator power users avoid making extra work for themselves. The trick is to press the Option [Alt] key *after* you start dragging and to keep holding it down until you release the mouse.

3. **With the second box still selected, choose Object⇨ Transform⇨ Transform Again.**

   As if summoned from another dimension, a third box appears.

The Transform Again command is another way that Illustrator power users avoid extra work. This command repeats the last transformation made on the currently selected object. Transformations don't have to be made using the Transform tools. Option [Alt] copying is considered a transformation, as is simply moving by dragging.

4. **With the Direct Selection tool, click the right side of the first square and drag it up and to the left.**

    This action creates the shape shown in Figure 20-29.

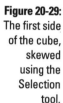 

Figure 20-29: The first side of the cube, skewed using the Selection tool.

5. **Click the right side of the second square. Choose Object⇨ Transform⇨ Transform Again.**

    The side moves the same way as the first square moved. Now you have two sides of the cube, but one is facing the wrong way.

6. **Click the second side with the Selection tool.**

7. **Choose the Reflect tool from the Toolbox. Hold down the Option [Alt] key and click the selected side.**

    The Reflect dialog box opens.

8. **Choose the Vertical axis option and click OK.**

    This flips the second side of the cube so that it is the mirror image of the first.

9. **Move the second side so that it touches the right side, as shown in Figure 20-30.**

Figure 20-30: The second and the first sides of the cube, together at last.

10. **Select the third square with the Selection tool; then choose the Rotate tool, hold down the Option [Alt] key, and click the square.**

    The Rotate dialog box appears.

11. **Rotate the square 45 degrees.**

    Type 45 into the Angle field and click OK.

12. **Position the square over the first two sides, as shown in Figure 20-31.**

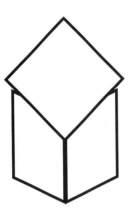

Figure 20-31: The cube is coming together. The fit isn't quite right, but that's easily fixed with the Scale tool.

13. **With the square still selected, click the Scale tool; then click in the center of the square to set the origin point.**

14. **Click and drag outside the square until it lines up with the tops of the other two sides of the cube.**

    There you have it! A stunning three-dimensional object that looks like it will pop right off the page, as shown in Figure 20-32.

Figure 20-32: The final cube, with shading added to the sides for dramatic effect.

Fill the three sides with appropriate colors, and you have a toy chest, a building block, or a *really* simple cube-puzzle in less time than it takes to tell about it.

Chapter 21

Ten (Or So) Ways to Customize Illustrator

*K*eyboard commands — ya gotta love 'em, finger-cramps and all, but what if you could make them easier to use? Or maybe you have some styles that you use all the time and you want them to be (gasp) *available* all the time. And how about that quirky default page size that each new document shows up wearing? Well, if you itch to tinker, adjust, and fine-tune (but you've misplaced your ball-peen hammer), you've come to the right place. This chapter shows you how to adjust, redefine, and yes, *customize* the way Illustrator works for you.

If you're like a lot of us, you may already be thinking, *Customizing! Cool! So where do I put the tailfins?* Whoa. Before you go on a feature-tweaking rampage, consider: *You're changing the way Illustrator works.* So a word to the wise: Read first. Then, if you like what you see, make a change and try it out for awhile before you change anything else. Return to default settings if you make a mistake.

Positioning Palettes

Illustrator saves all palette positions just as they are when you quit Illustrator. The next time you use it, the palettes appear right where you left them. This structure is handy most of the time, but your palettes can get a bit disorganized if you move them all over the place while chasing a creative inspiration. If you want to get them back to Square One with no fuss, read on.

Because Illustrator saves the palette positions in the Preference file, you can save a set or "sets" of palette positions for later use by saving a copy of the Preference file. Whenever you need to reset the palettes to their "best" locations, replace the active Preference file with the saved version.

Keep in mind that this shuffling of files may zap other Preference settings, such as your units of measurement or your Pencil Tool Preferences (see Chapter 8) that you may have changed.

On the Mac, Illustrator's Preferences file is inside the System folder, tucked inside a folder named (surprise) Preferences. Hey, sometimes obvious is nice. In Windows 98, this file is called AI Prefs and is located in the Windows/ Application Data/Adobe/Adobe Illustrator 9 folder.

Changing the Items on the Menu

You can customize all the Illustrator menu commands using the Keyboard Shortcuts dialog box, shown in Figure 21-1. You can get to it by choosing Edit⇨Keyboard Shortcuts.

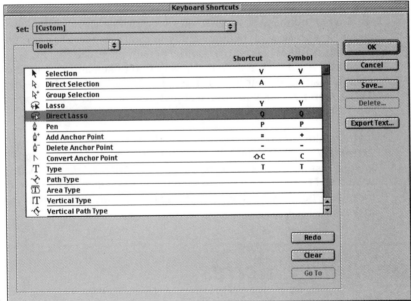

Figure 21-1:
The
Keyboard
Shortcuts
dialog box.

Even the most common commands, such as Open and New, can have different keyboard shortcuts, if you choose to redefine them. You can also print out a big sheet of all the keyboard shortcuts, even if you haven't changed any of them. To add a new keyboard shortcut, follow these steps:

1. **Choose Edit⇨Keyboard Shortcuts.**

   The Keyboard Shortcuts dialog box opens.

2. **Choose Menu from the pop-up menu at the top left of the dialog box (the default name is Tools).**

   A list of all Illustrator's menus appears. Click the arrow beside the menu name to open the complete list of items under that menu. If the item already has a keyboard shortcut, it is listed to the right of the menu item, in the column labeled *Shortcut.*

3. **Change the keyboard shortcuts by highlighting the current keyboard shortcut, typing a new shortcut, and pressing Enter.**

   If the item has no keyboard shortcut assigned to it, you can give it one: Click in the Shortcut column, to the right of the menu item, to highlight the empty space; whatever shortcut you type occupies that space.

To print out all the keyboard shortcuts, follow these steps:

1. **Choose Edit⇨Keyboard Shortcuts.**

   The Keyboard Shortcuts dialog box opens.

2. **Click the Export Text button in the lower right of the Keyboard Shortcuts dialog box.**

   A Save dialog box opens.

3. **Name the text file you want to contain your keyboard shortcuts, specify a location for it on your hard drive, and then click OK to save the text file.**

4. **Open any word processing program on your computer, choose File⇨ Open, open the text file you just created, and then print it as you would any word processing document.**

You can always return to the original keyboard commands by choosing Illustrator Default Settings from the Set pop-up menu in the upper-left corner of the Keyboard Shortcuts dialog box.

The Flexible Toolbox

Well, no, we're not talking rubber screwdrivers here, but you *can* give each tool its own keyboard shortcut. Then you can access any tool by pressing a key on the keyboard. For example, the V key brings up the Selection tool; the Z key brings up the Zoom tool.

To change the keyboard shortcut for a tool (or to add shortcuts for tools that don't have any), choose Edit⊅Keyboard Shortcuts. In the Keyboard Shortcuts dialog box, find the tool you want to change (or add) and then highlight the current command. Type a new shortcut; click OK to make the new shortcut available.

The Startup Document

You may notice that whenever you open a new document in Illustrator, the new document always appears the same way. For example, the Artboard and Page Tiling are always visible, the Swatches palette always has the same contents, and so on. The appearance of a new document doesn't happen by random chance. It is determined by a file called the *startup document*. This document controls the way each new document is created, and you can change it to make each new document open the way you want it to. Here are some items you can change in this document:

- ✔ **Number of layers.** If you only need three, this option makes it so.
- ✔ **Zoom percentage.** If you find the best balance of detail and readability at, say, a 63-percent zoom, that zoom is yours.
- ✔ **Artboard and Page Tiling.** You can show or hide these to suit your needs.
- ✔ **Window size.** This option is especially handy if you're working on several images at once.
- ✔ **Styles.** Add the styles you want, delete the ones you don't, and the result is exactly what you'll have for your new documents.
- ✔ **Swatches.** You can make the Swatches palette open with exactly the swatches you want — no more, no less.
- ✔ **Brushes.** New documents open with the brushes you have in the Brushes palette at the time you save the startup document. (How about leopard spots?)

To change the startup document, follow these steps:

1. Open the startup document in Illustrator.

Illustrator has two of these, titled *Adobe Illustrator Startup CMYK* and *Adobe Illustrator Startup RGB*. You can find them inside your Plug-Ins folder (located in your Illustrator Application folder).

CMYK documents and RGB documents (see Chapter 1) have separate startup documents. This arrangement lets you tailor each startup document to the specific work environment. For instance, RGB files are often used for Web graphics while CMYK is used for print graphics. In the RGB startup file, you can hide the Artboard and Page Tiling (which are print-specific features); you can also turn on Pixel Preview. In the CMYK file, you can add color swatches that represent your company's corporate color to the Swatches palette.

2. **Make changes to any of the items on the handy list that precedes these steps.**

   For example, if you want new documents to have three layers instead of one, put three layers in the Layers palette. The layers don't need any artwork in them; just the act of adding layers in the Layers palette is enough. If you want Pixel Preview turned on automatically, choose it from the View menu. Add or delete swatches from the Swatches palette, and so forth.

3. **Save the document and close it.**

Henceforth, each new document you create reflects the items that you changed in the startup document.

Not to worry. The startup document does *not* change existing documents.

Changing the Default Settings

Don't stop with the startup document — you can change the way the entire Adobe Illustrator application works. Assuming that you have a plan (handy to have at a time like this), choose Edit⇨Preferences⇨General. Behold: A dialog box appears, as shown in Figure 21-2.

Figure 21-2: The General Preferences dialog box.

Preferences
General ⬍
Keyboard Increment: `1 pt`
Constrain Angle: `0` °
Corner Radius: `12 pt`
OK
Cancel
Previous
Next
☑ Use Area Select   ☐ Disable Auto Add/Delete
☐ Use Precise Cursors   ☐ Japanese Crop Marks
☐ Disable Warnings   ☑ Transform Pattern Tiles
☑ Show Tool Tips   ☑ Scale Strokes & Effects
☑ Anti-aliased Artwork   ☐ Use Preview Bounds
☐ Select Same Tint Percentage
Reset All Warning Dialogs

The General Preferences dialog box is just the first of several preferences dialog boxes containing a multitude of options for you to change. Each change affects the way the application works, and Illustrator saves these changes when you quit the program, regardless of the documents that you're working in.

Don't start changing preference settings all helter-skelter when you first stumble across this dialog box. Doing so may cause unexpected behaviors in the application. Illustrator may start printing your letterhead in hieroglyphics or singing loudly in the shower. (Kidding. But you get the idea.) A better idea is to look at the list of items and only change one at a time, testing each item after you change it, even (gasp) writing down what you did so you can remember the changes. If the results of a change aren't up to snuff, then be sure to change the preference back to its original setting.

Changing Hidden Commands You Never Knew About

In addition to those nice, respectable, *visible* menu commands and tool shortcuts, all sorts of nifty shortcuts just hang around in Illustrator without a single menu item or tool associated with them. These shortcuts are handy commands such as "Increase Type Size" (⌘+Shift [Ctrl+Shift]). Even better, every one of these commands can be customized. Simply scroll through the Keyboard Shortcuts dialog box to find every command that exists in Illustrator. If you find one that looks as though it may be useful to you, give it a new shortcut.

Using a Master Document

Although the startup document enables you to customize certain items in your new documents, you're limited to one startup document (well, two actually, one for RGB and one for CMYK). If you're really clever (and of course you are), you can simply use multiple documents as your startup documents, without having to swap them in and out of the Plug-Ins folder.

Try keeping a folder full of seemingly empty documents that contain special sets of styles, swatches, brushes, and layers. When you open one that has the stuff you want, choose Save As. What you get is a "custom" document, without the process of loading or creating any of the styles, swatches, brushes, or layers you're using.

Action Jackson

Have you ever found yourself doing things again and again (such as typing the word *redundant* dozens of times)? Have you ever wished that your computer could do some of this tedious work for you? Well, that's where Actions come in. Actions make Illustrator do the grunt work, while you get to do all the fun stuff.

Illustrator comes with hundreds of Actions, although only a dozen are installed with the software. You can find the rest on your CD-ROM. Better yet — you can make your own Actions! *Actions* can be virtually any series of Illustrator activities, such as scaling, rotating, changing colors, or bringing selections to the front. You can even use Actions to select objects (if they have specific names).

One of the handiest uses for Actions is creating *compound keyboard shortcuts*. For example, you can perform a set of procedures such as Create New Layer, Place, and Scale at the same time, without even wrenching your back. Instead of performing all three keyboard commands individually, you can easily set up an Action to do all three simultaneously. Result: One keyboard command does three tasks! You just smile and watch. Choose Window➪Show Actions, and meet the friendly Actions palette in Figure 21-3.

Figure 21-3:
The Actions
Palette puts
power at
your virtual
fingertips.

To use any Action, click it in the Actions palette and then click the Play button (the right-pointing arrow) at the bottom of the palette.

Creating your own Action feels something like taping your voice or image and then playing it back. You may feel a little self-conscious the first time you create an Action, but after a few tries, you get the hang of doing so. When you record an Action, Illustrator watches what you do and records every step as closely as possible.

Computers have no imagination; you have to tell them exactly what to do. Therefore, your recorded Actions must use precise values. Anything that requires a level of human interaction does not get recorded. In effect, Illustrator says, "That's not my department. So there." For example, creating a one-inch rectangle is a precise action. Drawing a squiggly line is not. You can't always know in advance whether Illustrator can record all the actions you perform — but you know for certain after you play it back. Hey, it's not a program; it's an adventure.

To create your own Action, just follow these steps:

1. **Open a new document in Illustrator and choose Window⇨Show Actions.**

   The Actions palette opens.

2. **Click the New Action button.**

   The New Action dialog box opens.

3. **Name the Action and click Record.**

   For example, name the Action **Red Rectangle.** After you click Record, the Action records everything you do, tapping your phone, and transmitting that information back to Adobe where they're keeping a file on you. Just kidding. Honest.

4. **Perform a series of actions with the keyboard or the mouse.**

   For the example, select the Rectangle tool and drag out a rectangle in the document. Then choose a red swatch from the Swatches palette for the Fill color.

5. **Click the Stop button.**

   The Action shows up on the Actions palette, ready for, um, *action*. Great gung-ho attitude, eh? But hold on a minute....

6. **Prepare to test your Action.**

   In this case, delete your original rectangle. This finishing touch prevents the Action from creating *another* rectangle of the exact same size, shape, color, and position.

7. **Test your Action by clicking the name of the Action and then clicking the Play button.**

   If the Action does exactly what you planned, it's ready for duty.

The preceding example is a simple Action. With a bit of practice, you can create infinitely more complex Actions. This wonder results from a simple fact: An Action records (nearly) everything you do from the time you start recording to the time you click Stop. The Action can be a simple menu command or something as complex as the creation of some amazing artwork, as if by magic.

Sticky Settings

Some of the things that you do in Illustrator remain "sticky" until you quit the application. For example, if you create a rectangle that's 1 x 2 inches, the next time you click with the Rectangle tool the values are automatically set to 1 x 2 inches. All the dialog boxes in Illustrator remember what you did last during your current Illustrator session. (But don't worry; they won't tell a soul.)

Between sessions, the entries in the Preferences dialog box and the positions of the palettes are all that remains constant. Oh well. At least *something* does.

Index

• •

• *W* •

• *Z* •

Notes

Notes

Notes

FOR DUMMIES
BOOK REGISTRATION

Register This Book and Win!

We want to hear from you!

Visit **dummies.com** to register this book and tell us how you liked it!

✔ Get entered in our monthly prize giveaway.

✔ Give us feedback about this book — tell us what you like best, what you like least, or maybe what you'd like to ask the author and us to change!

✔ Let us know any other *For Dummies* topics that interest you.

Your feedback helps us determine what books to publish, tells us what coverage to add as we revise our books, and lets us know whether we're meeting your needs as a *For Dummies* reader. You're our most valuable resource, and what you have to say is important to us!

Not on the Web yet? It's easy to get started with *Dummies 101: The Internet For Windows 98* or *The Internet For Dummies* at local retailers everywhere.

Or let us know what you think by sending us a letter at the following address:

For Dummies Book Registration
Dummies Press
10475 Crosspoint Blvd.
Indianapolis, IN 46256

...FOR DUMMIES ™

BESTSELLING BOOK SERIES

RECEIVED NOV 1 9 2002
21.99